THE HORSE COMPANION

THE HORSE COMPANION

A comprehensive guide to the world of horses, including all you need to know about riding skills, equipment, healthcare, grooming, and diet.

Jane Holderness-Roddam

BARRON'S

A QUARTO BOOK
Copyright © 1997 Quarto Inc.

First U.S. edition published in 1997 by Barron's
Educational Series, Inc.

All inquiries should be addressed to:
Barron's Educational Series, Inc.
250 Wireless Boulevard, Hauppauge, NY 11788

Library of Congress Catalog-in-Publication Data

Holderness-Roddam, Jane.
    The horse companion / Jane Holderness-Roddam.
        p.   cm.
    Includes bibliographical references and index.
    ISBN 0-7641-5047-2
    1. Horses. 2. Horsemanship. 3. Horse sports. I. Title
SF285. H7236   1997   97-17645
636. 1—dc21   CIP

Designed and produced by
Quarto Publishing plc,
The Old Brewery, 6 Blundell Street,
London N7 9BH

Senior Editor: Gerrie Purcell
Copy editors: Mandie Rickaby, Chester W. Krone, Jr.
Indexer: Dorothy Groves
Art Editor: Sally Bond
Designer: Karin Skånberg
Photographer: Bob Langrish
Illustrators: Janos Marffy, Wayne Ford
Picture Researcher: Zoë Holtermann
Assistant Art Director: Penny Cobb
Art Director: Moira Clinch
Editorial Director: Pippa Rubinstein

Typeset by Central Southern Typesetters,
Eastbourne, Great Britain
Manufactured in Hong Kong by
Regent Publishing Services Ltd.
Printed in China by Leefung-Asco Printers Ltd.

CONTENTS

SECTION 1: *Horse Basics 10–55*

INTRODUCTION

Humans domesticated the horse 6,000 years ago, and people have had a passion for horses ever since. The horse that was tamed and put to human service had taken around 54 million years to evolve from a nomadic animal with four hoofed-toes and which stood no taller than 12 inches (30 centimeters).

The first section of this book, HORSE BASICS, includes the development of the horse and the ancestors of the modern horse that are described in detail in *Evolution*. The domestication of the horse was vital to human history for there were many human activities—war, transportation, communication, and sport, to mention just a few—that the horse profoundly influenced, as discussed in the chapter entitled *The Horse in History*.

The chapter on *The Horse in Art* clearly shows how artists and sculptors have been enthralled by the movement and beauty of horses, from the primitive artists who drew the wild horse on the walls of caves to the grand masters who painted masterpieces depicting it in all its myriad activities with people. Many of these activities are still being enacted today, such as ceremonial duties, recreational pastimes, and work in agriculture and industry as covered in *The Role of the Horse in Modern Times.*

The power and beauty of the horse have enthralled people for thousands of years and this fascination has led to poets and writers throughout the ages using the horse as a topic or literary metaphor in many works of literature. This literary influence and the horse's role as a performer in the movies, television shows, circuses, parades, displays, rodeos, and horse shows are dealt with in *The Horse in Entertainment*. There are few shows on earth more breathtaking and eye-catching than the Spanish Riding School's dancing white Lipizzaner stallions, France's Cadre Noir, or Britain's Household Cavalry Trooping the Color.

The *Directory of Breeds* section that follows deals with the horse since its domestication 6,000 years ago, and, in particular, with the 50 most popular breeds developed over the years in different parts of the world.

The degree of development, of course, varies greatly. The ponies, many indigenous to specific areas, are in a lot of cases relatively unchanged for centuries, whereas some of the horses have been crossed with other breeds in the last five hundred years to create a lighter-framed and faster animal more suited to improved roads, lighter carriages, and cavalry soldiers who saw the value of speed of attack over cumbersome and heavy armor.

Further refinement to today's horses also came about to satisfy people's ever growing interest and participation in sport and leisure activities—show jumping, racing, polo, eventing, showing, hacking, and trekking vacations, to mention just a few.

In Section 2, KNOWING AND CARING FOR YOUR HORSE, you will learn everything you need to know about your horse or pony. In *Points of the Horse*, you will understand the physical makeup of the animal and how to recognize its important parts. *Breeding* deals with the critical subject of horse reproduction and what to look for when you decide to take your mare to stud. *The New Foal* shows you how to look after your foal from birth and weaning to *Breaking In* a few years later. To improve your skill in handling your horse or pony, the general behavior of horses is treated in *Understanding Your Horse,* and a further chapter, *Vices,* gives you invaluable hints on how to cope with the bad habits some horses and ponies pick up or copy from other horses.

Choosing and Buying a Horse gives you advice on the most critical decision you will face as a rider—the purchase of your first horse or pony—and shows you what pitfalls to avoid. It is essential to know what you can reasonably expect and what to look out for when you purchase an animal if you are not to be disappointed later.

General Care, as the title implies, deals with taking care of your horse in both its stable and while out in its paddock. The following chapters then take the reader through the important aspects such as *Stabling and Bedding. Grooming,* an integral component of proper horse care, shows you how to improve your horse's appearance, and includes a description of the essential grooming kit. *Blankets* makes you aware of which of a large choice of blankets (rugs) best suits your horse or pony.

The companionship of horse and helper charmingly displayed at a horse show.

In *Braiding,* you will be able to follow the clear, illustrated instructions for both English/American and European (Continental) methods of making braids (plaits), while in *Clipping,* equally well illustrated, you will learn the best method of this vital grooming function for your animal.

Shoeing gives you the invaluable information you need in this area to keep your horse or pony sound, while *Exercise* and *Fitness* both present the many options you have for developing a program as well as using fitness aids.

◀ The tranquil grace of the horse has enthralled people throughout history. There can be an almost magical quality to the relationship between people and these beautiful creatures once a trust has been agreed on both sides.

▶ This fine Trakehner chestnut horse (see p. 39), has a blaze and white stockings. White feet generally go with white markings. Find out more about markings on page 26.

The subject of your horse's or pony's diet is dealt with in *Feeding,* in which the important point is made that as no two horses are alike in their food requirements, it is important for you to understand which feeds are available and how and when you should go about feeding your animal. This is followed by a useful chapter on how to work out a sensible *Daily Routine.* Then, *Transportation and Loading* covers both the loading and carrying of your horse or pony.

The Healthy Horse covers the signs of a healthy and unhealthy horse and acts as an introduction to the following sections that deal in detail with the important areas of *Teeth* care, *Worming and Vaccination, Leg and Foot Care,* and shows you how to recognize and treat the *Common Ailments* you are likely to encounter. In the two chapters on *First-Aid,* you will learn how to deal with the emergencies that may arise for either horse or rider. Keeping your head and knowing what to do if an accident occurs will hopefully minimize the consequences. Finally, there is a fascinating presentation on *Natural and Herbal Medicines* for your horse or pony—many of these "modern treatments" were once used by our ancestors centuries ago!

▲ This young rider has just gotten ready for a competition. Her horse is waiting expectantly in the background. When entering equestrian competitions you will be required to wear special clothes and follow certain rules, so refer to the *Competitions and Riding sports* section for basic information on your chosen sport.

◄ The western horse ready for action. A different style of riding is employed with this saddle which is covered in *Western Riding* and *Riding Western Style* on pages 172–179.

The third section, EQUIPMENT AND RIDING TECHNIQUES, concentrates on riding in all its forms. Starting with *Tack and Horse Equipment* and *Cleaning the Tack,* you will learn what tack you need for your horse and pony and how to care for it. *Tacking Up* shows how to put all the tack on correctly in easy-to-follow, step-by-step format.

Now the horse or pony is equipped, the next chapter deals with the *Rider's Equipment.* There is also invaluable information in *Rider Fitness* on the exercise programs *you*—not your horse or pony—might want to follow for better equestrian performance.

Straight-talking advice on *Mounting and Dismounting, Rider Position, Control and the Aids* is followed by easily-understood discussions of *Paces, Preparing to Jump,* and *Jumping.*

Western Riding is a subject of its own, with insights about equipment, tack, rider's clothes, position in the saddle and other topics discussed in detail—especially a guide to *Riding Western Style.*

► Olympic gold medals are the aim for many top competition riders, such as Germany's dressage star, Isabel Weth on Gigalo pictured here.

The final section, COMPETITIONS AND RIDING SPORTS, presents the wide variety of equestrian sport that can be enjoyed. The section includes *Dressage, Show Jumping, Eventing, Endurance Riding, Flat Racing, Steeplechasing, Driving, Harness Racing, Vaulting,* and *The Pony Club and Gymkhanas.* Each unit gives an indication of what is involved and how to do them. *Other Sports* such as polo, hunting, Western show, and rodeo are also dealt with.

▲ **Winning rosettes makes all the hard work, time, and effort worth every bruise and sleepless night.**

To compete at the top requires years of dedication (and often frustration), but nothing can surpass the atmosphere of major competitions. Nothing is more exciting for you or your horse or pony than the roar of the crowd, the commentator's announcements, and the sensation of entering the ring to do your round and performance, or the track for a race, after all those months of hard work and training. Sometimes things go wrong, but even these disappointments are compensated for by the successful moments when things go well and you secure a coveted prize, rosette, or trophy that will be a reminder for many years of what you and your horse or pony have achieved together.

Throughout the book there are *Question & Answer* boxes on common problems on caring for your horse or pony and riding it properly. Many readers will have already asked these questions to themselves; many others will not have to ask them in the future.

Interspersed throughout the book are information boxes and feature boxes, such as those on "star horses," in appropriate chapters. Many of these feature boxes include personal accounts from people who work with horses in order to give an extra insight into the equestrian world!

This book will be an invaluable source of information for the horse lover and horse-owner whether your interest lies in competitive sports or if your real pleasure may be a solitary trail ride or a day with friends and family who share a similar pleasure—seeing the world from the back of a horse. Whatever your choice of activity, there is no doubt that for all of us who enjoy horses and riding, the care of, and companionship shared with, the animal of our choice gives an amazing amount of satisfaction.

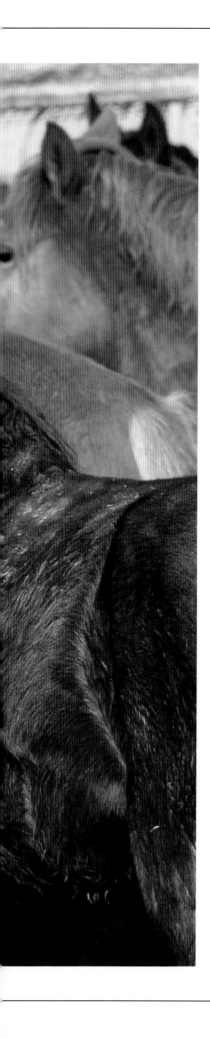

SECTION
1
Horse Basics

It was only in the last million years that *Equus caballus*, the forerunner of the modern horse, emerged—and developed into the animal we know today.

Eohippus, the first known ancestor of the horse, stood only three hands high (7.5cm), and it ate succulent leaves as it browsed through the swamp-like forests. Instead of hooves which we would recognize today, these creatures had four, weight-bearing pads, each with three hooved-toes. By 35 million years ago, this primitive animal had doubled in size to six hands (15cm) and became known as Mesohippus. It had also lost one of the weight-bearing toes and became faster.

Over the next ten million years, more changes took place. By 25 million years ago, Merychippus had evolved—now ten hands high (25cm) and running on central weight-bearing hooves with a reduced toe on each side of the cannon bones.

Early art such as this petroglyph, a carving into rock, found in Libya showing an early horse and rider have helped to build a picture of how our ancestors lived. This one may be using a bow to hunt for food.

EVOLUTION OF THE HORSE

Throughout history, we have long taken our partnership with the horse for granted. Both loyal friend and trusted servant, the horse has been used for everything from heavy agricultural work to sack races in the local gymkhana. Little wonder, you might think, that it has taken about 54 million years for the horse to develop from a small bear-like creature to the enormous diversity of breed and type that makes up the modern species.

At the same time, the jaw and teeth were changing. A definite gap was developing between the molars and tushes and Merychippus had teeth suitable for eating grass.

By ten million years ago, Pliohippus had appeared—characterized by single central hooves and no sign of the toes. The jaw line was longer, the teeth larger, and the animal was around 12 hands high (30cm).

EARLY "DOMESTIC" HORSES

Over the last one million years, dramatic changes have taken place. *Equus caballus* emerged and grew to a size that made domestication worthwhile. Horses appear to have been domesticated about 6,000 years ago, in Europe and Asia, although they are found in cave paintings from around 15000 B.C. Records exist that show man was riding the horse in 2637 B.C. Gradually, the horse's real worth started to be realized as the animal began to replace the ass for hauling loads and carriages, for entertainment, for war, and as a means of transportation.

Przewalski's horses are thought to be the ancestors of the modern horse. The massive head and spiky mane are typical of the breed. The pale muzzle and area around the eyes are also distinguishing features of other ancient breeds such as the Exmoor and Celtic pony.

By 1500 B.C., the Hittites (members of a great empire in North Syria and Asia Minor) had worked out how to deal with general horsemanship. The horse's presence spread throughout Assyria and Egypt, India and China, and its progress thereafter is well documented.

DIRECT ANCESTORS OF THE "MODERN" HORSE

Early evidence of *Equus caballus* appears to be confined to Asia and Africa where six distant species of wild *Equidae* still exist today or at least have been known in modern times. It is interesting to note that most equine fossil evidence exists in the United States, yet when the European colonists first reached the "New World" in the 15th century there were no live species to be found.

The main species of wild horse are:

Przewalski's Horse. This species roamed most of Asia. It still exists today (see Directory of Breeds, p. 52).

The Wild Ass. Originally from North Africa, the wild ass incorporates two subspecies—the Nubian Ass and the Somali Ass. It probably spread to Asia but did not reach Europe until the Middle Ages.

The Asiatic Wild Ass. Also known as a hemionid, it is a mixture between the horse and ass. Perhaps the best known is the onager of Persia, which was domesticated by the ancient Sumerians of Mesopotamia long before the arrival of the domesticated horse. Onagers are shown drawing chariots in carvings at The Royal Cemetry of Ur of Chaldees 2500 B.C.

Common or Plains Zebra. Found in Kenya and the Cape of Africa, this zebra has about five or six stripes on the flanks.

Mountain Zebra. Now confined to southwest Africa, this was the first zebra to be encountered by European settlers in Africa and is distinguishable by the "gridiron" striping over the base of the tail and about 12 stripes on the flanks.

The Quaggo. This animal once roamed Cape of Africa in huge herds but was completely exterminated by early settlers in the last century. It had no striping on the hindquarters.

Przewalski's Horses are the most likely ancestors of the modern strain of *Equus caballus*. In the early 1880s a group of hunters killed an unusual looking horse in the Gobi Desert, west of Mongolia. The skin and skull of this animal were sent to the Russian explorer, Nikolai M. Przewalski. After the specimens were examined, a new species was declared, named after Przewalski.

The Common or Plains Zebra with their spectacular markings roam in huge herds in parts of Africa. They have dark muzzles and a tufted end to their tails and spiky black and white manes similar to Przewalski's horse in texture.

HOW THE EQUUS HOOF EVOLVED

HYRACOTHERIUM OR EOHIPPUS
FORE AND HIND FEET Weight-bearing pad and 3 hooved toes

MESOHIPPUS
FORE AND HIND FEET Weight-bearing central hoof and 2 hooved toes

MERYCHIPPUS
FORE AND HIND FEET Weight-bearing central hooved toe. Two reduced side toes.

PLIOHIPPUS
FORE AND HIND FEET Weight-bearing central hooved toe. No recognizable side-toe.

EQUUS CABALLUS
FORE AND HIND FEET The final form of the hoof. The cannon bone is at its longest and no side-bone is apparent.

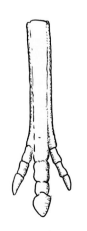

THE HORSE IN HISTORY

No one knows for certain when humans realized the potential of a close association with the horse. What is known is that this realization changed the history of humankind forever due to the use of horses in so many human activities, from transportation and use in agriculture to their deployment in warfare.

The drama and excitement of ancient chariot racing is depicted in this engraving which shows four horses pulling a cart from a single shaft. Much of the harness and leg protection is similar to that used today.

HORSES IN ANCIENT TIMES

Historians are still arguing over the region and the period when domestication of the horse took place, and by whom. It may well have been that several tribes had the same idea over a period of time, although one theory suggests that it was the nomadic steppe tribes of Eurasia, moving around the lands bordering the Caspian and Black Seas, who were first responsible. It is known, by depictions of working horses in ancient stone carvings, that the horse was being used to pull and carry in 2637 B.C., and it would not have been long before humans experimented by riding it.

By 1500 B.C., the Hittites were experienced horsemen, and stone clay tablets from this period have been discovered that give a comprehensive set of instructions on feeding, watering, exercise, grooming, bedding, and coping with problems. Shortly afterwards, people from other countries, such as China, India, Egypt, and Syria, became adept at coping with these new-found skills. In the centuries that followed, horses became trained in the skills of war. Suitable bridles for riding appeared gradually, making horses easier to handle, but as yet there were no saddles.

The great Greek general Xenophon (430–355 B.C.) was the author of one of the most complete books on horse management and training, much of which is still relevant today. His book gave details of breaking in horses, types of bits and tack for riding, as well as advice on feeding and general stable management. His thoughts and studies went on to influence future leaders such as the Macedonian prince, Alexander the Great, whose "civilization" of neighboring states was a remarkable feat of war. His faithful black horse, Bucephalus, was huge and extremely impressive, making it easier for the great leader to see around him. Thereafter, it became popular for generals and senior commanders to ride "high horses" to gain a better view of progress on the battlefield.

WAR-HORSES

Throughout history, horses have been instrumental in the development of new ideas and inventions. Body armor invented by the Romans to protect their cavalry became much heavier throughout the centuries, and meant that much larger horses were needed as mounts. So, for a time, heavy horses became popular in Europe, until the "age of chivalry" brought a period of relative peace.

During this period, in the Middle Ages, horses became used in entertainment. Jousting became a popular competitive sport, and also helped to increase fighting prowess for future battle. Tournaments took place involving knights on light Barbs or Arabs. While the strong war-horse had been ideal for carrying the heavy armor of the day, with the advent of fire power during the 17th century, warriors began to realize that lighter armor and speedier horses would be more effective. In time, the heavier horse was enlisted to pull the cannon and lighter breeds became popular for the cavalry.

FAMOUS HORSES OF WAR

Many horses throughout history have become immortalized from their performances in battle, from Alexander the Great's Bucephalus to the delightful Arab stallion, Marengo, ridden by Napoleon in so many conflicts. On the opposite side during the Napoleonic wars, the diminutive Copenhagen was the

▲ The heavy armor used in Europe in the Middle Ages must have made it very difficult for both the rider and horse to move quickly and effectively.

▼ Here you can see Napoleon, mounted on his famous white horse Marengo, in this dramatic wartime scene at Eylan.

The horse has been used in battle for centuries. In this scene, it is easy to see what vast numbers of riders made up formation line ups. When things went dramatically wrong, as in the Charge of the Light Brigade in 1854, hundreds of horses were killed. There have been numerous stories of great acts of courage on the battlefield by horse and human all through history.

favorite of the Duke of Wellington—despite lashing out at his master and nearly seriously injuring him after an exhausting day's fighting at the Battle of Waterloo.

In the United States, Robert E. Lee, commander of the Confederate forces and a great tactitian and master of military campaigns, rode his spirited gray—Traveler King—throughout the American Civil War.

The first American president, George Washington, was given the unbroken colt Firebrand for his 11th birthday. He trained him with sugar cubes, and soon it was said there wasn't a hedge high enough or a stream wide enough to stop this bold pair. Jackson, Lexington, Magnolia, Nelson, Ranger, and Royal Gift were all horses that were owned by Washington. It was on Lexington, who died at the Battle of Monmouth in 1778, that Washington was painted by John Trumbel.

BEASTS OF BURDEN

Just as horses have been invaluable in changing the face of war, their role in cultivating the land has been incalculable. Ever since the invention of the wheel, they have had to pull heavy loads and help till the earth, and frequently have been the only means of transportation. Even today, in some remote and mountainous regions, horses, asses, and mules are still performing the same essential functions.

The methods employed in plowing, harrowing, scything, and generally tilling the land were required to develop and improve and this necessity produced many ingenious inventions that enabled the horse to cope with the various types of work. Fundamental was the invention of the harness, which even in early times included a form of collar or breaststrap to enable the horse to pull against a large bearing area, however primitive the equipment. Eventually, breeching straps were designed to take the weight of vehicles when going downhill and to help prevent them from pushing up against the horse. However, it took a long time for these to be perfected, and no doubt many an accident occurred.

As roads were improved and upgraded, horse-drawn vehicles quickly improved in design and comfort. Many were adapted for different uses, such as stage and mail coaches.

The horse contributed so much to people's everyday way of life, it became a necessity.

Robert E. Lee, the American General who commanded the Confederate Army, was devoted to his horses, particularly his favorite Traveler King.

◄ The tranquillity of the mare and foal in the center of this study, highlights both the temperament we so admire and the reasons for our dependence on the horse. Everything from delivering mail to the turning of wheels is shown. Transportation, work, leisure, war—we should not forget that there are still many places in the world where we still rely on the horse.

▼ This carousel in the Winter Riding School by M. von Meytens in 1743 typifies the surge of interest in all things equestrian during the Renaissance in Europe. *Haute Ecole* or high-school movements were taught and many of the great classical riding schools trained riders to become teachers of the new art throughout Europe.

EQUESTRIAN SKILLS AND HORSE TRAINING

During the Renaissance, riding became recognized as a skill in its own right—alongside the classical arts of music, painting, and literature. Every nobleman was encouraged in the art of riding, and training schools sprang up throughout Europe. A remnant of these is still in existence in the world-famous Spanish Riding School in Vienna. Xenophon's high-school movements (or "airs" above the ground), devised for use in ancient battles, were rediscovered and used as an art.

There were many great teachers spreading the word during the Renaissance. Circuses were a popular form of entertainment and the Italian circus horse trainer, Piguatelle, from Naples, realized that kindness was more effective with the circus horses. His kind teaching methods spread around the great European schools, which were beginning to adopt a lighter type of horse for riding.

Piguatelle's student, De Pluvinal, carried on the teachings of his master, refining his training methods even more. He was the first to introduce work between the "pillars" to perform specialized movements, especially the famous "airs above the ground." Patience and quietness in breaking and all training were his watchwords, and he was instrumental in bringing many new ideas to the traditional training methods in Europe.

William Cavendish, Duke of Newcastle, was the only English master of classical riding. He had trained in Naples and started a school in Belgium, which he later transferred to Bolsover Castle in Britain. A perfectionist and hard taskmaster, this influential man realized that the horse had the capacity to memorize. In 1658, he published a book on training horses, in which he stated that, "often repetition fortifies the memory."

In France, the father of classical equitation, François

Robichon de la Gueniniere (1658–1751), was a major influence. His work, *Ecole de Cavalerie*, remains the basis for modern equitation, the "shoulder-in" being one of his most important exercises for straightening the horse. He also designed the modern low cantle and pommel saddle.

The French schools of Versailles and Saumur, and the Spanish Riding School, dominated classical teachings up until the World Wars, by which time equitation was already well established. The schools put on many equestrian entertainments, especially carousels and circus acts, which were enhanced by music and sumptuous clothes.

Today, it is in the world of competition that horses play their main role—from gymkhana games to Grand Prix dressage, from polo to horse racing. Horses may no longer fulfill a need on which humankind's very survival depends, but they are loved and revered as pets, and as partners in sport all over the world.

From earliest times, cave paintings have depicted horses, asses, and zebras. It is thanks to these early depictions that so much has been learned about the domestication of the horse and the lifestyles of those who used them. Certain characteristics, particularly those of Arab influence, can be seen in several cave paintings found scattered throughout Europe, Asia, and Africa, many dating back beyond 15,000 B.C.

The tombs of the Pharaohs offer a wonderful insight into how horses were used by the Ancient Egyptians, with detailed reliefs and friezes showing them in all kinds of activities. The clarity and detail are extraordinary in the various types of art demonstrated. The Greeks and Romans were particularly enthusiastic about depicting everyday scenes and battles on their friezes, and it is easy to see the tremendous influence played by the horse on these great civilizations. There are numerous magnificent statues of horses with or without famous riders in every great capital of the world.

Perhaps one of the most extraordinary historical finds was the army of terracotta horses and soldiers found in Xi An, the ancient capital of China, dating from around A.D. 700. Hundreds of these red-clay model horses were buried with the emperors to protect them on their journey to the next life.

Illustrated manuscripts and frescos have provided a wealth of information about how horses have been used in war, in agriculture, and in sport throughout the centuries. Most countries can claim to have superb examples in their museums and private collections, and much value is placed on the type of historical detail that they supply. Battle scenes give an indication of changes of weaponry, dress, and military tactics, as well as the type of horse used by the combatants—all frozen in one moment of time. Several artists specialized in depicting their famous subjects on horseback, especially monarchs, generals, and nobles—all looking magnificent with the clothes, tack, and horses of the day.

THE HORSE IN ART

It is not difficult to understand why the horse is so widely seen in paintings and sculptures in every corner of the earth. Not only its renowned beauty but also its contribution to world history have ensured that the horse has a special place in art.

GEORGE STUBBS

One of the greatest equestrian painters, George Stubbs, earned the label "Mr. Stubbs the Horse Painter" in his own lifetime (1724–1806). Largely self-taught, he believed that "nature is superior to art"— not always a popular assertion at the time. His passionate interest in dissection, which resulted in such natural and anatomically accurate drawings brought new dimensions to animal art. It also resulted in a certain vitality and dignity which were previously unknown.

His famous work on the *Anatomy of the Horse* not only required months of research but also included the physical dissection of several animals to enable him to study every aspect. He recorded each muscle layer, the internal organs, and the veins and arteries, right down to the skeleton itself. To achieve this, apparently he had to suspend his subject from a series of hooks on a hoist and iron bars to get a true representation. As he was a tanner by trade, it is easier to understand how Stubbs was able to perform this incredible work in what must have been unsavory conditions to say the

least. This work is considered to be one of the greatest contributions to animal knowledge and understanding in the last millennium.

Before Stubbs, it was common to see magnificent paintings depicting horses looking wooden or anatomically incorrect. He brought the knowledge to introduce real life and movement into equestrian portraits, and was one of the first painters to understand the horse's true action.

One of Stubbs' most famous subjects—"a horse attacked by a lion"—of which he painted several variations. Power, fear, beauty are all depicted in this dramatic picture.

OTHER ARTISTS

Lack of understanding of horse anatomy is evident in the work of artists such as Van Dyck (1599–1641), who was responsible for many splendid portraits of mounted kings and nobles on impressive steeds. Another artist, John Wootton, was unable to remove the stiff-legged appearance of horses at the gallop,

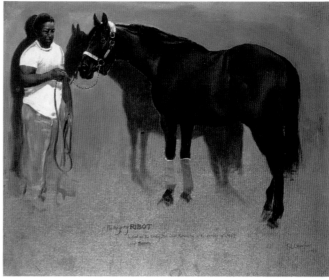

◄ *Philip II of Spain* by Velásquez is a charming picture in every way, but shows a relative lack of knowledge of horse anatomy when compared to Stubbs'.

▲ This delightful painting of the great Ribot by Susan Crawford charms by its simplicity and directness.

a pace too fast for accurate observation by the human eye. The common pose of horses galloping in "the rocking horse position" was to remain until the advent of movies could demonstrate the diversity of movement throughout the pace.

More modern artists, such as the celebrated Sir Alfred Munnings (1878–1959), produced an amazingly diverse collection of paintings—from racing scenes to fairgrounds and from work horses to portraits. Many of these can be found in Britain and the United States, where he worked regularly.

Snaffles—the British caricaturist whose hunting and wartime pictures were world-renowned—brought a certain thoughtfulness into his work.

Richard Stone Reeves's numerous portraits in the United States are popular, and Susan Crawford's exquisitely detailed works show how much the camera has enabled modern artists to study in minute detail every aspect of their noble subjects.

In bronze, the horse is equally well represented. Most major cities and racecourses in the world can boast magnificent statues in bronze. Small bronzes sell at huge prices at auction, perhaps the best known created by the great Mene.

Cecil Aldin's works were typical of many of the caricaturists who brought humor into their work at the beginning of the 20th century. This everyday scene was inspired by Dickens' Pickwickians outside "The Bull" in Rochester. Note the expressions of humans and horse!

In police work, the horse can be found standing patiently at public events, controlling crowds, monitoring traffic duty, patrolling national parks in the American West and in Canada, and carrying officers to places inaccessible to vehicles.

On most ranches, the horse is still the main means of getting about to check stock and to round up cattle, horses, and sheep. On plantations around the world, they still play a role in getting among the crops and finding out what is going on. Many a ranch or plantation manager still prefers to ride, insisting one can see and do more from the back of a horse than from a vehicle, and will often add a few words about the horse not running out of fuel—presumably taking a dig at those people who have relied on cars and trucks and not always thoroughly prepared themselves for the vast distances which can be covered in some areas!

This horse is "logging" in a National Park where vehicles could cause severe damage to the land.

THE ROLE OF THE HORSE IN MODERN TIMES

Today the horse still plays a major role in our everyday life. In spite of mechanization and hi-tech inventions, few machines can match the horse for its versatility, toughness, and maneuverability in many different situations throughout the world.

In the more remote areas, the horse is often found to be preferable to expensive machinery for tilling the land. Carefully handled by those experienced in the art of horse-drawn plowing, drilling, and harrowing, and used for carting hay, straw, and other crops, the horse can pay for itself ten times over. The heavy breeds, renowned for their strength, are regularly used to pull timber on hills throughout the world where access can be a problem or where vehicles could cause excessive damage to the land.

It is still a common sight outside developed countries to see deliveries of coal and other commodities being done with a horse and cart. In some of the less-well-off areas where roads are not kept up or have never been good anyway, the long suffering horse will trudge its way through the streets where many a truck or delivery vehicle would soon break down. The horse has also always been a favorite with tourists wishing to be driven in elegant carriages to local attractions and through fashionable areas as people were before the days of modern motorized travel.

Mounted police in Kentucky's famous Horse Park, in the United States, show the patience required of a horse that will spend many hours of the day standing and watching.

The cow horse is a vital part of the cowboy's way of life in North and South America, as well as to the stockmen of Australia. Here in Texas, cattle driving is a regular chore.

Trekking centers cater to tourists wanting to ride through the more beautiful open areas around the world—the Grand Canyon or the Rocky Mountains in the United States, the foothills of Africa's Mount Kenya and Table Mountain, and Snowdonia in Wales. There are so many venues where seeing the world around you from the back of a horse is something so special and different, it truly does make for that once-in-a-lifetime vacation.

The horse in sport has had a profound effect on many people's lives. There are so many different occasions where the horses give great pleasure to spectators regardless of whether they can ride or just enjoy watching them for their extraordinary beauty and versatility. For many physically challenged people learning and mastering horse riding skills gives a new dimension to life.

Few, if any, other animals give so much pleasure. From the child whose first pony has brought many months of happiness, frustration, and triumphs as different skills are mastered, secrets shared, and problems coped with, to the race-goers watching Thoroughbreds on the flat or over fences, trotters, or Quarter Horses—exciting events whether they've placed a bet or not.

Then there are the thousands who ride purely for fun and pleasure, the camaraderie, and the relaxation. They all testify to their belief that the horse is truly a person's best friend.

This heavy Belgium horse can pull this type of sleigh in Colorado across a partially snow-covered area with little, if any, difficulty.

THE HORSE IN ENTERTAINMENT

Throughout history, the horse has long been celebrated in entertainment—whether chariot racing in Ancient Rome or jousting in the Middle Ages. Horses still have the power to excite, enthrall, and keep us on the edge of our seats.

Today, there is more opportunity than ever to see this noble animal in action, whether it is in the flesh at sports events or shows, or on the screen in movies and on television.

HORSES ON DUTY AND DISPLAY

Additionally, there are shows or displays involving horses that have been trained to do a specific job, and for whom the task of performing is just a secondary function. Police horses, for example, are just as at home controlling fans at soccer and football matches as they are performing for fans at special displays. Similarly, the Royal Canadian Mounted Police—or "Mounties"—are recognized a long way from home by virtue of their displays set to music. Just for show, however, Britain's Household Cavalry demonstrate traditional—though no longer applicable—warfaring skills, which have made them a hit on parade grounds around the world.

▲ Two world famous scenes: the Canadian Mounted Police or "Mounties" who along with their everyday work appear in displays regularly, and the British King's Troop who give breathtaking displays pulling heavy guns. ▶

CIRCUS AND FIESTAS

Most circus horses tend to work closely with their riders, but Liberty horses are a riderless team of formation dancers who excel at dancing in a team. With feathered headdresses tossing, they will weave and re-weave the complex patterns of a waltz without any mistakes and this is where the ringmaster's whip really comes into its own. No one in the circus would ever use the whip to hit an animal. A spoken command would never carry over the music, so the Liberty horses wheel and spin to cues from the whip. Proud and beautiful, they are usually Arabs or small Thoroughbreds and up to 12 can dance in the ring at the same time.

Liberty horses spend years of gruelling training before they are finally allowed to perform in a professional circus. They are specially chosen for their skill in dancing and their calm characters. They must not be put off by the antics of the clowns who may perform alongside them, or be distracted by the cheers of the crowd.

The Haute Ecole or high-school horses are usually Spanish, Portuguese or Friesian in origin. They need to be large enough to carry their riders who perform spectacular dressage movements such as the "airs above the ground" as the high leaps are called, which take great strength. With muscles sliding smoothly under the velvet skin, these big, beautiful stallions can carry a full-grown man straight up into the air with a standing jump and land as lightly as a cat.

Rosinbacks are nearly always mares and are usually Shires or French crosses. They must have the strength to support the ballerinas who dance on them, with wide backs providing

These highly-trained Liberty horses are performing one of the carefully choreographed movements which are so popular with circus audiences.

space and support. These horses are known as rosinbacks because of the resin powder which is spread over their quarters to give a safe landing for the horse dancers.

In Spain, at the fiestas, the colorful scenes of horses and their riders in traditional costumes all add to the special sense of occasion. Similarly, there is a great degree of showmanship in the bullring, with the mounted bullfighters and their highly trained horses.

The colorful spectacle of the Spanish fiestas is enhanced here by the flared costume of the girl sitting beside her escort.

HORSES IN LITERATURE

In legend and literature, many great stories have been based on the exploits of man and horse—for example, Don Quixote and Rosinante, and Dick Turpin and Black Bess. Hunting yarns abound, the best loved including the John Surtees stories of Jorrocks and the poems of Siegfried Sassoon. Anna Sewell's powerful *Black Beauty* has probably done more for the plight of the horse than any other book, by highlighting the conditions in which many horses were expected to work in 19th-century England.

▶ *The Lone Ranger* with its hero mounted on his spectacular gray "Silver" was just one of the many wonderful Western movies where the horse was as much a star as its rider!

▼ The popularity of stories about the special relationship between children and horses were once again demonstrated by the huge success of the movie *The Black Stallion*.

HORSES IN THE MOVIES

The emergence of television brought with it a wealth of equestrian entertainment, including the thrilling depictions of life in the Wild West. Such favorites as the Lone Ranger on his rearing gray Silver, and Champion, the Wonder Horse, were awaited impatiently on a weekly basis by millions of young fans around the world.

Big feature movies in the 1940s, such as *National Velvet*, starring Elizabeth Taylor, were hugely successful at the time. Its more recent 1970s sequel, *International Velvet*, encouraged

"From the moment he first saw the stallion, he knew it would either destroy him, or carry him where no one had ever been before..."

FRANCIS FORD COPPOLA
PRESENTS
the
Black Stallion

generations of Pony Club riders to aim for stardom. *The Black Stallion* was yet another movie from the 1970s to provide a glamorous partnership between a young person and a horse.

More recently there has been a resurgence of the Western movie with the huge success of *Dances with Wolves* in 1992, which included fantastic riding sequences—especially the famous buffalo hunt scenes.

COMPETITION PARTNERSHIPS

However, it is not just in movies that audiences have the chance to see such partnerships. They exist in real life, with numerous combinations excelling in the competitive field. The elegant art of dressage, including such intricate movements as the *piaffe* and *passage*, is breathtaking in the power and precision displayed, with the horses literally appearing to dance to the music. In show jumping and eventing, the close cooperation between horse and rider is clearly evident when the two jump huge show jumps or plunge into the spectacular lake at the Badminton Three-Day Event. The endurance riders' determination not to overexert their horses, while maintaining a steady rhythm over such long distances, involves a well-organized team.

Here Elizabeth Taylor mounts Velvet in the all time classic MGM movie *National Velvet.* Such movies really tugged on the heartstrings of their vast audiences, many of whom had never even seen a horse close up.

The dual Olympic Gold Medalist in Eventing, Mark Todd and his horse, Charisma, have achieved their "stardom" through unrelenting dedication and hard work.

The partnership is critical to success in every equine sport, and it is the bond that makes for those special, much-admired winners at the top. These include the great showjumper Milton and his rider, John Whitaker; the eventer Mark Todd and his tiny horse Charisma; double Olympic Gold Medalist Nicole Uphoff and her exuberant mount, Rembrandt. In the racing world, the horses often came out on top as they had different jockeys on many occasions, but such stars as the great Man O' War, Native Dancer, and Secretariat have become household names.

DIRECTORY OF BREEDS

The 50 different breeds described include the three main types of equine animals— ponies, horses, and heavy working breeds. Each have specific characteristics which are unique; some are particularly pure while others have been adapted by selective breeding over the years to meet with modern requirements.

A horse's temperament is the most important attribute for the rider to consider, especially if the horse is to be ridden by children. Some will be ideal while others perhaps a little too quick for a young child, so it is essential to choose the right one depending on what role you have in mind.

The Thoroughbred or Arab being bred for speed and who possesses a very high degree of intelligence, is unlikely to be suitable for a newcomer to the sport. The small child needs a steady conveyance, and Britain's native ponies or one of the newer American breeds such as the Pony of the Americas are ideal for this task.

Size will also determine what might be suitable for a specific rider, but strength is also critical in choosing a horse or pony. The powerful Welsh Cob and Haflinger, to name two, make ideal riding horses even though they are not very big. Being over-horsed by riding something too large and strong can be a recipe for disaster.

Many of the breeds mentioned here are crossed with others, and often combine the best attributes of both parents. This works particularly well with some of the larger pony breeds put to small Thoroughbreds—the result being a really useful Pony Clubber for children or general riding horse.

After reading this section, you will soon be able to recognize certain unique features in the different breeds, such as the Appaloosa spots, the flared nostrils and flowing mane and tail of the Arab, the mealy muzzle and toad eyes of the little Exmoor, the spiky white edged mane with the black center of the Norwegian Fjord, or the golden color and white mane of the Palomino. You will also notice that the descriptions of color for the breeds are often very specific about what face or leg markings are permissible. These white markings are used in the descriptions of individual horses on documentation, such as their passports. The information below should help you identify these markings.

FACE MARKINGS

A star—a small white area usually fairly centrally placed between the eyes.
A stripe—a thin white strip down the center of the face.
A blaze—a broad white area down the center of the face.
A snip—a white area over one nostril or part of the nose.
A white face—most of the front of the face is white, and may even spread around the eyes.

1. Star

2. Stripe

3. Blaze

4. Snip

5. White Face

EUROPEAN BREEDS

This versatile and distinctively colored breed is becoming more and more popular for a wide variety of activities.

HAFLINGER

COUNTRY OF ORIGIN: Austria
HEIGHT: 13.1–14.2hh (135–147 cm)
COLOR: Palomino or chestnut with distinctive flaxen mane and tail.
CHARACTERISTICS: The Tyrolean mountains were the native home of this tough breed, and it remained fairly isolated for centuries at heights of up to 6,400 feet (2,000 m). Consequently, the breed evolved only gradually, but was originally probably a cross between local mountain ponies and Arabs brought back from the fighting in Italy in the 6th century. Haflingers have small heads with a slight "dish," strong backs and limbs, and a well-set tail. The distinctive coloring can be traced back to Folie, an Arab stallion used to upgrade the breed 150 years ago. The color is now 99 percent inherited.

Haflingers make ideal driving, trekking, and riding ponies. Their versatility enables them to take part in a wide variety of different activities.

LIPIZZANER

COUNTRY OF ORIGIN: Austria
HEIGHT: 15–16hh (152–163 cm)
COLOR: Gray (occasionally black). Born dark, they generally lighten with time.
CHARACTERISTICS: Famous for their high school work at the Spanish Riding School in Vienna, Lipizzaners were founded by Archduke Charles of Austria at the stud at Lipizza in 1580 from nine stallions and 24 mares, based on Andalusian stock. Since 1735, records have been kept, and it is known that all of today's Lipizzaners descended from six stallions still based on Andalusian breeding. The stud is now at Piber in Austria.

Lipizzaners have a high-stepping movement, a fine outlook, tremendous power in the quarters and a tractable temperament. They are used mainly for dressage but also make excellent driving and riding horses. They have been crossed with other breeds to produce combined-driving horses.

This magnificent breed are world-renowned for their fantastic dressage displays and "Airs above the Ground" performances.

ARDENNES (ARDENNAIS)

COUNTRY OF ORIGIN: Belgium and France (Ardennes)
HEIGHT: 15.1–16.1hh (155–165 cm)
COLOR: Bay or roan, occasionally bay or liver chestnut.
CHARACTERISTICS: This ancient horse has been bred up in the hills of the Ardennes for almost 2,000 years. Tough and energetic, it has been used as a war-horse throughout the ages – both Caesar and Nero having favored its ancestors. Napoleon, too, used a smaller version to mount his army, as did the Dutch during World War II. Over time, the infusion of some Arab blood has helped to refine the breed, which is renowned for its ability to cope with harsh climates.

The Ardennes is a stocky animal with short legs and little feather (long hair on the hocks). It has a small head and straight face, and is thick through the jowl. It is still used for draft (draught) work in France, Belgium, and Sweden, where it is considered "the best tractor for hill or forest work."

The power and strength of these horses is combined with a very tough constitution, making them ideal for hill and forest work.

PERCHERON

COUNTRY OF ORIGIN: France (La Perche)
HEIGHT: 15.2–19hh (157–192 cm)
COLOR: Gray or black.
CHARACTERISTICS: The Percheron is one of the most popular heavy breeds in the world, renowned for its power, temperament, and looks. It is also one of the oldest breeds and originates from the horses left by the Moors in A.D. 732 that crossed with the heavy Flemish horses. The influence of more Arab blood during the Crusades is probably responsible for the air of elegance so evident in the breed today.

The Percheron has a distinctive small head with prominent eyes and a strong, sturdy body with short legs and little feather. Percherons are remarkably tough and energetic workers, and survive on relatively little food for their size. Today, they are still used for agricultural purposes, as well as for showing and displays. They are popular in the United States, Argentina, and many countries in Europe.

The elegance of the Percheron's head gives this popular and ancient breed a special place in the show ring.

SELLE FRANÇAIS

COUNTRY OF ORIGIN: France
HEIGHT: 15.3–16.2hh (160–168 cm)
COLOR: Mostly chestnut, but other strong colors permissible.
CHARACTERISTICS: The Selle Français was formed from the amalgamation of half-bred hotblood and coldblood horses (see p. 55) in France in 1958. Everything other than the Thoroughbred, Arab and Anglo-Arab was brought together under this heading, which in reality has become the French warmblood. Most of the encompassed breeds were evolved from the Norman war-horse, with infusions of Arab, Thoroughbred and Trotter blood over the centuries. The majority have records tracing bloodlines back for many generations, and today they are refined to an even greater extent for their specific competitive roles.

The Selle Français now falls into three distinct divisions. The most famous is that of the competition horses. The second section comprises racehorses – mostly those that race over fences. These horses also make excellent eventers. The third section covers the non-specialist group used for general riding and trail riding.

The Selle Français is one of the most highly sought after competition breeds in all Olympic disciplines.

CLEVELAND BAY

COUNTRY OF ORIGIN: Great Britain (Cleveland area)
HEIGHT: 16–16.2hh (163–168 cm)
COLOR: Bay with black points (no white permitted).
CHARACTERISTICS: This clean legged bay horse with black points (legs, mane, and tail) combines substance, strength, and stamina with quality and an excellent temperament. It has very strong tough feet, which are always black (referred to as "blue" because of the special intensity of color). It is the oldest established breed of English horse, and was bred in the North East for centuries.

Often known as "Chapmans," because of their former popularity with traveling salesmen, they were used for riding and as carriage horses. Blood introduced from the Darley Arabian in the 18th century helped to improve speed.

Today, the Cleveland is renowned as a show animal, hunter, and carriage horse. Pure and part-bred Clevelands have excelled in all the Olympic disciplines.

Excellent as a driving horse, Clevelands crossed with Thoroughbreds have produced many outstanding sporthorses.

DARTMOOR

COUNTRY OF ORIGIN: Great Britain (Dartmoor)
HEIGHT: Up to 12.2hh (127 cm)
COLOR: Most solid colors but usually bay or brown – no piebald or skewbald. Few white markings.
CHARACTERISTICS: This small, sturdy, and attractive breed boasts a typically neat head with little pony ears and an intelligent outlook. It is medium-boned, and has good sloping shoulders and reasonable length of neck.

The Dartmoor's ancestors roamed the southernmost area of England for centuries – one was even named in the will of a Saxon bishop in 1012. Most modern Dartmoors, however, have been influenced by Arab blood introduced in the early part of this century.

Noted for its quiet, kind temperament, the Dartmoor is a perfect first child's pony. It has free-flowing paces, making it a comfortable, easy ride, and is a good all-rounder. Once upon a time you would have found it working in the tin mines, but these days it is more at home hacking, jumping, hunting, or being driven.

One of the nine native British breeds, the very versatile Dartmoor makes an ideal child's pony.

EXMOOR

This Exmoor is not showing much of the pale mealy coloring round its eyes and muzzle but this will be more apparent with its paler winter coat.

COUNTRY OF ORIGIN: Great Britain (Exmoor)
HEIGHT: Up to 12.3hh (129 cm)
COLOR: Bay, brown or dun with distinctive mealy markings around eyes, nostrils, and inside flanks. No white at all.
CHARACTERISTICS: The Exmoor is the oldest of the British breeds and is said to conform almost identically to the original British wild pony of 130,000 years ago. Extremely hardy, it has a unique hard and springy coat to help insulate the animal in the cold, wet weather, and has distinctive toad eyes. It is probably the ancestor of other British native breeds but is remarkable for the purity of type maintained in one area around Exmoor.

Registered ponies have to pass a rigorous inspection before they can be accepted by the Exmoor Pony Society. They are then branded with the society's star and a number.

A kind, amenable temperament makes the Exmoor an excellent child's pony, although its strength makes it quite capable of carrying adults as well.

CLYDESDALE

COUNTRY OF ORIGIN: Great Britain (Scotland)
HEIGHT: 16.3–18hh (170–183 cm)
COLOR: Bay or brown with white stripe or blaze on the face and white limbs often extending over the knees and hocks.
CHARACTERISTICS: This heavy horse was developed specifically to meet the demands of the Industrial Revolution that swept Britain in the 18th and 19th centuries. Local hardy mares were crossed with imported larger and heavier stallions, mostly Dutch or Flemish, to produce horses that were capable of various types of work. The result was an animal of tremendous strength, with powerful shoulders and well-muscled backs and quarters. The Clydesdale has a straight head, with kind, intelligent eyes and large ears, and there is an abundance of feather on the legs.

Clydesdales are still used for work on farms, for deliveries, for showing and breeding. They are exported in large numbers to the United States and other countries.

One of the most spectacular of the working horses, Clydesdales are widely used in the show ring as well.

DALES

COUNTRY OF ORIGIN: Great Britain (Eastern Pennines)
HEIGHT: 13.2–14.2hh (137–147 cm)
COLOR: Black, brown, occasionally gray or bay. A white star or snip are the only permissible markings.
CHARACTERISTICS: This strong, intelligent pony is a versatile all-rounder for children and adults alike. Similar to its close relative the Fell, the Dales has a neat pony-like head, good sloping shoulders, and a lush mane and tail, but it is taller and has less feather. Originally, it was used as a pack pony, particularly for transporting lead from the mines across the rough ground to the ports. It was crossed with various other breeds such as the speedy Norfolk Trotter, Scottish Galloway (now extinct), Welsh Cob, and the Clydesdale, which may have given it the extra height over the Fell. Only the toughest survived, as the largest and most powerful were used as pack animals or for further breeding. Some were used in the foundation of the Thoroughbred breed.

Popular for trekking and general riding, the Dales is also ideal for shepherding, endurance, and driving.

This tough and versatile breed has changed little since early times and is an ideal all-rounder.

The power of the Highlands has enabled them to transport game down mountain tracks inaccessible to motorized vehicles.

HIGHLAND

COUNTRY OF ORIGIN: Great Britain (Scotland)
HEIGHT: 13–14.2hh (132–147 cm)
COLOR: Dun, gray, brown, or black. Most have a dorsal eel stripe and may have zebra stripes inside fore and hind legs. White markings are not favored, except for a small star.
CHARACTERISTICS: The Highland has influenced Scotland's history for centuries, being the country's main source of transportation and of tremendous importance as a pack animal – particularly for sportsmen carrying game. Hardy and sure-footed, Highlands have neat, broad heads with strong necks, backs, and quarters, set on short limbs with little feather. An unusual coat of coarse hair over a soft down enables them to cope with the harsh Scottish climate.

Because of their strength and temperament the Highlands' use has extended from pulling felled trees to shepherding. They also make excellent children's ponies.

NEW FOREST

COUNTRY OF ORIGIN: Great Britain (New Forest)
HEIGHT: 12–14hh (122–142 cm)
COLOR: Bay and brown, but all colors except piebald, skewbald, or blue-eyed cream.
CHARACTERISTICS: The New Forest is a versatile breed that tends to be narrower in structure than most other British natives. It has an easy, straight movement and a good temperament.

Records show there were horses roaming free in the New Forest area in the 11th century, but it was not until the 1800s that serious efforts were made to improve and standardize the breed. These days, the New Forest is bred and exported worldwide for a variety of different uses, although it is also crossed with other native breeds, Thoroughbreds, and Arabs to produce a highly popular riding pony suitable for all the family.

These versatile ponies are great favorites worldwide as children's ponies and are widely exported.

FELL

COUNTRY OF ORIGIN: Great Britain (Western Pennines)
HEIGHT: 13.1–14hh (135–142 cm)
COLOR: Black, brown, bay, and occasionally gray.
CHARACTERISTICS: Closely related to the Dales pony, the Fell has roamed around the west side of the Pennine hills in Cumbria, Northern England, since earliest recorded times. As with the Dales, and probably the Shire as well, the breed was influenced by the influx of large black stallions brought in by Friesland labor during the building of Hadrian's Wall in A.D. 120. The mix this produced has remained virtually unaltered ever since, and is characterized by a pony-like head with a long, thick mane and tail and plenty of silky feather on the legs.

Fell ponies are well used in a variety of different activities, particularly as pack animals and for trekking, riding, and driving. Their energy is tremendous, but they lack the speed to outpace competitors in top-class driving competitions.

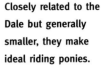

Closely related to the Dale but generally smaller, they make ideal riding ponies.

HACKNEY

COUNTRY OF ORIGIN: Great Britain
HEIGHT: Ponies – up to 14.1hh (144 cm)
Horses – up to 15.3hh (160 cm)
COLOR: Bay, brown, black, and chestnut.
CHARACTERISTICS: The combination of high-stepping action and tremendous presence is unique to the Hackney, whether horse or pony. Originally, it was bred from trotters in Norfolk, Yorkshire, and Cambridge, and the result was a carriage horse with elegance and a spirited temperament. The name is thought to derive from the French word *haquenée*, meaning "horse for hire," as hackneys were often used as taxis on city streets (and still are in many tourist areas around the world).

Hackneys can trot at remarkable speeds – often up to 24 miles (39 km) per hour – and were in their heyday during the mid-18th and 19th centuries before mechanized transportation superseded them. Today, they are still enormously popular. They are exported worldwide for driving and have been successfully crossed with other breeds to produce competition sporthorses.

Hackneys generally have a high tail carriage and carry their heads high too, giving an air of elegance to their already spectacular movement.

SHETLAND

COUNTRY OF ORIGIN: Great Britain
(Shetland Islands)
HEIGHT: Up to 10.2hh (107 cm)
COLOR: Black, bay, brown, chestnut,
gray, skewbald, and piebald.
CHARACTERISTICS: The smallest of the
British breeds, this tiny animal
remained untouched in its native
islands for centuries until taken to the
mainland in the 19th century. It is the
strongest "horse" in the world relative
to its size, is extremely tough, and has
played a unique part in the islands'
history – carting huge loads of peat,
minerals, seaweed, and other heavy
loads. Its "dwarf" features are unique
to the breed, although it is similar in
type to the Exmoor.

Now, the Shetland is used for
driving, as a pet, and as a child's
pony. It is also regularly ridden by
adults as well in the Shetland Islands

being used as a working animal. In the
U.S. the Shetland is popular for adult
purposes for driving and halter classes.

**Although a children's favorite, it is the
strongest horse for its size in the world and
capable of carrying adults. It is the smallest of
the nine British native breeds.**

**Shires have profuse
feather which needs
careful tending to
ensure the legs and
heels remain
healthy especially in
wet conditions.**

SHIRE

COUNTRY OF ORIGIN: Great Britain
(Midlands and Fens)
HEIGHT: 16–18hh (163–183 cm)
COLOR: Black, sometimes bay, brown,
and gray.
CHARACTERISTICS: Gentle giant is an
apt name for this massive, impressive
horse, with its slightly roman nose and
long neck on strong back and quarters.
It has short, strong legs with copious
amounts of feather and is a good,
straight mover.

Shires are thought to have
originated from Old English Black
Horses of the Middle Ages or the Great
Horses on which knights rode into
battle. They were used for carting
during Britain's industrial heyday,
but now they are more likely to be
found being driven under magnificent
harness at ceremonial or show displays.
For breeding purposes, they have
been successfully crossed with
Thoroughbreds to produce
high-class hunters.

THOROUGHBRED

RED RUM

Red Rum's Grand National wins at Aintree are legendary and unlikely ever to be repeated. He had a narrow win in 1973, an easy one in 1974, followed by two seconds in 1975 and 1976. Then he won again in 1977 and created a unique record. His pricked ears and superb jumping endeared him to the British public in a way never seen before or since.

Retired shortly afterwards, Red Rum became a national institution, appearing at fund raising events.

COUNTRY OF ORIGIN: Great Britain
HEIGHT: 14.2–17.2hh (147–178 cm)
COLOR: All solid colors.
CHARACTERISTICS: The Thoroughbred is the fastest and (since it became a breed in its own right) most influential breed in the world – renowned for both its intelligence and wonderful sweeping action. It is finely proportioned, with no feather on the legs, yet it is extremely tough.

The breed originated in 17th-century Britain, thanks primarily to the reigning monarch, King Charles II, and his great passion for horse racing. He wanted to improve the quality of animals available for the sport, and so imported Oriental stock to breed with the horses used in Britain at the time. Records were kept, and finally the breed became established from three important stallions from which every Thoroughbred can trace its ancestry. First was the Byerley Turk, who left life on the battlefield for a stud in the North of England in 1689. Then came the Darley Arabian, who was brought from Syria to Yorkshire in 1704. Lastly, the Godolphin Arabian was bought from the King of France in the early 1720s and used with the emerging better types of mare to consolidate the breed.

Flying Childers, born in 1715, was the first "great" British racehorse, unbeaten in all his races. Later, Eclipse, also undefeated in 18 races, became a legend and his progeny inherited much of his talent.

Originally, races were over distances of anything up to 12 miles (19 km), and demanded tough, weight-carrying animals. Gradually, speed took over as the all-important factor. Races became shorter, because of the enthusiasm for using younger horses, so stamina became less significant. Short races known as sprints developed into the "classic," "middle distance," and "stayer" events we know today. Jumping races also evolved, and branched off into events ranging from timber races and amateur point-to-points to steeplechases – the Maryland Hunt Cup and Britain's Grand National being two of the most famous.

Thoroughbreds excel at other sports, such as dressage, eventing, and show jumping. They have also been crossed successfully with numerous breeds including the various warmblood breeds, to produce versatile horses for various sports.

This outstanding breed is fundamental to the sport of racing worldwide, both on the flat and over fences. It is also an excellent cross with other breeds for producing sporthorses.

WELSH

COUNTRY OF ORIGIN: Great Britain (Wales)

HEIGHT: Section A—up to 12.2hh (127 cm)

Sections B and C—up to 13.2hh (137 cm)

Section D—13.2hh (137 cm) and above

COLOR: Any color except piebald and skewbald.

CHARACTERISTICS: Renowned for its beauty, toughness, intelligence, and versatility, the Welsh breed has been divided into four distinct types and sizes.

Section A—the Welsh Mountain Pony—is the most beautiful. It probably descended from the Celtic pony, which lived in the Welsh Hills for over 1,000 years (and benefited from some Arab blood in Roman times).

The larger Welsh Pony—Section B—is a little stockier. Originally, it was bred by Welsh farmers to provide transportation in the hills for herding their sheep. The Section B Welsh is the largest of the breed in the United States.

The Welsh Pony of Cob type—Section C—is a stocky but smaller version of the Welsh Cob, which is one of the most versatile breeds in the world.

This spectacular breed is divided into four distinct types based on size and shape. Its beauty and movement is spectacular. This is the Section D— Welsh Cob—type.

The Welsh Cob—Section D—is a powerful, proud animal that has been used to mount armies, pull agricultural implements, as a driving horse, for trail riding, and in every aspect of horse sports. It has influenced many breeds, such as the Morgan, Hackney, Dales, and Fell, and is renowned for its powerful, elevated trot.

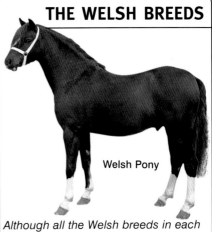

THE WELSH BREEDS

Welsh Pony

Although all the Welsh breeds in each category owe their origins to the Welsh Mountain Pony, the Welsh Pony and Cob Society stud book split into the four sections: A, B, C, and D by which the breeds are now categorized.

Welsh Pony of Cob Type

This Section A— Welsh Mountain Pony—shows how the intelligence, and energy of the type makes it a great favorite as a child's pony.

SUFFOLK
(SUFFOLK PUNCH)

This purely chestnut breed is the smallest of the British heavy horses, but is still used for agricultural work, as well as showing.

COUNTRY OF ORIGIN: Great Britain (Suffolk)
HEIGHT: 16hh (163 cm)
COLOR: Chestnut with no white except a small star. There are seven shades recognized, from dark to the most popular—bright.

CHARACTERISTICS: The Suffolk is the smallest of the British heavy breeds, showing great depth and width, and set on short, powerful limbs with little feather. It lives to a great age—often into its thirties—and is able to survive on less food than most other horses of equivalent size and type.

Thought by many to be the original war-horse, it is undoubtedly the purest of the British coldbloods (see p. 55). There are advertisements in existence that show that the Suffolk was taking part in "pulling" competitions in 1760, although an encyclopedia from the period, *Camdens Britannia*, claimed that its ancestry could be traced back even further, to 1506. It is known to have won the Best British Breed class 14 times out of 23 at the Royal Show in the 1800s. It is mainly used for agricultural work, breeding, and showing.

HOLSTEINER

COUNTRY OF ORIGIN: Germany (Schleswig – Holstein)
HEIGHT: 16–17hh (163–173 cm)
COLOR: Most solid colors.
CHARACTERISTICS: Bold is a word that is commonly used to describe this tall, elegant horse. It is probably the oldest of all the German breeds, and there are monasterial documents to show that they were bred along the Elbe in 1225.

The Holsteiner was well known as a war-horse in the Middle Ages, and was exported all over Europe in the 16th and 17th centuries. After the Napoleonic Wars, however, demand fell for this large, high-stepping horse and the numbers started to dwindle.

In 1960, efforts were made to modernize the breed for competitive use. Thoroughbred blood was introduced at the Elmshorn stud, and these efforts were so successful that many members of today's German international competition teams are mounted on Holsteiners. A good mover and jumper, the modern Holsteiner is used in all disciplines.

This ancient breed has been refined to make it a highly popular sport horse which has excelled in Olympic events.

HANOVERIAN

DEISTER

This powerful big bay ridden by Paul Shockemohle was typical of his breed—a wonderful athlete with a big jump and bold heart. He made it all look so easy and his show jumping record was outstanding —three European championships and countless Grand Prix. Deister was strong and impetuous; with pricked ears he would soar into the air over the highest fences in the show jumping world and surge around the courses in spectacular fashion to mark up countless wins.

COUNTRY OF ORIGIN: Germany
HEIGHT: 15.3–17hh (160–173 cm)
COLOR: All solid colors.
CHARACTERISTICS: The versatile Hanoverian is probably the most famous and prolific of all the German breeds and has been adapted through the ages to meet the demands of the day. Originally a powerful war-horse type, the breed was organized by a royal decree in 1735 from George II, King of England and Elector of Hanover, who ordered the establishment of the Celle State Stud in Germany. Using selected stallions, local farmers could bring their mares to produce lighter carriage horses and agricultural animals capable of moving loads much quicker. By 1867, the breeding policy had been highly successful, with injections of Thoroughbred, Cleveland Bay, Andalusian, Prussian, and Neapolitan stock, and a society was formed for selected stallions. In 1899, a stud book for mares with outstanding characteristics of the breed, good temperament and movement was introduced. These selected breeding mares produced excellent offspring and resulted in Hanoverians being used widely in Europe and Scandinavia.

This was followed in 1928 by the establishment of a stallion training station. All young stallions had to undergo 11 months of intensive training, during which time records were kept to determine character, disposition, endurance, ability, jumping technique, speed, and attitude. As a result, only the best were passed for breeding. This scenario still stands today, and now the breed is much lighter and specifically bred for competitive use. Hanoverians are particularly successful in the dressage and show jumping worlds, but are also used for driving and general riding thanks to further refinement from Thoroughbred, Arab, and Trakehner blood.

The stringent breeding policy adopted to trace good blood lines has ensured that the best attributes are produced in this breed.

TRAKEHNER

COUNTRY OF ORIGIN: Germany
HEIGHT: 16–16.2hh (163–168 cm)
COLOR: Mostly dark colors.
CHARACTERISTICS: One of the oldest and most elegant of the German warmblood breeds (see p. 55), the Trakehner is noted for the quality of its conformation—its long neck sloping down to strong shoulders and an athletic body.

The breed was founded at the Trakehnan Stud in 1732 by Frederick William I of Prussia on well-drained marshlands that proved ideal for horse breeding. These tough little local Schweiken horses were crossed with Arabs, Thoroughbreds, and some Turkmen blood to produce high-class cavalry and coach horses. Breeding was well organized and documented, with young stock carefully trained and tested before being used at stud.

Despite the devastation of World War II, some Trakehners were kept safe and survived. Today the Trakehner are truer to type than any other warmblood. It makes an outstandingly successful sporthorse, excelling at dressage and show jumping. The Trakehner stallion Abdyullah won an Olympic Silver Medal for show jumping.

The elegant Trakehner has been produced through carefully documented breeding policies, and is highly sought after as a sporthorse.

OLDENBURG

COUNTRY OF ORIGIN: Germany
HEIGHT: 16.1–17.2hh (165–178 cm)
COLOR: Bay, brown, or black.
CHARACTERISTICS: Oldenburgs were developed in the 17th century in the northwest of Germany, near to their close neighbors, the Friesians—with whom they have much in common. Much of their origins are owed to Count Anton von Oldenburg (1603–1667), who had arranged for the importation of Spanish and Italian blood to improve the local horses. The results became known as Oldenburgs.

A breeders' society was formed in the 19th century, and more upgrading continued through importation of Thoroughbreds, Cleveland Bays, Yorkshire coach horses, and some Hanoverians. These produced good warmblood types capable of being ridden or driven for the army, working in the fields, and pulling coaches. Today, the Oldenburg has been lightened even more to become suitable for equestrian sports.

The Oldenburg was upgraded from a war and driving horse at the turn of the century and is now a popular sport and riding horse.

WESTPHALIAN

COUNTRY OF ORIGIN: Germany
(Westphalia)
HEIGHT: 15.2–16.2hh (157–168 cm)
COLOR: All solid colors.

The second most prolific of the German breeds, the Westphalian is extremely popular as a dressage and show jumping horse.

CHARACTERISTICS: International competition has long known the presence of the superb Westphalian, the second most numerous of the German breeds – after the Hanoverian. It stands alongside the Hanoverian and Thoroughbred at the Warendorf State Stud. Over the years, additions of Hanoverian blood have helped the Westphalian to evolve from a popular farm and army animal into a strong, high-quality sporthorse. It is a heavier animal than the Hanoverian, but it has an intelligent, alert outlook, good bone, and has a rather flat croup.

Westphalians have an excellent competition record and can boast outstanding major wins at world and Olympic levels in both dressage and show jumping.

FRIESIAN

COUNTRY OF ORIGIN: Holland/
The Netherlands (Friesland)
HEIGHT: 14.3–15.3hh (150–160 cm)
COLOR: Black—a small star is permissible.
CHARACTERISTICS: This ancient breed has played an important role in Dutch history and has influenced many British breeds such as the Dales and Clydesdale. It is tough and stocky, has great presence, and a wonderful, high-stepping action.

Used in medieval times for mounting knights in armor, Friesians became highly valued as a means of travel and for use in trotting races. Mechanization, however, caused the decline in their usefulness and it is only recently that their fortunes have changed for the better. This is due to the success of carriage driving, where their uniform color is an added asset for pairing of teams. Their spectacular action and spirited way of going have made them extremely popular once again, for riding, dressage, driving, and circus displays, as well.

This ancient black breed is extremely popular for driving, has spectacular action, and is sometimes used for circus displays.

ICELANDIC

COUNTRY OF ORIGIN: Iceland
HEIGHT: 12–14hh (122–142 cm)
COLOR: Most colors, but dun and chestnut—including those with flaxen manes and tails—are most common.
CHARACTERISTICS: The agility and hardiness of this sure-footed animal made this native pony the backbone of the Icelandic economy—it provided meat as well as the only means of transportation for a millennium. Even today, with few roads, it is used as a pack horse and for shepherding.

These stocky, well-made ponies have large heads on short, muscular necks, and combine docility with strong independence. Their tremendous homing instinct means they can find their way back if turned loose even after a long trip. They also have an unusual four-beat gait known as the *tölt*, a type of running walk that is extremely comfortable. Although traditionally very much a work animal—even used as pit ponies in British coal mines—they are popular today for riding, trekking, and sports.

The Icelandic is one of the purest of the ancient breeds. Its location on its island homeland ensured there was little chance of any cross breeding.

CONNEMARA

COUNTRY OF ORIGIN: Ireland
HEIGHT: 13–14.2hh (132–147 cm)
COLOR: Mostly gray but also black, bay, brown, dun, and occasionally roan.
CHARACTERISTICS: This tough and versatile breed has lived for centuries on the mountains and bogs of the Connaught region. It is sensible and calm and used extensively for riding and driving. It may have crossed with either horses of Oriental blood being transported by traders from Spain or animals shipwrecked from the Spanish Armada in 1588 to produce the definite aura of class and beauty not often seen in mountain ponies.

Crossed with the Thoroughbred, the Connemara has produced some outstanding competition stock, boasting great power and true, free action. Its temperament has made it ideal for competition driving, but it is as a children's riding pony that it is universally acclaimed.

The versatility of this popular breed from the West Coast of Ireland makes it an ideal mount for all children's riding activities.

IRISH DRAFT

COUNTRY OF ORIGIN: Ireland
HEIGHT: 15–17hh (152–173 cm)
COLOR: Bay, brown, chestnut, or gray.
CHARACTERISTICS: This relatively light-framed draft (draught) horse was bred to work on the land and transport goods—as well as fulfill the Irish passion for hunting. It evolved from Irish ponies being crossed with horses of Arab and Spanish blood in the 18th and early-19th centuries.

Its conformation, especially its powerful sloping quarters, make it a good jumper. The Irish Draft has an excellent temperament and is very popular as a cross with the Thoroughbred to produce top competition horses, and the hunters for which Ireland is renowned.

A popular cross for hunters and competition horses, the Irish Draft is an excellent jumper and good mover.

NORWEGIAN FJORD

COUNTRY OF ORIGIN: Norway
HEIGHT: 13–14hh (132–142 cm)
COLOR: Dun with a dorsal eel stripe and zebra marks. The coarse mane is dark in the center with silver hairs on the outside.
CHARACTERISTICS: The ancient Fjord shows little crossbreeding and breeds very true to type. Many historians believe it is closely related to the primeval pony. The Fjord is very similar to the horses used by the Vikings in war and those used to pull the plow. It has a small, concave head, is extremely hardy and strong, and has a calm temperament. The Fjord is most distinctive for its spectacular mane, which becomes tougher as it matures.

For centuries, it has been used as a work and pack animal, as well as for riding. These days it is also popular as a driving pony.

The distinctive mane is an unusual feature of this tough ancient breed. It is generally trimmed to accentuate the colors.

This ancient high-stepping breed from Spain has a calm temperament and elegance ideal for high riding school work.

ANDALUSIAN

COUNTRY OF ORIGIN: Spain (Andalusia)
HEIGHT: 15.1–16hh (154–162 cm)
COLOR: Gray and occasionally bay, black, or roan.
CHARACTERISTICS: The eye-catching, high-stepping Andalusian is an ancient breed and shows similarities to horses depicted in cave paintings dating back 20,000 years. Its blood is found in many breeds, including Lippizaners and Lusitanos, as well as in such American breeds as Paso Finos and Mustangs.

Its elegance and easy temperament made the Andalusian hugely popular for high school work in the European courts of the Renaissance, until the French Revolution caused a decline in riding. Luckily, the Carthusian monks maintained their studs, keeping the breed pure, and the breed is now promoted by the Spanish government. Andalusians are used for dressage, jumping, and in the bullring, as well as for general riding.

BREEDS FROM THE AMERICAS

FALABELLA/ MINIATURE HORSES

COUNTRY OF ORIGIN: Argentina
HEIGHT: 8.2hh (86 cm) or slightly above
COLOR: All colors, including spotted.
CHARACTERISTICS: The Falabella was produced more than a century ago from a tiny stallion discovered roaming in South America by an Irishman named Newton. Although the animal was said to be suffering from "dwarf sickness," it was found to produce others similar in size and the dwarf features were passed on. Other peculiarities include two fewer ribs and vertebrae than most other breeds, and a gestation period of 13 months instead of 11.

Today, the Falabella is bred at Senor Falabella's ranch in Argentina and at the Kilverstone Stud in England. It is extremely delicate and takes a few generations to "shrink" down to the

average height of 8.2hh (86 cm). Falabellas and Miniature Horses are used as pets or for driving.

The Falabella is not strong enough to be ridden and requires a specially adapted harness for driving to cope with its tiny size.

PERUVIAN PASO (PERUVIAN HORSE)

COUNTRY OF ORIGIN: Peru
HEIGHT: 14.2–15.2hh (147–157 cm)
COLOR: Bay, chestnut, brown, black, and gray. Occasionally roan, palomino, and dun.
CHARACTERISTICS: This stocky but elegant gaited horse ("stepping horse") is noted for its distinctive lateral gait. Generally larger than its relative, the Paso Fino, the Peruvian Paso has long, sloping shoulders and strong bone. It carries its head high and its tail rather low.

The breed was developed from the same blood as the Paso Fino—the Arab, Barb, Adalusian, and Spanish jennets brought over to South America by the Spanish conquistadores. The broken pace, which is inherited, was developed through selective breeding for more than 300 years. It enabled the Peruvian Paso to carry its rider over vast estates of the country, keeping up speeds of as much as 18 miles (29 km) per hour for long periods of time without tiring.

These days, it is used for parades, endurance, pleasure riding, and showing.

This slightly larger horse has similar characteristics to the Paso Fino, to which it is closely related.

PASO FINO

The attractive Paso Fino has a distinctive lateral gait which is much admired in the show ring.

COUNTRY OF ORIGIN: Puerto Rico
HEIGHT: 13–15hh (132–152 cm)
COLOR: Most colors.
CHARACTERISTICS: This attractive little horse has a tremendous presence that belies its small stature. It is particularly distinguished by its broken four-beat pace, which has come to be known as the Paso gait.

The breed is believed to have originated in the Caribbean from horses brought from the Dominican Republic by Christopher Columbus. He is reputed to have had Andalusians and Barbs on board his ship, as well as Spanish jennets with a broken four-beat gait. Breeding took place on several of the Caribbean islands, and the resulting tough, strong-backed animals were used by the Spanish conquistadores during their conquests of Mexico and other parts of South America.

Today, Paso Finos are used for trail riding, showing, driving, pleasure, and for exhibitions. They can be found in the United States and Colombia, as well as in Europe.

DUALLY

Monty Roberts, the Californian who has made "Horse Whispering" so popular, thinks the world of his 16hh brown Quarter Horse gelding, Dually. On him, he has won numerous championships for cow cutting and has traveled the world to demonstrate how he trained the horse to perform all the normal activities without a bridle.

Dually is no beauty! He has quite crooked front legs—nevertheless, his superb courage overcame this fault. Monty liked Dually's determination to succeed, so he set about training the horse in his quiet and understanding way that relies on imitating a horse's own body language.

Dually had a sense of the big occasion and gave his utmost at every performance before acknowledging the crowd's applause by nodding his head and pawing the ground.

AMERICAN QUARTER HORSE

COUNTRY OF ORIGIN: United States
HEIGHT: 14.3–16hh (150–163 cm)
COLOR: Most colors, including Palomino.
CHARACTERISTICS: Tremendous strength and speed mean that the American Quarter Horse can stop, turn, and start with extraordinary ease. The power comes from its broad, deep, and rather heavy quarters, and its muscular thighs and gaskins. Its stop-start ability and "cow sense" makes it the perfect animal for working cattle, although it was also developed to fulfill one of the few sources of leisure in ranch life—racing.

The breed owes its development to Spanish and British stock imported during the 17th and 18th centuries, but in particular to a small chestnut stallion, named Janus, which arrived from Britain in 1752. This grandson of the Godolphin Arabian was said to possess "great bone and muscle and round, very compact large quarters, and was swift." Janus was able to reproduce near replicas of himself. His blood spread rapidly and crossed with the Native American Mustangs, resulting in horses that were ideal for racing— particularly in the popular sprint over a quarter of a mile (0.4 km).

Over time, people recognized the value of producing a horse that could be used for ranching, rodeo work, and racing—and yet retain its calm, easy temperament. So the American Quarter Horse was developed and went on to become the largest breed in the United States. Exported worldwide, it is used for numerous sports outside its traditional role, including trail riding, eventing, and pleasure.

The most popular breed in the United States, it is famous for its speed over a quarter of a mile (0.4 km) and its tough strong quarters and thighs.

AMERICAN SADDLEBRED

COUNTRY OF ORIGIN: United States
HEIGHT: 15–16hh (152–163 cm)
COLOR: Bay, chestnut, or gray, also roan, pinto, and palomino.

This popular American breed with its three- and five-gaited paces is also used for pleasure riding, driving and jumping.

CHARACTERISTICS: This spirited, showy horse used to be known as the Kentucky Saddler because of the area in the southern states in which it was bred. Developed by the pioneers to be a versatile all-rounder, it was fast and comfortable enough to ride around the plantations, yet fancy enough to pull buggies smartly. Not only was it strong enough for farm work but it was also fast enough to race on special days – owing its heritage to Thoroughbreds, Morgans, and Trotters.

The American Saddlebred's inherent ability to perform the two man-made gaited paces, the "rack" and the "slow gait," make it extremely popular for showing. There are three divisions: the three-gaited, the five-gaited, and the Fine Harness Horse, which are then subdivided into performance, pleasure, and equitation classes.

MISSOURI FOXTROTTER

COUNTRY OF ORIGIN: United States
HEIGHT: 14–16hh (142–163 cm)
COLOR: All colors.
CHARACTERISTICS: What makes this breed absolutely unique is the peculiar, ambling gait from which it takes its name. In the so-called "fox trot," the horse walks with its front legs but trots from behind. Selective breeding combined this unusual gait with a gentle, reliable temperament.

The breed was developed at the beginning of the 19th century by the pioneers who settled in the area around the Ozarks of Missouri. It was mainly bred from Arabs, Morgans, and Southern Plantation Horses, which were later crossed with the Saddlebred, Standardbred, and Tennessee Walker. This produced a horse that was quiet, fast, and comfortable.

Today, the Missouri Foxtrotter is used extensively for trail riding because it is so comfortable to ride.

46

APPALOOSA

COUNTRY OF ORIGIN: United States (but spotted horses are found worldwide)
HEIGHT: 14.2hh (148 cm) and over
COLOR: Spotted (eight different patterns), not gray or pinto.
CHARACTERISTICS: The Appaloosa is descended from the ancient spotted horses, many of which were depicted in cave drawings (the most famous being those at Lascaux in France). In Persia,

Prince Rustran's spotted horse, Rukash, led the Persian armies to victory in 400 B.C. It is also thought that Spanish spotted horses arrived in North America in the 17th century, and it is from here that the breed developed. Some of these horses were captured and bred by Native Americans, notably the Nez Percé tribe based near the Palouse River—from which the name evolved.

In 1938, thanks to efforts by Claude Thompson of Oregon, the Appaloosa Horse Club was founded and the Appaloosa is now one of the foremost and most prolific breeds in the United States.

In appearance, the Appaloosa is most unusual, and its spectacular spotted coloring makes it popular for demonstrations and exhibitions at shows. Its skin is mottled with spots, particularly around the eyes and nose; it has white sclera around the eye; and its hooves are striped vertically with black and white. As far as conformation is concerned, it is well made, with a deep body and strong limbs. It has good paces and is extremely versatile, used for anything from trail riding and ranching to competition work and racing.

APPALOOSA

The eight basic coat patterns are:

1. **Spotted Blanket**—*dark head with white blanket over loin and quarters with spots.*
2. **White Blanket**—*dark head with white blanket over loin and quarters without spots.*
3. **Leopard**—*pure white base with evenly distributed spots over the whole body.*
4. **Near Leopard**—*leopard markings at birth but these fade as the horse ages.*
5. **Marble**—*dark base color, which fades with maturity, with "varnish" marks on face and legs.*
6. **Few Spot**—*basically leopard with just a few odd spots, but some roan (blue or red) marks.*
7. **Frosted Tip**—*dark base color with either frost or white spots on loin and quarters.*
8. **Snowflake**—*base color is dark with white spots, which often appear later.*

The spectacular coloring of this breed is most unusual and is not unlike the mottled skin of horses in prehistoric cave paintings.

STANDARDBRED

COUNTRY OF ORIGIN: United States
HEIGHT: 14–16hh (142–163 cm)
COLOR: Bay is most common but all colors found.
CHARACTERISTICS: The Standardbred is the fastest breed for harness racing in the world and was developed mainly from Thoroughbred blood imported in the late 1700s, with a little trotter influence. As the sport of harness racing developed, selective breeding for the sport became even more important. Hambletonion 10 (1849), who traces back to the three foundation sires of the Thoroughbred, became the father of the modern Standardbred by producing no less than 1,335 offspring.

Nowadays, harness racing is enormously popular in the United States, where trotting horses are almost as valuable as flat racehorses. Harness horses either trot (move their legs conventionally in diagonal pairs) or pace (move them laterally). Some, including the Standardbred, are capable of both. So successful is the American Standardbred that it has been exported worldwide to improve other harness breeds.

The Standardbred is the fastest harness racing breed in the world. The breed has been developed to have extremely hardened legs which can withstand the intense strain of harness racing.

PONY OF THE AMERICAS

COUNTRY OF ORIGIN: United States
HEIGHT: 11.2–13.2hh (117–137 cm)
COLOR: Appaloosa coloring.
CHARACTERISTICS: This completely new breed of pony looks like a miniature version of an American Quarter Horse and an Arab, but with Appaloosa characteristics. In fact, it's the result of a cross developed by Leslie Boomower of Iowa in the 1950s, who bred a Shetland stallion to an Appaloosa mare.

The Pony of the Americas (POA), as it's known, often has an Arab-like head, a good, rounded conformation, and a free-and-easy movement. It inherits all the Appaloosa characteristics of mottled skin and white sclera around the eyes, as well as striped hooves. The POA is popular with children and adults alike and makes a versatile mount for all riding activities.

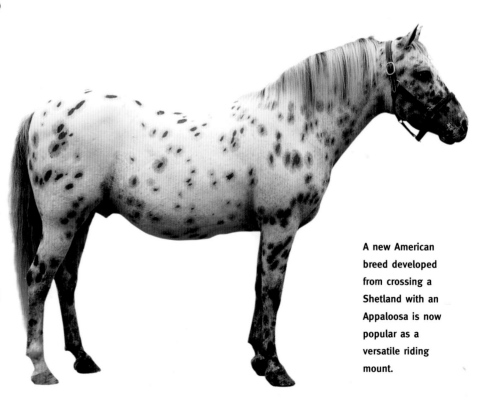

A new American breed developed from crossing a Shetland with an Appaloosa is now popular as a versatile riding mount.

PINTO/PAINT

COUNTRY OF ORIGIN: United States
HEIGHT: All heights and types (ponies and horses).
COLOR: Colored (two main patterns of colored horse—Overo and Tobiano).
CHARACTERISTICS: Originally considered a color—horses sporting pinto patterns today fall into four distinct conformation types. The color is prepotent and tends to reproduce itself unlike those of pure breeds such as the Thoroughbred or Arab.

Pinto types are registered by three registries in the United States—the American Paint Horse Registry covers Quarter Horses and Thoroughbreds of stock-horse type. The Pinto Registry covers four types—the stock-horse types, hunter, saddle type, and those of Morgan or Australian breeding. The Moroccan Spotted Horse Co-operative Association registers the gaited horse as well as Hackneys, Saddlebreds, Tennessee Walkers, Morgans, Arabs and some Thoroughbreds. Although horses in Europe, Asia, and Canada are included, it is in America that the breed is best known.

This colored horse is considered a breed in America and comes in all heights and types, with skewbald and piebald being two main colors.

TENNESSEE WALKING HORSE

COUNTRY OF ORIGIN: United States
HEIGHT: 15–16hh (152–163 cm)
COLOR: Chestnuts (some with flaxen manes and tails), bay, black, and roan.
CHARACTERISTICS: Known as "the world's greatest show, pleasure and trail horse," the Tennessee Walking Horse was developed by 19th-century plantation owners as a comfortable hack to ride around their expansive estates. The horse needed to be agile and placid to pick its way through crops without damaging plants. Exceptionally good natured, it was bred from Pacers crossed with Thoroughbreds, Saddlebreds, Standardbreds, and Morgans—perhaps the most influential stallion being Black Allen, a Standardbred foaled in 1886.

The Walker's unusual and extremely comfortable gaits are all natural to the

breed. These include the flat-foot walk, running walk, and rocking chair canter. These gaits are accentuated by specialized shoeing for the show ring.

The practice of using specialized shoes to enhance the gait of the Tennessee Walking Horse has proven to be quite controversial in the past few decades.

MORGAN

COUNTRY OF ORIGIN: United States (Vermont)
HEIGHT: 14.1–15.2hh (147–157 cm)
COLOR: Black, bay, or chestnut, with very little white.
CHARACTERISTICS: This small, clean-limbed, and versatile horse is renowned for its tremendous presence, tractability, and strength. What makes it so unique is that it originated from one dark bay stallion in the late 18th century, named after its owner—Justin Morgan—a singing teacher from Vermont. The founding stallion stood just 14.1hh, was believed to be of Arab or Barb descent (possibly with some Welsh or Friesian blood), and possessed exceptional talents of speed and strength in pulling, racing in-harness, and under saddle. As his fame grew, so did the demand for his services as a stallion.

His ability to reproduce his own characteristics, regardless of the type of mare, ensured the emergence of a whole new breed.

Now, the Morgan is divided into "Park" and "Pleasure" horses, both of which are used in harness or under saddle. The Park Morgan has greater animation and elevation, whereas the Pleasure Morgan possesses a more manageable temperament and a lower action.

Descended from one very dominant stallion, this highly popular breed is used for showing and driving.

MUSTANG

COUNTRY OF ORIGIN: United States
HEIGHT: 13.2–15hh (137–152 cm)
COLOR: Any color.
CHARACTERISTICS: The unsung hero of just about every Western movie, the Mustang is the original horse of the Wild West. Tough and agile, its apparent inner "cow sense" made it the ideal ranch animal.

Originally, the breed was based on Andalusian and Barb horses imported by Spanish settlers in the 16th century. Many of these ran free, to mix with local horses, eventually forming feral herds that roamed the western United States. These horses were first used by Native Americans, then taken up by cowboys for ranch work. As the settlers moved west, they crossed the Mustangs with bigger, heavier carriage horses to increase their size. The Chickasaw Mustangs from the southeast were crossed with Thoroughbreds and produced what became the forerunner to the Quarter Horse. Wild bands of Mustangs still roam the American West, and since the 1970s have been afforded federal protection.

This popular breed has been used as a cow pony since the American settlers first realized the value of horses for transportation and cow herding.

AUSTRALASIAN AND ASIAN BREEDS

AUSTRALIAN STOCK HORSE

COUNTRY OF ORIGIN: Australia
HEIGHT: 14.2–16hh (147–163 cm)
COLOR: Most colors.
CHARACTERISTICS: This tough, good-natured horse has evolved over the last 200 years from the Australian Waler used by the Australian Army. It is of mixed breeding and includes blood from Arabs, Barbs, Percherons, Dutch, and American Quarter Horses, as well as a fairly recent infusion of Thoroughbred. The mix has produced a breed that combines endurance and good temperament – qualities that are much in demand in all the major equestrian sports.

The World Three-Day Event Champion, Regal Realm, ridden by Lucinda Green, placed the breed firmly among the top sporthorses in the early 1970s.

The toughness and versatility of this breed has made it extremely popular as a top sporthorse.

AKHAL-TEKÉ

COUNTRY OF ORIGIN: Turkmenistan
HEIGHT: 14.3–15.2hh (150–157 cm)
COLOR: Golden bay, occasionally black, brown, chestnut, and gray.
CHARACTERISTICS: The ancient, pure lineage of the Akhal-Teké can be traced back 4,000 years to the mountains of Central Asia, where it was bred by Turkmen tribes. Only the toughest could survive in these harsh desert regions, and so this fine breed is extremely robust despite its small, light frame. It is thin-skinned, with little hair in the mane and tail, and capable of withstanding dramatic changes in temperature. However, its rather long body sometimes lacks strength, and it has a tendency toward bad hocks.

The breed is noted for its shiny golden coat and its ability to cover huge distances. It is very fast, and it is a good jumper and mover. An Olympic Dressage gold medallist, Absent, was a purebred Akhal-Teké. The breed is often used for racing, endurance, and to influence other breeds around the Caucasus areas.

A fine tough breed, renowned for its stamina, it has excelled in many equestrian sports as well as racing.

The King of Morocco keeps a large stud of Barbs, and they are used in many ceremonial displays.

BARB

COUNTRY OF ORIGIN: North Africa: Algeria, Libya, Morocco
HEIGHT: 14–15hh (142–152 cm)
COLOR: Any solid color.
CHARACTERISTICS: The Barb is an ancient breed which is believed to have existed in the region of North Africa since prehistoric times, but it has mixed with Arab blood over the centuries. Unlike the Arab's fine features, the Barb has a straight face and muzzle, lower set tail, and sloping quarters. It is quick tempered and is very fast and agile.

Barbs played an important role in the further development of the Thoroughbred, following the work done by Charles II of England in introducing Oriental stock to create the ideal racehorse. Around 200 mares and stallions of Barb, Arab, and Turk breeding were imported in the 1700s to improve and upgrade existing stock.

PRZEWALSKI'S HORSE

COUNTRY OF ORIGIN: Western Mongolia
HEIGHT: 12–13hh (122–132 cm)
COLOR: Yellow dun with mealy muzzle, dorsal stripe, and zebra markings on legs.
CHARACTERISTICS: Przewalski's Horse is the only known true wild horse. It is not of the same species as today's domestic horse but from a closely related subgroup. Przewalski's Horse and *Equus caballus* (the modern horse species) can be crossed and reproduce. The Przewalski's Horse has a massive head with small ears, a big jaw and teeth, and a tufted mane. The body is broad and short with a straight shoulder. These animals are extremely wild and timid.

Almost extinct in the wild, where they were killed for meat by nomadic Turks, these horses were named after the Russian explorer Nikolai M. Przewalski. This was in recognition for his efforts in their identification and preservation in 1881. Most are kept and bred in captivity in zoos around the world but attempts have been made to reintroduce them into their native homeland.

Many believe that this breed is of the same strain as the modern horse but has retained some equine features from prehistoric times.

EGYPTIAN KHALIFA

Endurance riding is all about stamina, and that is what Egyptian Khalifa is renowned for and what made him Individual Champion with his rider Jill Thomas in 1993. Wiry, strong, obstinate yet generous, this tough little Arab excelled in the show ring originally, then progressed to the endurance side of life where he became even better known with his determination and stamina ensuring he reached his goal in good shape.

Starting in a 25 mile (40 km) ride, he progressed to 50 mile (80 km), then 60 mile (96 km) rides, recording low heart rates at the all important veterinary checks, before, during, and after each ride. His flowing stride, indomitable spirit, and careful, patient buildup to his training program meant he completed the courses sound and happy.

Egyptian Khalifa loved the exciting atmosphere and attention of competing as much as his rider enjoyed the fun of the parties afterwards. Egyptian Khalifa must have been amazed at the strange goings on at parties that followed such rides—but being the star attraction he always behaved impeccably himself!

ARAB (ARABIAN)

COUNTRY OF ORIGIN: Arabian peninsula (Yemen Arab Republic—Saudi Arabia)
HEIGHT: 14–15.2hh (142–158 cm)
COLOR: Most strong colors—black, chestnut, bay, and gray.
CHARACTERISTICS: The Arab has a noble and proud outlook; its short head combines a concave, "dished," face with a small muzzle. The nostrils are prominent; the eyes are large and expressive; and the ears are small and alert. The jowl is deep and wide. The tail is carried high and has a distinctive flaring carriage. The Arab has one less lumbar vertebra and rib than other breeds.

The Arab is the oldest pure breed in the world and drawings of it have been found dating from around 6000 B.C. Numerous legends abound, including one that claims Noah's grandson, Baz, was the first to capture and tame one of its ancestors. The prophet Mohammed used the Arab to expand the Islamic faith, claiming that Allah had helped to create it. Solomon is reported to have had more than 40,000 Arabs in his stables.

Arab blood has been used to improve nearly all breeds and was particularly influential in the development of the Thoroughbred. There are many lines within the breed, but the Original or Elite are from desert stock mostly bred by the Bedouins. They used tough, selective breeding methods for centuries and can claim to have achieved one of the purest lines. The Persian and Egyptian lines are also old, with statues and paintings depicting Arabs dating back to 2000 B.C. Polish, Hungarian, and Russian Arabs also boast early histories.

Today, a World Arabian Horse Organization has been set up to ensure the purity of the Arab. Now an international breed, it is found in major studs worldwide and is popular in the United States and Australia.

The Anglo-Arab has been developed from crossing the Arab with the Thoroughbred, and this has been particularly successful in France. Anglo-Arabs make superb competition horses in many spheres.

The Arab is the oldest pure breed in the world and has very distinctive features, particularly the dished face and flaring nostrils, and high flowing tail carriage.

PALOMINO

COUNTRY OF ORIGIN: Worldwide
HEIGHT: All sizes – more than 14hh (142 cm) in the United States.
COLOR: Pale gold with light/white mane and tail. White only on the head and lower limbs.
CHARACTERISTICS: One of the most beautifully colored horses in the world, a Palomino shimmers like a newly minted gold coin. It is actually a color found in most breeds of the world and not a true breed in the strictest sense, but in the United States, two Palomino Registries register Palominos as a color breed.

Known from ancient times, these brightly colored animals were common in Spain during the 15th and 16th centuries. Queen Isabella I presented Cortés with Palominos to take to the Americas. He in turn presented one to Juan de Palomino, a fellow conquistadore—and so the name stuck.

These days, the "Golden Horse of the West," is popular worldwide but nowhere more so than in the United States. Palominos are to be found in all horse sports, but they are particularly popular in the show ring and parades.

In America, this is classed as a color breed. Its spectacular golden color and white mane and tail is found in many breeds.

TRIGGER

This 15.3hh Palomino stallion shot to stardom in the 1940s as the four-legged friend of Roy Rogers, "King of the Cowboys," and achieved a legendary notoriety.

Together, the pair made 88 movies and 104 television shows, becoming household names worldwide. At one time they had 2,000 fan clubs around the globe, the largest—in London—boasting 50,000 members.

On one occasion, an adoring fan chopped off most of Trigger's white tail as a souvenir. It took nearly two years to grow back again, and Trigger had to wear a false tail in the meantime.

This lovable horse was a character in every way. He adored stardom and could perform innumerable tricks. Bowing, counting, nodding, and blowing kisses were just a small part of his repertoire, which helped to keep The Roy Rogers Show at the top of the TV ratings for 12 years. Trigger died peacefully in his sleep at the age of 33. Roy Rogers said of him: (sic) "Trigger was my partner and my pal and part of nearly everything I did. Never once let me down."

DUTCH COURAGE

Dutch Courage, a handsome brown Dutch Warmblood colt, was spotted by Britain's Jennie Loriston-Clarke late at night during a trip to the Netherlands. "I noticed this lovely head looking out in the car headlights," she said. On enquiring about the horse, she was told he'd failed the stallion grading because he was too immature, so was thus considered "no good."

Undaunted, the colt was brought to Britain by Jennie and Mrs. Gyll Steele and allowed time to mature into the magnificent stallion who was to prove the most influential sire during the 1970s in the formation of his breed in Britain.

Nicknamed "Bill," he became Britain's number one dressage stallion, winning the National Championships seven times, and was the first horse to win a dressage medal for Britain—the World bronze award in 1978, a medal which raised the profile of dressage in Britain. His dressage displays at home and abroad enthralled thousands, and it was with him that Jennie started her outstanding long-rein displays set to music, which became a feature of so many shows.

As a stallion, Dutch Courage produced Olympic, World and top-class stars in all three disciplines, passing on his athletic paces and generous nature to his numerous offspring. He was a great character who loved to work. He was the perfect gentleman but was quick to react to anything he disliked—the horse dentist being his greatest hate!

WARMBLOODS

COUNTRY OF ORIGIN: Worldwide (but especially Germany, Britain, Denmark, Sweden, and the Netherlands)
HEIGHT: 16hh (163 cm) and above
COLOR: Usually bays, browns, chestnuts and grays.
CHARACTERISTICS: The Warmblood horse has been created in several countries this century to meet the modern demand for competitive sports. Many of the old established breeds have been enhanced by fresh blood to make them lighter and more suitable for today's needs.

There are only two "hotbloods:" the Arab and Thoroughbred. Warmbloods have been developed by mixing the hotbloods with other breeds, occasionally with "coldbloods," the heavy draft (draught) horses, to create the sporthorse required.

The versatility bred into many other sporting breeds has made the Warmblood a successful modern sporthorse.

These horses have been produced to have the temperament, movement, speed, and athletic ability to excel in dressage, show jumping, or similarly international horse trials. Warmblood breeding has been spectacularly successful in show jumping and dressage, and the right type is now being produced for horse trials and driving.

With few real distinguishing features, it is their performance that has made these sporthorses so popular. Today the German, Swedish, Dutch, British, and Danish Warmbloods in particular have excelled in Olympic, European, and World Championships, as well as in many other international competitions.

SECTION
2
Knowing and Caring for your Horse

POINTS OF THE HORSE

To be able to understand how to identify different parts of the horse, it is important to know the names of what are collectively described as the points of the horse. A horse that is described as having black points indicates it has dark or black legs, mane, and tail like those seen in horses of bay or brown. Some have white markings on their faces (see p.26) and on their lower legs, referred to as socks or stockings.

Certain breeds have their own definite distinguishing features which make for easy identification, such as the Arab's dished face, the Exmoor's toad eyes, and the Norwegian Fjord's striking black and white mane. Some heavier breeds have excess hair on their lower legs, referred to as feather. This feather can be very fine and silky on some breeds, or profuse on others, such as on the Clydesdale and the Shire. Some plain-colored horses with no obvious markings are identified by small twirls in their coats often found around the head, neck or chest areas. These are known as whorls.

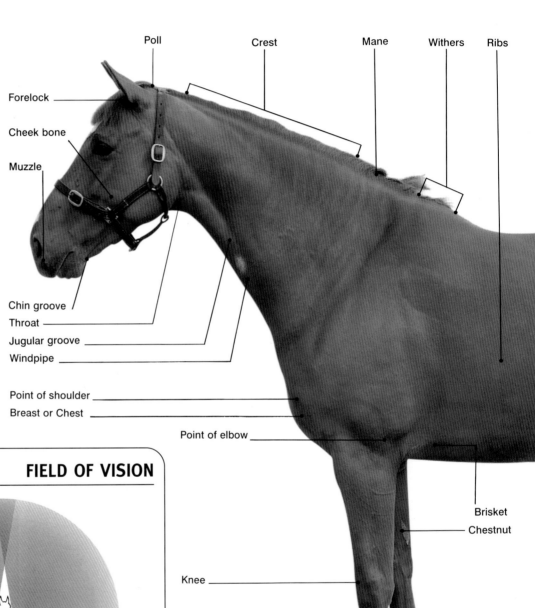

Poll · Crest · Mane · Withers · Ribs · Forelock · Cheek bone · Muzzle · Chin groove · Throat · Jugular groove · Windpipe · Point of shoulder · Breast or Chest · Point of elbow · Brisket · Chestnut · Knee · Back (flexor) tendons · Cannon · Ergot · Fetlock joint · Bulb of heel · Pastern

FIELD OF VISION

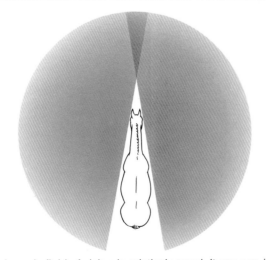

The horse's field of vision is relatively good. It can see in front of it very well and judges distance from ground level, which is important when it tries to assess heights of fences.

MEASURING

The horse is measured in "hands," one hand is equal to the width of an average hand of 4in (10cm). A measuring stick is placed beside the horse next to its forelegs with the measure taken horizontally across the highest point of the withers. (See also p.78.) Generally, horses measure from over 15hh (152 cm), while ponies are those measuring under this height (typically at or under 14.2 hands in the USA).

A horse is considered to have stopped growing and to be mature at six years of age.

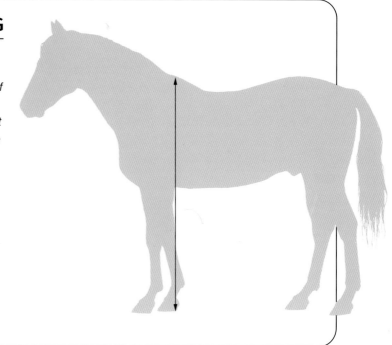

Loins

Croup

Hip joint

Hindquarters

Dock

Point of buttock

Flank

Tail

Hamstring

Gaskin

Point of hock

Hock

Cannon

Fetlock joint

Coronet

Hoof

FOOT AND HOOF

The foot is the most important part of the horse, and it is vital to keep it well trimmed and regularly shod if the horse is to remain sound (see pp.96–97). Get to know the parts of the foot both on the outside and the underside so that you are able to identify the area should problems occur. The outside wall is made of very hard horn and cannot expand should there be any inside inflammation caused by an abscess. The veterinarian will cut a small hole in the sole to release the pressure in some cases.

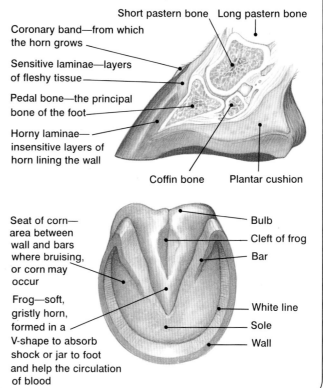

Short pastern bone   Long pastern bone

Coronary band—from which the horn grows

Sensitive laminae—layers of fleshy tissue

Pedal bone—the principal bone of the foot

Horny laminae— insensitive layers of horn lining the wall

Coffin bone   Plantar cushion

Seat of corn— area between wall and bars where bruising, or corn may occur

Frog—soft, gristly horn, formed in a V-shape to absorb shock or jar to foot and help the circulation of blood

Bulb

Cleft of frog

Bar

White line

Sole

Wall

BREEDING

If you have a healthy mare, plenty of room, good facilities, and sufficient funds, breeding is a fun and rewarding pastime. But too often animals are bred for all the wrong reasons. Sadly, little thought has been given to the end product and the resulting offspring may not be suitable for the role envisioned. If all is carefully thought through, however, there is nothing nicer than to watch your foal grow up into something special.

To be successful, there are many considerations to take into account when deciding whether to breed your mare:

- What you hope to produce.
- The temperament and soundness of the mare.
- The facilities available to keep a mare and foal.
- The time and expense involved.
- Choosing a suitable stallion.

When the mare is "in season," she may lean toward the stallion (seen here on the opposite side of the teasing board). If a mare does not appreciate a stallion's advances she will kick out and squeal, so the teasing board acts as protection for both animals.

WHAT DO YOU HOPE TO PRODUCE?

Although a foal may not necessarily conform to your ideal when it arrives, in most cases you can plan to produce something near to what you have in mind by careful choice of a stallion. Think of size, type, and what you have in mind, and remember that breeding is a long-term commitment. It will be 11 months before the foal arrives. After two years, you can begin to break it to ride, but then it will be another four or five years before you can think of it working seriously in a worthwhile career.

THE MARE

The temperament of your mare (also called a dam) will have a major bearing on your choice of stallion. You must choose your stallion to balance out any unfortunate traits. If the mare is naturally calm and easy in every way, then you will have few worries. If, however, she is quick and flighty, you would be wise to put her to a docile stallion whose offspring are known to have inherited his calm disposition.

Soundness is another important consideration. Is your mare tough enough to stand up to the work you ask of her? If she has always had lameness problems, you should think twice about whether to breed from her as her foal might inherit the same characteristics. All the best breeds have been developed by breeding only those horses tough enough to do the job expected. Breeding your mare because she is lame is the worst possible reason, unless her condition has been caused by accidental injury.

The covering of a mare at a stud is always supervised.

FACILITIES

You must decide how and where you are going to keep and produce your foal. Do you have a large enough stable for a mother and foal if the weather is bad? If the climate is mild, the mare and foal can live out as nature intended—especially if they are a tough breed. Do you have enough land for this? An absolute minimum of two acres (0.8 hectare) would be necessary if you use excellent paddock management and have an open shed to shelter them in as well. The paddock fencing must be completely safe and secure, and clean, fresh drinking water must be freely available. See pp. 80–85 and 102–105 for more information.

EXPENSE

Breeding can be a costly affair. First, think of the top range of stud fees, the price you pay for the services of the stallion. If everything goes well, you get your foal at the end as hoped. Sometimes, however, problems occur and your mare does not hold the foal. The whole process then starts all over again. The mare may be difficult to get in foal, so more veterinary fees will be added to your account. In all cases, there will be veterinary fees, as well, for swabs that are taken for culture examinations, pregnancy scans, and routine prenatal care.

The charges for the keep of your mare while at stud can mount up. Think about the timing of when you want a foal and when to take the mare to stud. Taking the mare to stud between five and ten days before she is due to come in season is ideal as this will give her a chance to settle into her new environment. Generally, mares come into season every three weeks for about six to eight months a year.

CHOOSING A STALLION

Choosing a suitable mate for your mare can be a fun process. The stallion (also called a stud or entire) must complement the mare's attributes and make up for failings on her side. If she is rather long in the back (mares often are because they need room to hold a foal) and has poor hocks, it is best to choose a more compact stallion with good strong hocks. If she is a mediocre mover choose a stallion with good action.

Temperament is important. Choose a kind, mannerly stallion and ask what his offspring are like. Talk to people who have bred from him recently and find out about his offsprings' temperaments and saleability; go and see the offspring in person, if possible.

Ask about the stallion's fertility too. It's a great waste of time and money if you hear later that your chosen stallion is not very fertile and gets few mares in foal.

In some cases, the mare can be inseminated artificially—distance, injury, and transportation expense being some reasons for this choice. Here the semen is being collected from the stallion using a dummy mare. This will be stored and then inseminated into the mare when she is in season.

Where is the stallion? Be sure that he is within a distance that you can cope with or arrange easily for your mare's transportation.

Are you satisfied with the way the stud is managed and confident that your mare will be handled properly? Is the facility well run and organized? Do the horses look contented and happy? Ask to see the stallion out of his stable, walked and trotted in hand so that you can assess his conformation, movements, and temperament. Stallions are usually a bit playful and should have plenty of presence—or star quality—but they should not look vicious or mean, or be dangerous.

The stud fee is likely to be a major deciding factor. Investigate this before you even go to see the stallion, and make sure you are clear about the terms.

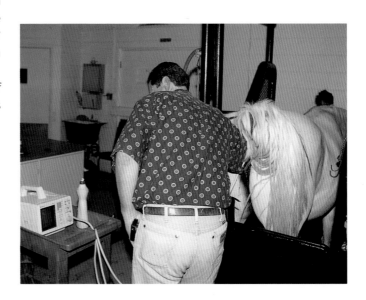

The veterinarian is inserting a scanning probe into the rectum to ascertain if a fertilized egg is in the uterine horn and if the mare is in foal—usually possible after 16 days from the date of service. It is advisable to repeat this procedure a month later if all is well as pregnancies can sometimes be aborted in the early stages.

THE NEW FOAL

After 11 months of preparing for the big day, your foal could be born into the world at any time.

Keep everything as natural as possible for your mare—you are much more likely to be stressed about the event than she is, but keep an eye on her to ensure all is well.

The "in-foal" mare will need a little extra care during the last two to three months before foaling unless she is on really good pasture. Extra feed will be required if the pasture is poor, as this is the time when the foal inside really starts to grow. Lack of food at this stage may affect the unborn foal's chances of reaching its full height later on.

In the majority of cases the mare copes admirably on her own, especially with the hardy and long established breeds. Still, you should keep a close eye on her and watch for any changes. If you are not experienced, it is wise to have a knowledgeable person on hand, preferably a veterinarian, to assist or advise in the latter stages of delivery.

PREPARATION FOR THE FOAL'S ARRIVAL

In preparation for the event, the mare should be up-to-date with her routine health maintenance (worming, vaccines and farrier care) the month before she is due. If she will be foaling inside, have a large stall with plenty of clean straw kept ready. Although indoor foaling is preferable, in good weather, and if alone, the mare can foal outside perfectly happily if the paddock is safe and not too big. Remove any other horses, who may become too inquisitive and harm the foal.

The mare's udder (teats, also known as the milk bar) may begin to enlarge any time from six weeks to just a few hours before foaling. Usually about 24 hours before the birth, she will "wax up" (show a little pale, waxy substance of colostrum on the teats). She may become a bit restless, and the muscles around the anus and vagina will slacken to allow an easier passage for the foal.

DELIVERY

Most mares lie down for the actual birth. They may also lie down for the breaking of the waters and then get up once or twice before the birth itself. First to be "born" are the foal's forelegs, which should appear with one slightly behind the other so that the shoulders can get through the pelvic arch. The head should be pointed forward, resting along the forelegs. The hind legs are tucked underneath the belly, and appear last in a normal delivery.

The whole event usually takes from 20 minutes to an hour before the birth is complete. Left alone without too much interference (as long as the foal's mouth and nose are free of the amniotic covering [sometimes called the birth sack]), it is best to allow both to rest for 20 minutes or so. The mare needs time to recover as her womb begins contracting back to shape and she expels the afterbirth. In most cases, this should be expelled within the next hour or so.

The birth is a very emotional and exciting moment. Here the mare looks around at her newborn offspring foaled in a stable. The head is out but the rest of the foal is still covered in the protective amniotic covering within which it has been living inside the womb. The mare will usually lick the foal dry and pull off any excess covering. Should it be necessary you can remove excess covering—especially if still over the foal's mouth or nostrils—by hand.

DEVELOPMENT OF UNBORN FOAL

Days from Conception	Approx. Length	Approx. Weight	Brief Description
28	1¼" (3 cm)	—	First heartbeats seen on scan.
56	4" (10 cm)	⅓oz (9 g)	All internal organs present, limbs distinct, and sex recognizable.
112	11¼" (28 cm)	2½oz (70 g)	Some fluids in fetal stomach, first traces of hair around lip.
224	22½" (56 cm)	20lb (9 kg)	Hair much more apparent, external sex organs formed.
280	33½" (84 cm)	42lb (19 kg)	Mane growing, hair all along spine.
340 (full term)	39" (97 cm)	99lb (45 kg)	Coat and long hairs fully grown, milk molars through gum.

SIGNS OF MARES BEING IN SEASON

- Marked change in temperament.
- Lifting of tail.
- Winking of vulva.
- Leaning toward teasing boards.
- Receptive to stallions and some geldings.
- Mares usually come "in season" 7–10 days after foaling.

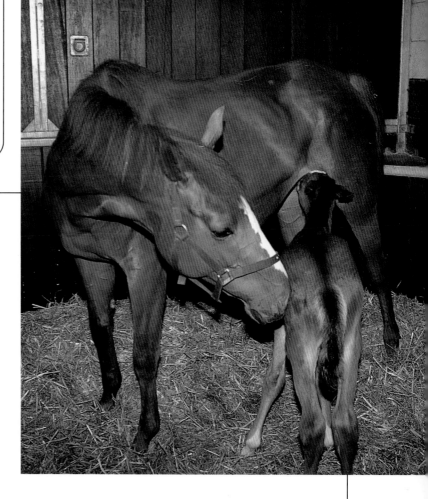

A delicious drink from the milk bar! The mare is gently nuzzling her offspring to encourage it to stay in position. She herself is looking a little thin following the birth. After two or three days, the mare will have filled out again.

DUSTIN MAKES AN ENTRANCE

The foal's first day

3:30AM I arrived into my new world and suddenly felt very cold. It was a big surprise to see my mother for the first time, after only feeling her heartbeats and hearing her comforting noises over the last few months.

4AM Mom licked me all over and I felt much warmer. My coat dried off and became fluffy and cozy. Mom made me stand up, which felt very strange. I told her she had made my legs too long because I kept falling down.

4:30AM I found the udder (teats) between her hind legs. It was difficult to drink at such a funny angle but Mom helped me to get there—delicious!

5AM Exhausted but content, I collapsed beside Mom and slept.

8AM I woke up to such a strange world. It was light and creatures called humans with just two legs came and looked at me. I got up and had another drink, then went off with my mother to have a look at everything. Exhausted by all this effort, I fell asleep again.

12PM Another drink and more excitement. The humans were back again, putting down clean bedding and making sure Mom had food and water.

2–6PM More drinks and lots of new experiences. My legs are much stronger and I have found out how to move around without getting tangled up by them.

8PM Mom takes me for a trot around the field. It is starting to get dark and other animals are wandering about and saying hello. After my nightcap of more milk from Mom, I fall asleep exhausted, but pleased to have arrived into this big, exciting new world.

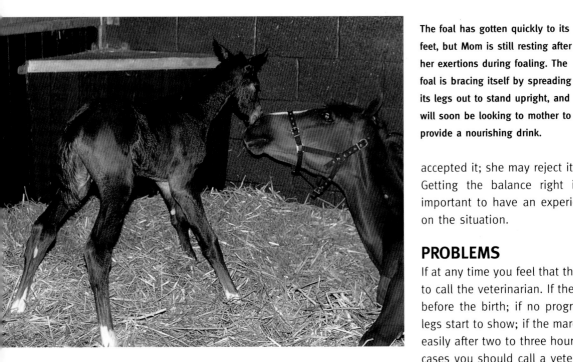

The foal has gotten quickly to its feet, but Mom is still resting after her exertions during foaling. The foal is bracing itself by spreading its legs out to stand upright, and will soon be looking to mother to provide a nourishing drink.

FIRST STEPS

The foal will try to move around and get up, usually with comical results to start with. The mare may continue to rest or get up and start to lick the foal dry—all part of the bonding process. Left to nature, most mares and foals will be up, with the foal having taken its first milk, or colostrum, within an hour and a half of the birth. If the foal cannot manage, it may be necessary to assist it to its feet and guide it to the udder. Some young mothers tend to follow the foal around, never allowing it the chance to find the teats for itself. Be careful not to bother the mare, and always make sure that she can see her foal. Do not overdo handling of the foal until the mare has accepted it; she may reject it if there is too much interference. Getting the balance right is tricky and this is why it is important to have an experienced person on hand to advise on the situation.

PROBLEMS

If at any time you feel that things are not right, do not hesitate to call the veterinarian. If the mare is getting up or down a lot before the birth; if no progress is being made once the fore legs start to show; if the mare's afterbirth does not come away easily after two to three hours following the birth—in all these cases you should call a veterinarian for professional advice.

Watch to see that the foal passes the meconium (the tarry substance expelled from the bowels), too, before the paler milk-based bowel movements get started.

THE NEWBORN FOAL

Most healthy foals are up on their feet within an hour, usually less. Although uncoordinated to start with, they quickly gain strength after just a few hours. If they have foaled inside and are strong, it is best to put them out for a few hours if the weather is mild. Foals born outside will spend hours sleeping beside their dams, after a little cavorting about and periodic nursing, at which they quickly become very experienced.

CARING FOR NEWBORN FOAL

Q Do I need to give my foal anything extra to eat or drink after foaling?

A No. The foal should get all it needs from its mother, but the mare will need extra food if grass is short or of poor quality. Mares and foals should be wormed (see pp. 116–117) after approximately six weeks.

A young foal will start to graze grass, by following its dam's example, while it is still being given milk.

Generally young foals will stay near their mothers to start with, but will gradually become more inquisitive and adventurous. Be sure that the paddock is safe, well fenced, and free from poisonous plants. If it is possible to have two or more mares and foals together, the youngsters can then play and mature together.

LEAVING MOTHER

From those first gangly steps, it is no time at all before a foal can achieve full independence from its mother. This is nature's way of ensuring survival in the wild.

Foals grow very quickly in the first month, as they fill out and strengthen each day. Their energy is boundless and they soon begin to explore and gain independence, especially if they can share a field with others. Their legs appear absurdly long to start with, and if they try to eat grass they have to buckle at the knees to get down there! Most mares provide more than adequate milk so long as they are on good pasture or receiving enough food to make up for poor pasture. This will involve an extra one or two feeds of special mix for lactating mares, depending on your mare's age, type, and condition—your veterinarian will advise you.

Generally, foals stay with their mothers until they are four to six months old, by which time they are independent enough to cope on their own. They quickly learn to eat grass and should be fed a suitable, specially prepared mix for a few weeks before weaning. This ensures that there is no sudden change in diet.

Newborn foals are best led with a stable rubber or cloth round their neck, or a foal halter, and a guiding hand on their rump either before or beside their mother depending on how she feels happiest.

It is important to get the foal used to being handled from an early age. This one seems unperturbed about having its feet picked out—a good sign to the farrier who will soon trim its feet.

Thereafter the weaned foal should continue on the mix through the winter months. It is important to reduce this before the foal/yearling is turned out on lush new pasture in the following spring.

WEANING

There are two ways of separating mares from their foals, both of which are easier in a group as the companionship of others helps to minimize the inevitable stress caused.

If the horses have been coming in at night and going out during the day, it is best to take the mares out in the morning and remove them far enough away from the foals so that neither can hear each other. This may require arrangements to be made with neighbors or friends. Keep the foals in until they have settled. It may be best to leave them quietly for 24 hours and then turn them out together. The mares will need time for their milk to dry up, so they should be kept on a restricted diet for a few days.

The other method of weaning is to keep the mares and foals in a field together with a suitable old retired mare as a nurse. Take the mares away and leave the foals with the nurse. Large stud operations take two mares away at a time, every few days.

Weaning is a stressful time for both sides. The foals inevitably lose weight at this time but quickly readjust, especially if they are with other horses. If you cannot find other foals to share weaning, find a sensible nurse as a companion.

GROWING UP

Full of boisterous fun, your youngster will spend its first few years enjoying a life of careless "freedom." Sensitive handling now will pay off when more starts to be expected of your rebellious "teenager" later on.

Once weaned, the foal adapts to its independent life, and with correct feeding (never overfeed) and regular worming it should continue to mature. As a yearling, it may lose its looks a little. Horses tend to grow by fits and starts, often looking a little higher behind and becoming angular as height takes over from roundness. All the temporary teeth will have been in place since the age of nine months (see p. 114 for more information on aging by teeth development), and the tail will still look foal-like.

At the age of two years, the animal grows into a more rounded and mature horse. The first permanent teeth, the central incisors, appear at two and a half years, as do two permanent molars on the top and bottom jaws. The mane grows long and the tail loses its foal appearance.

By three years of age, there is a look of maturity and the

CARING FOR WEANED FOAL

Q I have found a friend's foal to go with mine. How should I look after them once my foal has been weaned?

A The youngsters should have had a chance to get used to hard feed while still with their mothers. Continue to give two feeds a day and either keep them out or bring them in at night if the weather is bad. Youngsters should be wormed every six to eight weeks (see pp.116–117) and have their feet trimmed as necessary (see pp.96–97). Lead them around once or twice a week and practice picking their feet out periodically (or daily if inside). Basically all youngsters need plenty of fresh air, good food, and exercise to grow and mature into strong healthy animals.

These four handsome yearlings look happy and interested in what is going on. Being herd animals, they will thrive much better in groups than on their own.

mane and tail are filled out. The teeth become more mature, with permanent incisors and four permanent molars in place. Only one temporary molar of the original six remains in each jaw. At the age of three, most horses and ponies should not be asked to do anything too strenuous. Not until they reach the age of four will they be ready for more arduous work.

From weaning onward, it is important that youngsters are well handled and accustomed to the general day-to-day chores. They should be used to a halter and lead rope. They should be groomed (see pp.86–89) and have their feet picked out regularly so that they are accustomed to this sort of attention when the farrier comes. They should be led in and out of paddocks and handled calmly yet firmly to get used to human contact at least once a month, even if out at pasture throughout the summer. Confident, quiet but firm handling is essential if youngsters are to become well-adjusted adults.

Leading out in hand in quiet surroundings gives a very good grounding for when the time comes for breaking in and hacking out. This youngster led in a bridle for a stroll on a quiet lane looks quiet and happy.

BREAKING IN

The special bond you have built with your youngster should make it a willing partner in the first hesitant steps toward its career. How you have done your early work will prove invaluable during this next important stage. If the horse is obedient and understands words of command early in life and has been regularly handled, then the next stage should be most rewarding.

Breaking in becomes the next important milestone in the young horse's career. The trust and confidence built up between horse and humans during the first few years should pay off now with few problems, so long as the horse is given time to understand the role it is expected to play—that of being ridden.

LUNGE WORK

Lunge work, or lunging, involves the horse moving around the trainer on an outside circle attached to a lunge line. The trainer must stay in the center and encourage the horse forward with a lunge whip. This must not be used to frighten the animal, but only to encourage it forward. A triangle is formed between the trainer, the horse, and the whip.

FIRST USE OF A BIT

The first stage, if you have not done so already, is to get the horse used to a bit. Start with a mild rubber or snaffle bit, which can be put into the horse's mouth for 20 minutes each day. Then a stable roller and large comfortable pad can be

This horse has been lunged for some weeks off long reins (two reins used instead of one). This enables the handler to have a little more control and the horse to get used to reins around its legs.

introduced at the same time (as a forerunner to a saddle), and the horse led about until it is confident. The saddle can then be introduced. Prevent the horse from becoming frightened by securing the stirrups so they do not flap against its sides.

VOICE COMMANDS

The horse must learn to obey the voice so that you will be able to talk to it when it is ridden. Keep commands simple, such as "walk on," "teerot" for trot, and "whoa" for halt. Animate your voice when you want the horse to move faster, slow your commands when you want to reduce the pace. Horses learn by repetition, so practice each day until the horse begins to understand. Reward the animal when it does well.

Some people prefer not to lunge young horses, fearing that the small circles can strain immature muscles. You can still teach the horse to obey the voice by walking it up and down tracks in hand or long-reining with two lunge lines, one on either side. When long-reining, it is important to have a helper for the first few sessions. That way, the other person can hold the horse's head until it becomes accustomed to the reins and you can maintain control from behind at a safe distance. The horse can be "driven" like this all over the place if it is safe to do so, which will help it to get used to all the different sights and sounds in its environment.

HORSE WHISPERING

Horse whispering is a modern term for communicating with horses using skills and techniques which have gone on for centuries but until recently have never been understood or documented. Now this system has been made world-famous by Monty Roberts from California. Monty, a part Cherokee, used his Native American background to show to the world that it is possible to bond or "join-up" with horses by emulating equine body language.

At his ranch in California, Monty runs courses to train people to become "whisperers" and has given spectacular displays of how it is possible to communicate

This horse is ready to be backed (see below), and has been taken quietly through the lungeing stage and driven around in long reins while showing no fear or worry. Note the neckstrap around the neck for the rider's use in case the horse moves quickly.

with horses and dispel any fears they may have by empathizing with the horse's mind. Some horses respond quicker than others, but once the "whisperer" has been accepted, they usually respond quietly and willingly.

There are several people who have worked on difficult horses with kindness and understanding and have had equally good results. Either way, the secret is to gain the animal's confidence. If this has already been lost, the need to establish a bond becomes even more important. As with any training, patience and time are vital to success, and this is one of the keys to "whispering."

THE FIRST RIDER/"BACKING THE HORSE"

Ideally, you need three helpers to mount a horse for the first time, but it is quite possible with one. Your horse should still be on a lunge rein. When the horse is relaxed and quiet, bring it into an enclosed area that is familiar—a small paddock, for instance. The rider must wear a helmet and be calm and confident. With two helpers, one can hold the horse, talking to it quietly, and the second can give the rider a leg up across the saddle. Take plenty of time and be patient to ensure that the horse does not become worried at any time. When there is only one helper, that person must hold the horse's head and give the rider a leg up at the same time—making sure that the horse looks completely calm before starting.

Once the horse has felt the weight, it can be moved a step or two and then stopped and rewarded. Let the horse tell you when it is ready to progress. Some will be totally unconcerned, others may need a day or two just doing this before they can progress further. For the next step, lead the horse a few steps and then mount the horse without banging a foot on its rump. Talk all the time in reassuring tones and then progress to walking around the area, doing a little more each day. Allow between one and three weeks to break a horse. Each horse will vary, but with confident and sympathetic handling there is rarely a problem.

Lead the horse out and about and show it the sights, all

The rider has been lifted up onto the horse two or three times to ensure the animal is unconcerned. The horse is now being led forward for a few steps to get used to the weight of the rider.

the time teaching it to obey commands. The rider must talk to the horse and ask it to walk, halt, and trot as and when required. Once obedient, it can come off the lunge rein and start out on its own. Riding out with another quiet horse will help to improve the young animal's confidence. Most people break horses and ride them for a few weeks, then give them a rest before starting serious work.

THE MATURE HORSE

From four years on the horse is usually ready to do a variety of work, and by six years it is considered to be mentally and physically mature. Some, however, especially large horses, may take a year or so longer to mature—some less.

Generally horses are at their best from 6–12 years, but there are star Olympic horses who are 12–16 years old. Thereafter,

The horse is being led around with the rider on top, who must sit relaxed and calm to give the horse confidence. An assistant is walking beside the horse to give it some words of encouragement.

DAY IN THE LIFE OF A TRAINER

Up early this morning to travel 140 miles (224 km) to run a clinic at a barn in Pennsylvania.

On arrival the riders are introduced—six in all for the morning session. Some of the group were novices but some had ridden a little before. I decide to have them two at a time for one hour each. We work on the paces and transitions creating a better understanding of the methods used to obtain smooth obedient changes within the gaits. I found the riders respond well to the use of poles to supple

their horses first. One or two needed help with their position on the lunge.

After a great barbecue we did the jumping part. Worked on their position over fences and made different distances at combinations for them to practice.

Although this job is hard work I get a real sense of achievement when my students have practiced a skill over and over again and then get it right.

they need treating very much as individuals. With proper care and individual attention, they may continue to work happily until they are around 18, but some age earlier than others.

The horse must learn to go out on its own and be quiet in traffic. If it has been taken slowly and not rushed in its training, it will be confident and willing to do everything expected of it.

KEEPING CONTROL

Q What should I do when my horse won't move away from my friend's horse when we are out riding together?

A It is very important that you make your horse go where you want by effective use of your legs and short enough reins to keep it under control. (See Control and the Aids pp.158–163 for more information.) A stick correctly used behind your leg once or twice and maybe some sharp words from you should do the trick. The horse must respect your wishes and you must persevere every time it argues if you want to come out on top.

Riding the horse out first in company helps to build up confidence. These two are enjoying a splash in the river which will prove invaluable if they later jump cross country.

UNDERSTANDING YOUR HORSE

In the wild, horses use body language to communicate with the rest of the herd. If you take the time to study their behavior and try to understand what they need, it won't be long before you'll be convinced your horse is "talking" to you!

The longer you own your horse or pony, the more you will get to know its likes and dislikes. This is important, as you will be able to recognize if it begins to act out of character (there is usually an underlying reason). Horses may not be able to talk to us literally, but you can tell a lot from their expression and body language. Eyes, ears, and position of the body are the main ways we have of knowing what our horses are thinking.

Ears forward or relaxed denotes a happy or contented horse. Flicking back and forth could indicate nervousness or worry and uncertainty. Ears back usually means anger, pricked very far forward can indicate interest, surprise, or expectation. The eyes in conjunction with the ears give a good indication as well, and often will tell you what mood the horse is in!

The stance of the horse will also be informative. A stubborn animal will dig its toes in just like an obstinate child! It may hold a leg up in pain or point out a front one to relieve pressure. Many rest a hind leg, but this does not necessarily mean they are uncomfortable.

▶ The tired horse will generally look rather listless and sleepy, and its eyes will periodically close. It may hang its head or even lie down if excessively tired.

◀ A horse may show the white of its eye and tense its muscles away from sights and sounds that scare it. Reassuring talk and a pat on the neck will often calm a nervous or frightened animal. Be positive in your approach when your horse encounters frightening objects.

▲ The horse may indicate it is unhappy by frequently flattening its ears back and possibly wrinkling its nose. Try to vary its day with a spell in the paddock or a change in routine.

REACTING TO A THREAT

The horse will react by raising its head to look and listen intently. It may back off in a nervous way and start pawing the ground while still trying to figure out what is going on. It may also snort, raise its tail, and prance about, then either wheel around on its hind legs and gallop away or stand and face the threat. If the "threat" is another horse, it may kick out viciously if it dislikes what it sees—or do a few playful bucks and kicks and invite the other horse to join in and play!

Interested

Unsure—Go away

Go quickly—I don't like you

Play time

▼ The angry horse may flatten its ears back in a menacing attitude. If it is angry enough to attack it will open its eyes wide and bare its teeth. Some will threaten to turn their quarters toward you and even kick out.

▶ The questioning look which may follow something strange that has caught the horse's eye. Its head is raised and alert, and its ear flicks suspiciously.

▼ Suspicious horses will usually back away from anything they are unsure of while flicking their ears back and forth. They may also show a bit of white of the eye and be rather tense near any frightening object.

BEHAVIOR

Because the horse is a herd animal, it will often behave in a different way on its own than when in company. The motivation of the other horses will often encourage a nervous or easily intimidated horse to do things that it would be too timid to do on its own.

Other horses might become a little hyperactive in company, which makes it difficult to control, and therefore more suited to working alone. So much of how a horse reacts, however, will depend on its early handling as a foal and the confidence it has built up from an early age with human beings. The method of backing the horse during the breaking-in period is another time in the horse's life when knowledge and understanding of what the horse is feeling and thinking may well affect its future progress.

The horse is never happier than when running loose in a paddock—preferably with company. This fine Thoroughbred is enjoying a relaxing play in its field.

TEMPERAMENT

The temperament of the horse is genetically controlled. It is up to us to handle each type with the same care that we would when dealing with humans of different temperaments.

It makes sense to try to seek a suitable "match" between the temperaments of the horse and its rider. A very nervous rider requires a straightforward confident horse that will take things as they come. An experienced confident rider with a no-nonsense attitude will help a timid horse by instilling boldness.

KICKING OUT

Q When I come and see my pony, it sometimes turns its behind toward me and tries to kick me. It never used to do this!

A Maybe you have spoiled it with too many tidbits which is the ruination of so many nice animals. The occasional treat is fine, but once horses start to "expect" a goodie, they will feel let down like children if it's not there and respond in such a way as to show their displeasure. Walk slowly toward your pony without a tidbit and wait for it to come to you, then pat it and talk to him. A sharp "No" and standing still is the best way to stop its bad behavior. You could give it a break—it may be fed up with humans and enjoy a spell on its own for a while.

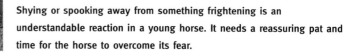

Shying or spooking away from something frightening is an understandable reaction in a young horse. It needs a reassuring pat and time for the horse to overcome its fear.

An inexperienced, reckless rider on a very overconfident horse is a recipe for disaster as they encourage each other to go dangerously fast. However, such a horse in the right controlling hands could be a champion.

INTELLIGENCE

The horse has a small brain in relation to its size, and to humans, its intelligence appears to vary tremendously. Some horses appear remarkably clever, others much less so. All, however, have a special animal cunning which can easily outwit a human in certain situations unless you learn early on to stay "one jump ahead" of your equine friend.

Many horses will find ingenious methods of opening their stable doors or gates. Others will soon learn the quickest route home, and it is up to the rider to ensure the horse goes where directed and is never allowed to take over. Some unfortunately realize that after three jump refusals, they must retire from a competition. A great way of getting out of doing something! When taken back for "a school" to cure this habit, they pop over the jump first time!

Many times after a fall, however, it is the pony who finds its way home to alert others that help is required. For that the animal can be forgiven a lot of their less endearing traits!

The horse is a herd animal and as such learns much better in company. If loose, most horses tend to follow one another, which is worth remembering when catching. Lead another in and its difficult friend will usually follow!

REARING

Q I went to see a horse to buy and viewed it in its large paddock. It seemed very high-spirited—running around the enclosure and rearing up. I'm worried about the horse rearing. Will it do this when I'm riding it?

A There are many reasons why horses rear—it may be startled, displaying its dominant qualities, playing or simply excited and full-of-life. Stallions are particularly fond of showing off in this way! Rearing while turned out is not necessarily a sign that the horse has developed the vice of rearing while being ridden. But, to be on the safe side if you are thinking of buying any horse or pony you should see the horse being ridden by the vendor to check that it is well-behaved and manageable for you to ride.

Rearing is often an expression of freedom and well-being for a horse.

VICES

Most horses love company and enjoy the stimulation of working. Unfortunately they can get bored easily, and confinement in a stall can lead to vices (bad habits) that are hard to break. Unfortunately horses with known vices are devalued when it comes to selling on so any attempt to prevent a vice is worth trying.

Horses are much happier in a group and are at their best browsing through pasture choosing what they like to eat. This means that stabling—an unnatural environment for a horse—can lead to boredom, which can then lead to the development of vices. Apart from being unpleasant, vices are also easily copied by other horses at the barn or stable yard.

Turning a horse out on a daily basis alleviates boredom, provides rest, and allows the horse to return to a more natural state. Turning out for a few weeks may even give a horse time to forget a vice that it has only just started to acquire—before it becomes too entrenched.

WEAVING

Weaving is a vice whereby the horse rocks from side to side, weaving its head from left to right. It is not too much of a problem in itself, but it is copied by other horses. It devalues a horse's sale price, so many stable owners don't like a weaver at their facilities. An anti-weaving grill is the most effective way to stop the practice. Hanging toys from the top of the door or inside the stable can help to alleviate the problem.

▲ Weaving can usually be controlled by using an anti-weaving grill or by hanging toys in a net from the top of the doorway.

◄ This horse is wearing a bib to prevent it chewing its blanket. These can also be helpful to stop the horse chewing bandages, such as those holding a dressing in place.

BLANKET TEARING

Q My pony keeps grabbing her blanket with her teeth. How can I stop this?

A This is a tiresome habit which can become very expensive if too many blankets get ruined. The use of a bib as shown attached to the back of the headcollar will usually solve this problem because the horse is prevented from getting hold of the blanket.

CHEWING

Q My horse chews the top of his stable door. What can I do to prevent this?

A There are two things that should help. First, you can paint the door with creosote or an anti-chew paste and see whether that works. Better still, cover the top, front area, and any other vulnerable parts of the door with a thin strip of metal sheeting. Make sure this is nailed down securely so that the horse cannot get his teeth caught in it.

Chewing the stable door is just as bad a habit as crib biting because it can damage the horse's teeth and this will lead to feeding problems.

CRIBBING AND WINDSUCKING

With crib biting or cribbing, the horse tends to grab hold of things with its teeth—especially the tops of stable doors. Unfortunately, this can lead to windsucking, where the horse gulps in air as it grabs the top of the door. Apart from being unattractive, this can lead to colic (see p.127) if too much air is taken in. Often, a cribbing strap can help solve the problem. It is attached around the top of the horse's throat and, so long as it is correctly fitted, prevents the horse from tensing its neck muscles while gripping the stable door. In most cases this effectively stops it from sucking in air. A confirmed cribber will continue its habit out in a field, using fence posts and rails.

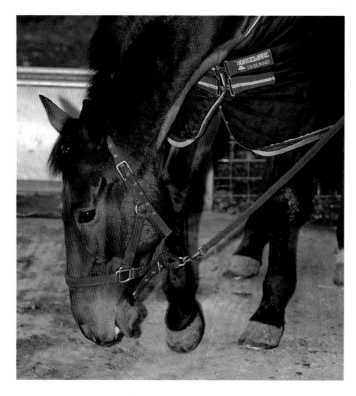

Pawing could be a sign of an impatient, greedy horse or of boredom and the onset of stall walking—so break the habit early.

STALL WALKING

Stall walking is the term used when a horse is restless and constantly moves around in its stall. This problem tends to affect horses who, for one reason or another, have been cooped up in their stalls for long periods or who do not spend enough time as nature intended, out free. Freedom is what they crave, and the more they can be out the better. Some are content to be tied up during their stressful periods —giving them a hay net at such times will help to occupy their minds. Some like music and a few may find a toy helpful.

Horses that stall walk tend to lose their condition quite easily, so any diversion that works should be employed. The best remedy, though, is to turn the horse out as much as possible.

PAWING THE GROUND

Q Is pawing a problem?

A This can be a maddening habit, and will tend to wear out shoes unevenly and may increase farrier bills. A sharp "no" every time the horse paws may help. If it does this at feed time, be sure to give the horse its feed first. Some become hungry and start pawing as soon as they recognize the sound of the feed being prepared. It may be a good idea to premix or prepare the feed when doing the earlier meal so that it will be ready to be taken straight to the horse without its hearing the preparations!

Pawing can also be a sign that the horse is in pain.

CHOOSING AND BUYING A HORSE

Before considering buying a horse or pony, it is essential to think everything through to ensure that you really can cope with owning one. Horses are both time-consuming and expensive, but, if you are prepared to put in the necessary hard work, they make wonderful companions and are a joy to own.

The first question you must ask yourself is whether you can afford a horse. Horses and ponies are fairly expensive to buy, but the cost of upkeep can be enormous also. Year-round feed, stabling, shoeing, veterinary care—such as worming, vaccinations, and dental care—schooling costs, tack and equipment, your own riding gear, transportation, and insurance—all of these add up to substantial expenses.

Do you have the facilities? Do you have a suitable paddock and stabling, or will you have to pay to stable your horse? If you can't afford to pay for full-time care, do you have the time to spare to look after the horse? How often will you be able to ride it?

Who is going to help you if you are a beginner? It's unlikely that basic riding lessons from a local barn or stable will be enough to prepare you to own your own horse. However, if you have also helped to care for horses on weekends or over vacations, then you are probably experienced enough to deal with one at home.

WHAT TO LOOK FOR

Choose a horse that is suitable in temperament, height, and type for you and what you plan to do with it. If you are not an experienced rider, you will need a horse that is quiet and sensible to give you the most pleasure. Go for a calm, well-schooled animal that is confident and happy in its work, and easily controlled. Depending on what it is you want to do, choose a horse aged somewhere between five and ten years. If you want an experienced, sensible horse that will get you

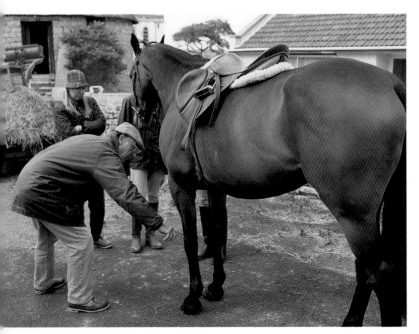

SUGGESTED SIZE GUIDE

The height of the horse or pony is important, as nothing is worse than being over-horsed. If buying for children, choose one that is small enough to be handled well, and check that it is not too big or too wide. If your teenager is outgrowing a much-loved pony make sure he or she intends to continue riding before you commit to the expense of buying a horse. Remember that size and shape—of people and horses—will play a key role. Heavy people, for example, require strong horses, such as those of a hunter or cob type. Below is a general guide but much depends on skill and experience.

If you are choosing a horse that needs to be a specific height for a certain activity, have it measured or see its height certificate before deciding to buy.

12.2hh (127 cm) pony—*suitable for average size children of 12 or under*

13.2–14.2hh (137–147 cm) pony—*suitable for average size children of 14 to 16 years*

14.2–15.2hh (147–157 cm) horse—*suitable for average size children of 14 to 18 years or adults*

15.2hh (157 cm) horse and over—*suitable for competent riders of all ages*

Always get your horse vetted to ensure that what you are buying is basically sound in eye, wind, heart, and limb. Consider your veterinarian's findings if there are any problems and be realistic about how you would cope.

going and give you confidence, go for something around eight or older. Choose a breed that is suitable for the tasks you require of your horse; such as for endurance or trail riding you need a strong, tough breed such as the Arab (see p.53). Some breeds are particularly capable at specific roles.

Of all the different factors governing your choice of horse, temperament is the most important of all. Only choose a horse or pony that fits in well with the job you have in mind. And never overwhelm yourself with a flashy animal you simply cannot control.

See the horse ridden first before you try it yourself, and take a knowledgeable person with you to see if he or she thinks it is the right horse for you.

AVOIDING PROBLEMS

- *Make a list of questions to ask regarding the horse's size, color, sex, and whether it is quiet to ride and able to perform those aspects of riding you are interested in.*
- *Ask the owners if the horse or pony is quiet in traffic, with children, with dogs, other animals, and so on.*
- *Why are they selling? Do their reasons seem genuine to you?*
- *Will there be someone there to ride it for you? This is very important: You must ensure the animal is quiet to ride before you get on. Many an accident has occurred by failing to see what type of animal you are about to ride.*
- *Always check the price they are asking and if not in your range, thank them and cross the horse off your list.*

WHERE TO FIND YOUR HORSE/PONY

When you decide to have your own pony or horse and have weighed all the factors involved—where and how to keep it, whether it is affordable—you will need to ensure you have a knowledgeable person to help you choose the right animal for you.

- *Reputable dealers may be able to find the perfect animal but you must first tell them what you want, what you hope to do with the animal, and how experienced you are. Your size, weight and age, and your price range will also be needed to assess your requirements accurately.*
- *Asking friends may be another method, especially if it is a pony you are looking for, as friends may well know of one that is outgrown or no longer required. Check carefully what work the pony has done before.*
- *Looking at the "For Sale" pages in horsey magazines and local papers will usually provide a mass of possibilities.*
- *Auction sales are not generally recommended for the first-time buyer because of the difficulty in trying out horses and ponies properly before the hammer falls and you are committed to buying subject to vetting. If you do go, know what you are looking for and do not get carried away by the occasion or your emotions. Take a knowledgeable person with you and find out all you can. Try to see photographs and ask everything possible about any animal that catches your eye.*

Buying at auction is best left to the professionals.

If it is possible, try to see the horse ridden or at least a photograph of it in action.

If you buy at a sale, you will be expected to produce appropriate funds or banking arrangements on the day and to arrange transportation from the sale. Go prepared for this in case you find what you want right away.

It is essential to know the pitfalls when buying or looking for a horse or pony, as sadly, not everyone is as honest or fair as he or she should be. Make sure you ask plenty of questions and never get drawn into something you do not feel confident about. Take a number and call back later to give yourself time to think before making a final decision.

GENERAL CARE

Your horse or pony relies on you to take care of its everyday needs. Whether a top eventer or a favorite family pet, all deserve the best attention you can give to ensure their health and well-being. Food, shelter, and exercise are vital to all horses, and, while geographical locations will inevitably dictate different ways of doing certain things, the basics remain the same worldwide.

Horses thrive on routine, so try to plan a schedule of care that is realistic on a daily basis. How you can achieve this all depends on the type of arrangement you have for stabling and/or where the animal is kept. If you have your own stable and land, obviously you can work out a routine that suits your own lifestyle or you may keep your horse at a boarding stable, in which case you will be paying someone else to look after it full time. The horse will even be exercised and turned out into a paddock area for you by the staff during the week and those times when you are unable to do so yourself. The expense varies according to the individual arrangement you have with the owners of the facility.

Do-it-yourself arrangements also exist, where you literally pay for the rental of a box stall and perhaps the use of a paddock and look after it yourself. It's worth bearing in mind that if your horse is likely to be fed by other people, you should display its feed chart prominently. Keep it up to date with any changes, and let everyone know if your horse is on medication (and whether any side effects are likely).

If the animal is kept out at grass, or even just turned out every day, you must make sure there is adequate fodder and fresh water. Pastures must be safe and securely fenced, and free from poisonous plants and trees. Check for potential hazards such as deep holes and broken wire. The emphasis on safety cannot be overemphasized.

Some horses and ponies are difficult to catch unless you take some food with you. Be careful doing this if the horse shares the field with others as they may crowd around you. Keep a handful for your horse or pony and tip the rest along the ground. As your horse goes to eat with the others, approach it and offer the separate food. (Left) Gently put on the halter and lead rope (see p.138) and lead your horse away. (Right) Keep the bucket in your spare hand—away from your horse or pony.

SAFETY PRECAUTIONS

Fire can be one of the main hazards at a stable and every effort should be made to ensure that safety precautions are taken. These should include a strict "No Smoking" policy and regular checking of all electrical appliances and wiring (which mice can be especially fond of!). The barn and grounds should be kept free of junk, cans, and bottles, which can ignite (especially in the summer months) and there should be fire extinguishers readily available.

SECURITY PRECAUTIONS

Security is another priority. All fencing should be regularly checked to ensure it is safe and stock-proof, and gates onto roads should be padlocked. If the facility is not guarded 24 hours a day—the ideal—security will need special consideration. All stable doors should have extra bottom kickover locks or other horse-proof fixtures, as some animals can become expert escape artists. Consider the various means of horse identification available, just in case of theft. As well as freeze branding, there are other precautions such as microchip implants, lip marking, and hoofbrands (these grow out eventually). Take photographs of your horse or pony, clearly showing both sides, and keep these in a file along with the horse's vaccination card, registration papers, and health records.

Security lighting may be a sensible precaution, and regular checks on the yard cannot be overemphasized. All tack rooms need to be very secure and the contents realistically insured and cataloged.

STABLE FITTINGS

Q What type of electrical fixtures should I use in my horse's stable?

A Ideally there should be no electrical fixtures inside the stable, except for lighting. All wires should be encased in piping, and the switch should be outside the stall and out of the horse's reach. The switches should be encased or incapable of causing shocks on touch. There are many safety fixtures available. (See pp.82–83 for more on stable features.)

A well maintained barn or yard will ensure that all safety features such as fire hoses and extinguishers are in place and that any electrical fixtures are protected and safe. Door fastenings and gates must be secure.

SAFETY KNOT

When tying up your horse, always use a safety knot which consists of a special quick release knot tied as shown. Some horses tend to pull back when tied up. This can cause an accident if the ground is slippery and the horse falls while still tied. To avoid this, it is safest to tie your lead rope with a piece of string to the tie ring, which will then break if the horse starts to struggle.

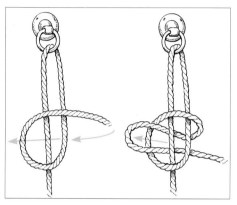

▲ **Make a loop and pull a loop of rope up through this, but not too tightly.**

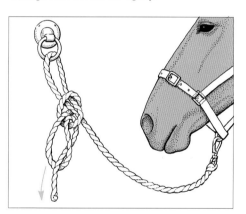

▲ **The end can be looped back through the loop, but must be pulled out before the loop can be released.**

YARD SURFACING

Q My pony is frightened of slipping on the concrete at our barn. What can we do?

A Some concrete can become slippery, especially if it has been around for a long time. It may be possible to groove lines or squares into it. Rubber matting can be sealed on top of concrete along the route out of the yard. Alternatively, some non-slip materials, such as rubberized coating or gravel can be poured over existing areas of worn concrete to give greater grip. Never hurry horses on slippery surfaces, especially on turns. Allow them time to adjust their pace to the new footing.

STABLING AND BEDDING

The stable needs to be safe, sheltered and well sited to make it as easy to manage as possible. Running water and storage space for feed and bedding are just the basics, as is an area set out for the muck heap. This needs to be far away enough to reduce the smell and flies, without becoming a major trek every time you clean out the stall or stable.

In Britain, the most typical arrangement in a stable yard consists of a single row of buildings incorporating loose boxes (stables), tack room, and feed room side by side. In the United States, however, you're likely to find everything under one large roof. In this "barn" system, box stalls face each other across a central walkway and all elements of the traditional stable yard (except the muck heap!) are enclosed against the extremes of weather. This all works extremely well, as long as adequate ventilation has been planned into the construction. Similar systems are in operation at the big stud farms in Europe, and are starting to be incorporated into existing agricultural buildings in Britain.

IDEAL STABLE REQUIREMENTS/FIXTURES

▼ The diagram below shows two loose box style stables side-by-side, the one on the left showing the ideal external features and the one on the right showing the internal features.

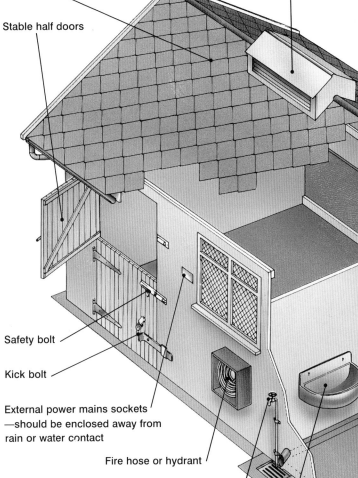

Ridge ventilator

Sloping roof

Stable half doors

Safety bolt

Kick bolt

External power mains sockets —should be enclosed away from rain or water contact

Fire hose or hydrant

Water faucet (tap)

Self-filling drinking bowl or water bucket

Doorway should be opposite feed manger so that the horse will walk straight into the stall and not be tempted to stop for a snack!

◄ There are two main types of stabling: those that look out with an overhanging roof to protect horses and helpers from the elements (top); and the internal or "barn" system which tends to have the horses inside under one roof (bottom). This latter system is popular in America and Europe.

STABLE SIZE

The size of the stall is important to the horse—the bigger the better, to allow more room for movement. The minimum recommended size for box stalls is 10 ft (3 m) square for a pony and about 12 ft (3.7 m) square for a horse. Height, of course, is another consideration. To allow enough head room, ceilings need to be 7 ft (2.1 m) high. Doorways need to be at least 6 ft (1.8 m) high and 4 ft (1.2 m) wide to get the animal in and out safely. Ideally, the roof should overhang the front by about 3 ft (0.9 m) to protect the horse and bedding in bad weather.

Generally, these stalls are constructed of wood, concrete, or brick, or a combination of all three. Many consist of wooden partitions built on top of a brick or cinder block floor surround to eliminate the problem of wood rotting. Some are made entirely of concrete blocks or brick with just a wooden door. Whatever the construction, allowance should be made for ventilation to ensure a free flow of air without drafts. Any windows should open outward for safety.

Just as important is a good floor base with adequate drainage. Many have slightly sloped concrete floors running into a gully outside the stalls, which then leads into a drain outside the stable area.

STABLE FIXTURES

Internal stable fixtures vary tremendously but at least one tie ring is essential for tying up the horse and another to secure a hay net. Many stables will have hay racks and possibly mangers fitted as permanent fixtures. Piped water may also be in place, providing water from special drinkers. These need to be kept scrupulously clean and adjusted so that they do not overfill. Otherwise buckets should be used and kept in a corner out of the way, or hung on clips if the horse is liable to knock them over—some do this as a pastime! It makes good sense if the faucet (tap) is in a convenient location. (Keep it covered if freezing weather is expected.)

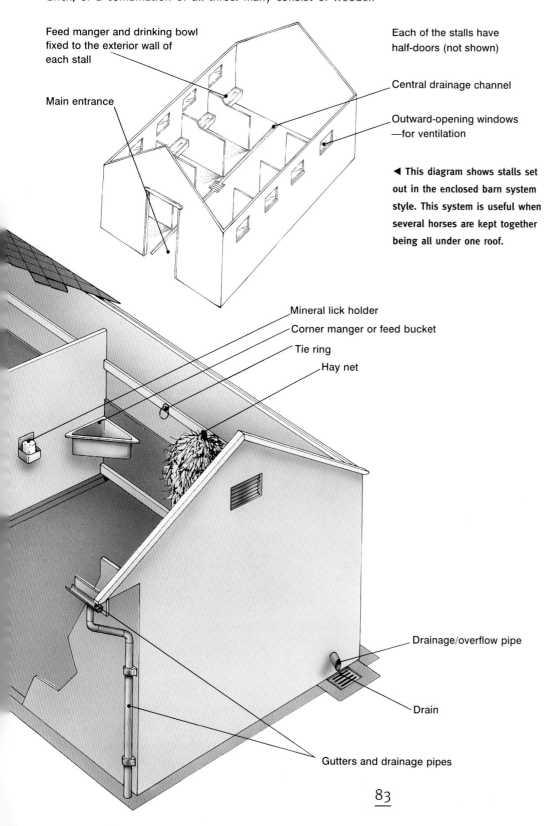

Feed manger and drinking bowl fixed to the exterior wall of each stall

Main entrance

Each of the stalls have half-doors (not shown)

Central drainage channel

Outward-opening windows —for ventilation

◄ This diagram shows stalls set out in the enclosed barn system style. This system is useful when several horses are kept together being all under one roof.

Mineral lick holder

Corner manger or feed bucket

Tie ring

Hay net

Drainage/overflow pipe

Drain

Gutters and drainage pipes

TACK ROOMS

Tack rooms should be easily accessible to the stall or stable area and big enough to accommodate all the necessary bits of equipment. Bridle hooks and saddle racks need to be high enough to ensure that the tack is kept off the ground, and no more than two saddles should ever be placed on top of one another. Western saddles require a rack of their own. A centrally hanging hook is useful for tack cleaning—many are adjustable to different heights. A tack "horse" is a good investment too. It helps to keep the saddle properly supported while it's being cleaned.

▲ A well-kept tackroom is a pleasure to use.

▶ Keep all tack in good condition by cleaning regularly and storing on appropriate bridle hooks and saddle racks.

FOOD STORAGE

Storage of food, hay, straw, and other bedding needs careful thought. They have to be as close as possible to the stable area but with consideration to the fact that they pose a fire risk. Hay is normally kept with the bedding, in a barn perhaps, and the feed room itself contains just the grains, concentrates, any supplements and vitamins, and feed buckets. Feed buckets should be dry, and always kept extremely clean. Any storage bins must be vermin-proof.

FUSSY FEEDER

**My horse is a very timid feeder. What should I do?**

Always ensure the feed bin in the stable is scrupulously clean and well drained and dry before use. Only give small feeds so as not to overwhelm the horse. Experiment with different types of feed and see what it likes or dislikes. Add any succulents such as carrots and apples to its feed as a "tempter." Feed little and often.

If you do not have a hay rack in the stall or loose box (stable) then you can tie a hay net up on a tie ring—ensure that it is kept at the horse's head height. Fix the net securely in place with a safety knot (see p.81).

BEDDING AND CLEANING OUT

Cleanliness is an absolute essential throughout the yard, but nowhere more so than in the stall or stable itself. Some types of bedding make this easier to achieve than others, but it's often a matter of personal preference or even a case of what is readily available in your area. Straw, wood shavings, and rubber sheeting are the main types used, although paper and peat are possible alternatives.

Straw. The most commonly used bedding, straw comes in three types—wheat, barley, and oat. Wheat is the most resilient and springy; barley is a little softer; oat straw is softer still, but some horses like to eat it. The main drawback to straw is that it can exacerbate respiratory difficulties.

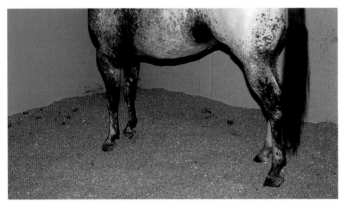

A bedding of wood shavings.

Wood shavings. This popular bedding is light and easy to work with, and useful for horses that eat straw or have allergies. If plastic wrapped, it has the advantage of being able to be stored outside. The only disadvantage is that it can be difficult to dispose of because it takes a long time to rot down.

Rubber sheeting. This is becoming increasingly popular as an alternative to the above. It can be labor-saving but opinions are divided on whether it is comfortable enough to be used without a light covering of conventional bedding. If bedding, such as wood shavings, is not used, the horse's droppings must be removed frequently to prevent the animal from becoming very soiled when lying down. Without other bedding rubber sheeting can be hosed down daily. It is expensive in the short term but because it is hard wearing works out well over a year or so.

A bedding of straw.

SHOW DAY—A BUSY TIME FOR A GROOM

When the alarm goes at around 3AM, I often wonder why I chose this job! A quick cup of coffee and out into the gloom of the emerging dawn to get everything ready, muck out and get Weasel ready for the show. We are leaving at 4.30AM!

Weasel looks out with a surprised expression as I bring him his early breakfast and rush off to put all the tack into the trailer. I've made a list and check it off, then quickly braid (plait) Weasel's mane and tail—his mane is a bit difficult to see in the glare of the overhead light. I then put on his travel gear—protective boots, bandage on the braided tail, and blanket (rug) (see pp.108 and 110). Another groom, Susie, starts up the truck's engine after making all the safety checks (see p.108) and we are all set to go the 100 miles (160km) 2½ hour trip. Crazy!

The show was great—Weasel was 3rd in one class and got a lovely yellow rosette. I was proud of his gleaming coat and polished tack.

At the end, we packed everything up and set off on what always seems like a long trip home because everyone is so tired. During the trip Weasel was munching his hay from the net I tied in the box, and Susie and I had our sandwiches. Home at last and a flurry of activity to unpack, clean out the trailer, unhitch the truck, and feed Weasel who was feeling very pleased with himself.

Finally a bit of supper and the longed for shower—then bed. I was too tired to even dream of the next show!

GROOMING

Grooming is one of the most rewarding chores. Not only does it help to clean the animal but it also stimulates the circulation of the horse or pony. It is the perfect time to really get to know your horse, as a good grooming session will take up to three-quarters of an hour.

Grooming should be done on a daily basis with the stabled horse. Grass-kept horses and ponies should not be over-groomed, however, as this will remove the natural oils that are keeping them warm. It should be enough just to pick out their feet and remove any mud and stains before tacking up.

THE BASIC GROOMING KIT

1. Hoof pick This is used from heel to toe for picking out dirt from hooves.

2. Hard brush (Dandy brush) This stiff brush is for initial cleaning of mud or dirt from unclipped horses. Do not use on clipped or sensitive-skinned horses or on the tail where it will pull and tear the hairs. Use with short, sharp strokes.

3. Soft brush (Body brush) This is used for removing grease and dust from the coats of fine-skinned or clipped horses, and for cleaning the head and the insides of the legs. Care must be taken in these areas not to knock the prominent bones around the eye, the knees, and hocks—which are extremely sensitive. The soft brush is used in conjunction with a metal curry comb (a cleaning device for the brush). The sequence is, one brush of the horse, one scrape across the metal curry comb with the soft brush to remove dirt, one brush, one scrape, and so on.

4. Metal curry comb Actually a cleaning device, this is used for removing grease from the soft brush only and *never* used on the horse. Grease can be tapped out of the curry on the floor as necessary. It is held in the opposite hand to the soft brush.

5. Stable rubber This acts like a dust cloth and is used all over the horse to give a final shine to the coat.

6. Water brush Used wet, this helps to lay the mane and tail at the end of the grooming session. A separate water brush is useful for washing the feet.

7. Sponge A most important part of the kit, the sponge is used for wiping the horse's eyes, nostrils, and under the dock. Always keep a separate sponge for the horse's face and for the dock or tail area.

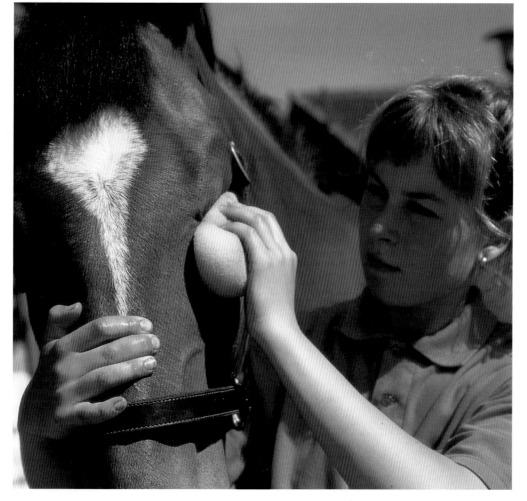

▶ A basic grooming kit with items most commonly found. It should be kept clean and washed approximately once a week.

You should ensure that you use clean cloths or sponges when wiping your horse's eyes and muzzle as infections spread to these areas can be irritating to the animal and troublesome for you to clear-up.

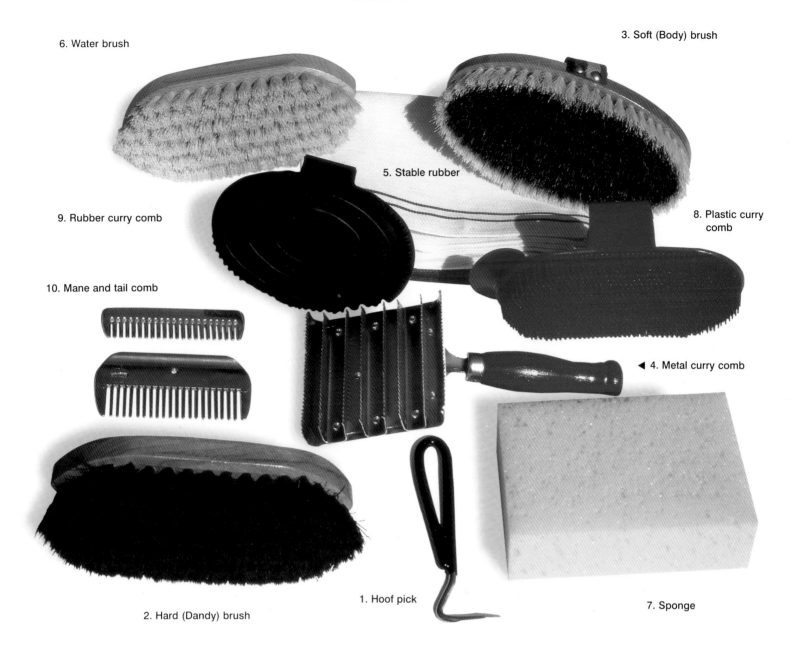

6. Water brush

3. Soft (Body) brush

5. Stable rubber

9. Rubber curry comb

8. Plastic curry comb

10. Mane and tail comb

4. Metal curry comb

1. Hoof pick

7. Sponge

2. Hard (Dandy) brush

OTHER USEFUL GROOMING AIDS

8. Plastic curry comb This makes a useful substitute for the metal curry comb, especially for children to use. This one can be used on the horse for removing mud and loose hair and tidying manes and tails.

9. Rubber curry comb This is a softer curry, designed for all-over use on the horse. Applied in a circular motion all over the coat, it will help bring the grease to the surface.

10. Mane and tail combs Such combs are useful for removing minor tangles and for "pulling" the mane and tail (which are usually tidied up during grooming sessions).

Grooming mitt Rubber or cactus and rubber mittens can be used to remove grease, sweat, and mud from the coat. The mitten is rubbed in a circular fashion all over the coat.

Cactus cloth Similar to a grooming mitt, this cloth is used damp and will help to promote shine to the coat.

Trimming scissors Large scissors can be used to tidy the horse's heels, in conjunction with a mane comb, or to trim a small area of mane behind the ears as a "bridleway" for the bridle to rest comfortably.

Grooming machines These labor-saving devices are to be found in some of the larger stables and can be hand-held or strapped to the waist. They act like a mini vacuum cleaner, loosening dust and grease. They are best used on the horse once or twice a week with manual grooming in-between.

Electric clippers Used for trimming excess hair on the horse's head, feet, or, at the end of winter, its entire body. Great patience—as well as positive reinforcement—must be used to accustom most horses to the sound and feel of the clippers.

Sweat scraper Used for removing excess water after the horse has been washed down after riding.

TIPS FOR GROOMING

- *Always tie up your horse or pony before grooming and ensure that it is dry before you start. If the coat is damp you will not be able to groom properly so it is best to wait until the coat has dried.*
- *Position yourself safely at all times, never directly in front of or behind the animal. Even the quietest horse or pony can react to an irritating fly or a sudden noise.*
- *Make sure your grooming kit is washed regularly—once a week is usual to keep it clean and fresh.*
- *Always be vigilant if you see any unusual skin problems or scaly round areas that could indicate ringworm (see p.123) which would be contagious. Grooming kits can spread infections from one horse to another very quickly, so if in any doubt wash the entire kit in disinfectant. Keep one brush or kit for the suspect horse until the situation has been clarified.*
- *Grooming time gives you a good chance to check the horse's feet thoroughly so that you may notice any foot problems developing (see pp.118–121) and whether shoes are coming loose.*

OILING HOOVES

Q **When should I oil my horse's feet and what does it do apart from improving their appearance?**

A Oiling the feet has little effect on the actual hoof but helps to keep the surface moist. In dry weather, hooves tend to become brittle. If there is serious hoof brittleness, it is best to discuss this with your farrier who will recommend a specific supplement to correct the condition.

You should make sure your horse or pony gets used to you picking up its feet so that you can oil the hooves and pick out dirt. To pick up the foot of the horse, slide your hand down the leg and, if necessary, gently tap the side until it is raised.

GROOMING ROUTINE

Grooming is one of the most rewarding moments of horse care and gives you the best chance of getting to know your horse and all its little eccentricities which make your animal so special to you. Some will be very ticklish in a certain spot while others are headshy or hate their ears being touched. It is the perfect opportunity to really study your horse or pony.

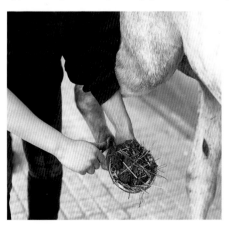

Picking out feet should be done daily before and after exercise. Oil the feet two to four times a week with a small brush in order to keep them moist and in good condition.

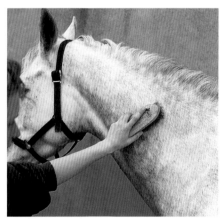

The dandy brush should only be used to remove dirt from long coats. It is too tough to use on fine skinned animals except with very gentle strokes.

The body brush is used with a sharp scrape through the curry comb to clean it of dust after each stroke or after every two or three strokes.

Great care must be taken not to pull out tail hairs when brushing. Hairs are best separated gently by hand. Only brush the tail once a week.

Two sponges are needed—one to wipe around eyes and nostrils, the other to sponge under the tail and dock area. This is most refreshing for the horse and should be done daily.

The mane (if not too long), is best tidied with a plastic curry comb or a body brush, but this will have little effect unless the mane is kept short and neat.

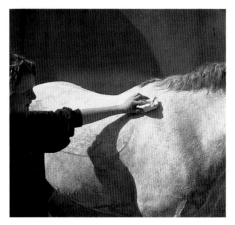

The stable rubber removes any excess grease or dust on top of the coat for a final shine. Dampened with hot water, it is excellent for cleaning a recently clipped horse.

SENSITIVE UNDERBELLY

Q My horse kicks out and tries to lie down whenever I touch his underbelly. How should I handle him?

A It would probably be best to give him a fresh hay net to occupy his mind before starting. Ensure he is a bit hungry first! Maybe you're being a bit too vigorous with your grooming, especially if he is a thin-skinned horse, so make your grooming strokes softer and slower. Be firm with your voice. The horse may understand a sharp "No." Reward him with praise when he's good.

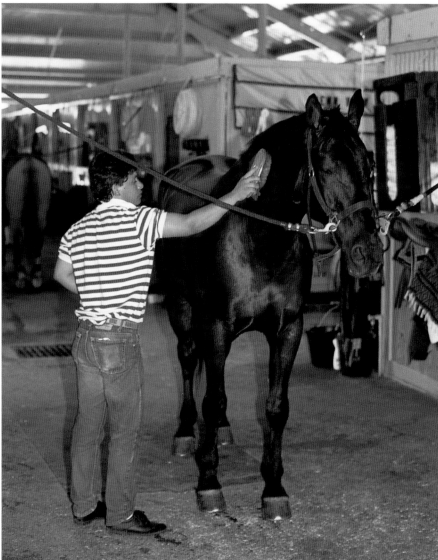

The use of "rack chains" allows the handler to keep the horse straight and work on both sides. They are attached to either side of the halter. Never attach to a bit. Quick-release chains are recommended in case the horse panics.

BLANKETS

Stabled horses need some form of blanket (rug) to keep warm, depending on the weather conditions, the breed, and whether or not they have been clipped (see pp.94–95). Keeping your horse warm will help the animal keep in good condition as the horse will not be using its energy stores just to keep warm.

These days, there are numerous types of horse blankets (rugs) available, catering to all horses and ponies. Most are designed so that they stay in place through careful shaping and are "self-righting" if the horse rolls. A variety of fastenings and/or leg straps assist in this. Choose a blanket that is suitable, easy to put on and adjust, and not too heavy.

TYPES OF BLANKET

There are several different designs to use for different situations.

Stable blanket This is a warm blanket, usually made of cozy quilted material of different weights, for use in the stable. Often there are special fittings to keep them in place, or they can be used with a "roller" (a special strap to stop slippage).
Under blanket This is a generally shaped basic

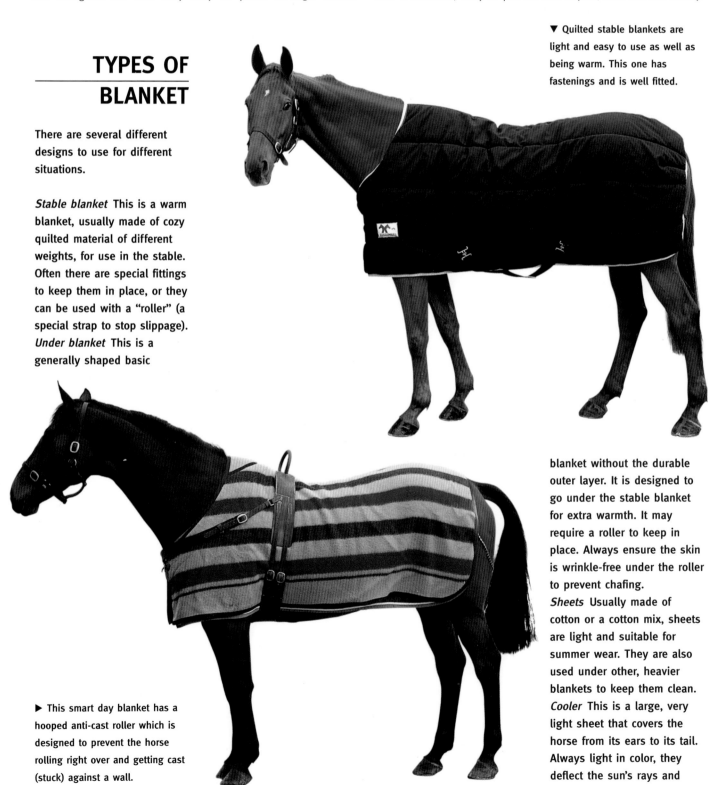

▼ Quilted stable blankets are light and easy to use as well as being warm. This one has fastenings and is well fitted.

▶ This smart day blanket has a hooped anti-cast roller which is designed to prevent the horse rolling right over and getting cast (stuck) against a wall.

blanket without the durable outer layer. It is designed to go under the stable blanket for extra warmth. It may require a roller to keep in place. Always ensure the skin is wrinkle-free under the roller to prevent chafing.
Sheets Usually made of cotton or a cotton mix, sheets are light and suitable for summer wear. They are also used under other, heavier blankets to keep them clean.
Cooler This is a large, very light sheet that covers the horse from its ears to its tail. Always light in color, they deflect the sun's rays and

protect the horse from flies. They also keep the horse dust-free.

Anti-sweat sheets These meshed sheets are designed to allow the horse to cool down without catching a chill or to prevent sweating. Made of various types of loose cotton-based mesh materials, they are especially useful for travel and after exercise. They are extremely effective at keeping warmth close to the horse when used with other blankets placed on top.

Heavy winter blanket (sometimes called a New Zealand blanket) Horses kept outside in inclement weather

◀ This lightweight cotton sheet is secured with criss-cross straps to hold it in place.

usually need to wear a New Zealand blanket. They are designed to be weatherproof and non-slip, and have a variety of harness leg straps to ensure they remain in place. It is important to ensure that the leg straps are kept soft and supple to prevent chafing and soreness and to monitor carefully the horse wearing it to prevent blanket-related accidents.

FITTING BLANKETS

You must ensure that whatever blanket (rug) you choose to use is fitted properly and has all the buckles or ties fastened securely. An ill-fitting blanket or loose strap could cause the horse or pony to get tangled up and fall badly.

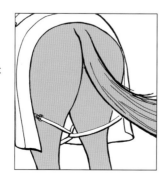

The top diagrams show how to fold a woolen Witney blanket, which has a day or night blanket (rug) placed on top and is then folded back and kept in place with a roller. ▶ Leg straps on New Zealand blankets must be crossed over between the hind legs to prevent any chafing.

▶ The all weather New Zealand blanket gives the horse great protection against bad weather. It has special leg fastenings.

BLANKET PROBLEMS

Q My pony gets very sore on her shoulders when she wears her heavy, winter blanket. What can I do about it?

A The continual motion of your pony moving around her paddock is causing friction rubs. These can be prevented by getting the pony a specially designed shoulder vest or bib, or by attaching some thick plastic to the inside shoulder area of her blanket. Always check that the blanket is the right size for the pony. Some designs are better suited to certain shapes than others.

BRAIDING

A braided (plaited) mane and tail show off your horse to its best advantage and are regarded as part of a neat turn-out. Although you will not need to braid every day it is a good idea to get your horse used to it by practicing regularly. It is usual to braid your horse for the show ring, when entering large competitions, and for hunting.

It takes a lot of practice to achieve perfect-looking braids, so don't be disheartened if your first attempts are a disaster! The starting point is a well-pulled mane—if it's too thick, it will not braid well. Similarly, the tail needs to be full and not rubbed. Do not shampoo the mane and tail beforehand—it will make the hair too slippery and flyaway.

MANES

Study your horse's neck to see how to present the mane at its best. A thick cresty neck will look finer with neat braids pulled down into the crest. A rather weak neck will be enhanced with larger braids placed on top. There is no limit to how many braids you can do in the mane, as long as they are evenly spaced. You can finish off with the English method, which is a "button" effect, or the continental style of a long fold of braid usually taped in white. The forelock is done separately in the same style as the mane. The braids can be secured with thread, which should match the color of the mane, or rubber bands.

This running or Arabian braid is also known as a Gypsy braid and is used on horses with unusually long flowing manes.

BRAIDING PROBLEMS

Q When I braid my horse's mane it seems to fall apart very quickly. Where am I going wrong?

A Always dampen the mane first, then take three even sections of hair and braid together tightly before securing the end with thread or rubber bands. It will remain tight for you to either roll or loop the braid into the form you require. No mane will braid well unless it has been pulled to the same thickness and length down the full length of the neck.

HOW TO BRAID THE MANE

Braiding is an art that needs plenty of practice to achieve really good results. The secret is to separate the sections of mane to be braided into even sections, dampen these well, and make each braid firm and secure. In the English method, the braid is folded once or twice, depending on the length of the mane, and secured with thread, which looks best, or tightly-twisted rubber bands.

Start by separating a section of mane and braiding it firmly down to the end. It is best to start at the top.

After securing the end with thread or rubber bands, fold up once or twice and secure with the same method on top of the neck.

After completing all the braids down the neck, finish off by braiding the forelock, taking care to keep it straight.

If there are any wisps of hair left they can be gently plucked out to leave a neat and tidy head and neck.

BRAIDING TAILS

To achieve the best results you need a full, untrimmed tail with plenty of length to the hairs at the top of the tail. The secret of success is to keep the hairs evenly spaced. Try to include an even amount of hair from each side, all the way down the length of the dock. The braid formed down the center of the tail must be kept straight and tidy for maximum effect.

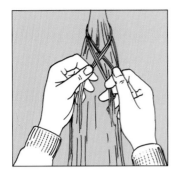

Take sections from both sides.

Braid down center for two thirds of dock.

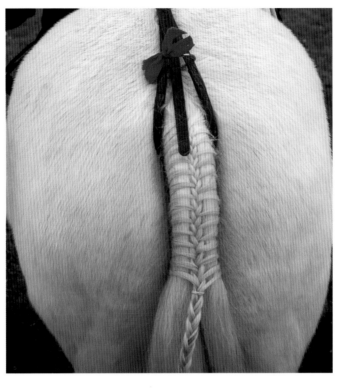

PROBLEMS "PULLING" TAIL

Q My horse clamps its tail down and kicks out whenever I try to "pull" his tail. Should I leave it?

A A full tail looks nice on many horses and can always be braided if it is suitable. Twitching the horse (see glossary) will usually work to ensure that he does not kick but do watch out for unpredictable behavior. Gently pat him on the rump several times and try to reassure him by pulling just a few hairs at a time from his tail.

The finished tail looks neat and tidy with the actual braid kept centrally spaced down the tail.

HOW TO BRAID THE MANE: CONTINENTAL STYLE

Continental braids can look very effective if done well with small, even braids secured with white tape down the neck (as shown). They are quite eye-catching when used with the white numnahs seen on dressage horses in particular. Continental braids can be difficult to get right but with a little patience you will achieve a good result.

The start is exactly the same with the mane divided into even sections. Braid tightly and loop the mane up once.

Leave approximately 1–1¼in (2–3cm) of mane as a loop and secure with thread or rubber bands.

Take white tape and wind around the braid, leaving a neat bud of mane showing at the end.

Keep the white tape at the same width up the neck to give a really good, even effect.

CLIPPING

Nature provides the horse with a new summer and winter coat according to the season, but that does not necessarily suit an animal that's working all year round. To ensure your horse or pony stays in top condition you should choose a clip that suits its lifestyle.

You can't expect a horse to be ridden, driven, or compete with a thick winter coat, especially if it's being stabled the rest of the time. Removing the coat has many advantages for the well-being of the horse.

- It enables the animal to work hard without undue stress (and so loss of condition) from sweating caused by a heavy coat.
- It prevents chills. Horses with a thick coat tend to dry slowly, particularly in cold weather.
- You are able to assess the horse's condition much quicker with a clipped coat. You can see at a glance if there are any medical problems.
- It is easier to keep clean and looking attractive.

The coat is removed with a set of clippers, and these come in various designs. Most common are electric clippers, which usually consist of a hand-held motor with blades attached. Always clean the blades after use and keep them well-oiled and in good order for the next time. Sharp blades are a must for a clean, neat cut. It is best to have two sets so that if one is blunt and requires sharpening you have a spare set on hand.

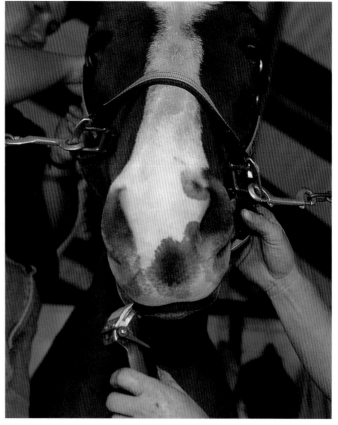

Trimming whiskers may prove a ticklish job. The careful use of scissors or a razor may be an alternative.

The head and face are the most difficult parts to clip. Make sure the horse is kept calm and its head is held still while clipping this area.

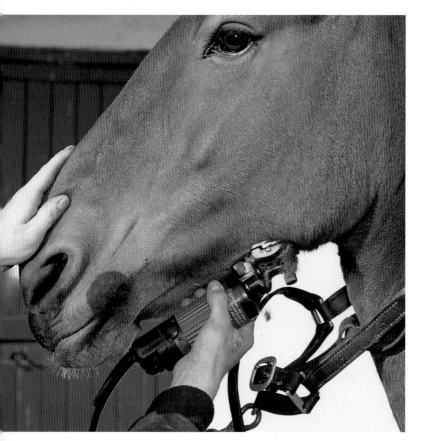

PREPARING TO CLIP

Choose a safe area with good light and a non-slip floor. Give your horse a thorough grooming and ensure that it is dry before you start—clipper blades will not run through a dirty or wet coat. Ideally, the horse should have been stabled and groomed for a few days beforehand. If the horse has never been clipped before, it is a good idea to let it see another horse being done. Let it see, hear, and smell the clippers, and feel them against its coat several times.

Always have an assistant hold a young or nervous horse until it is settled and accustomed to the procedure. Patience will really pay off with the first clip. Some horses may require twitching—usually just for the head area—but avoid doing this if at all possible. Often patience is all that is required—or a handful of food to occupy the mind. Have a blanket on hand to place over the clipped area to prevent the animal from getting cold. Wear overalls and head gear to prevent the hairs from sticking to your clothes.

Start at the front—the lower neck is usually a good starting point. Allow the horse to settle, then work your way back in sections. Go over any areas that need it two or three times until all is smooth.

Always clip against the lie of the coat and use long sweeping strokes whenever possible. Do one area at a time, keeping the blades close and flat to the skin so as not to produce "lines" in the coat from uneven pressure. Keep the blades well-oiled during the clip. This stops them from getting too hot and burning the horse's skin. If they do become overheated, turn them off until they cool down. Only do sensitive areas such as the head, under the belly, and inside of the legs when the blades are very cool.

Clip the main body of the horse first and, if cold, cover with a blanket before starting on the more sensitive, difficult areas (where you will need to gently stretch the skin to give a flat surface to clip). The front legs will need to be lifted and pulled forward to enable a successful clip around the chest and girth areas. Avoid nicking the skin.

When you have finished, quickly brush the horse all over (rubbing the coat with a hot, damp towel will remove surface grease). Then, blanket the horse immediately. If the horse seems a bit unsettled, take it for a nibble of grass or a short walk before putting it in the stall. Check that the horse is warm enough, especially if a very thick coat has been removed.

TYPES OF CLIP

The various clips are designed to suit different horses and the kind of work they are expected to do.

Full clip All the hair is removed with a full clip. It is used for fit, stabled horses in hard work.

Hunter clip The legs and saddle patch are left on but the rest of the hair is removed with a hunter clip. Used for hunters and many competition horses because the leg hairs give extra protection, it is suitable for all horses in work.

Blanket clip This leaves hair on a blanket-shaped area on the back and the legs. It is suitable for stabled horses that feel the cold or those in medium work.

Trace clip Hair is removed below a horizontal line running from the buttock through to the shoulder and up the lower neck with a trace clip. The legs are left on. This is popular for working horses and ponies ridden occasionally during winter months.

Hunter clip

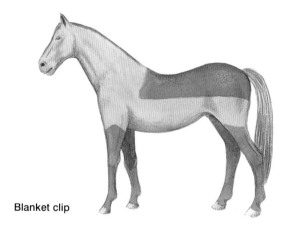

Blanket clip

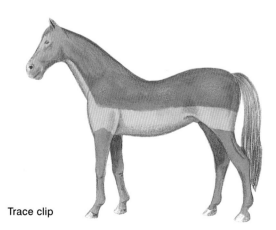

Trace clip

There are many other variations on these clips, depending on owners' preferences or on how much and where the horse tends to sweat. Some people leave half the head unclipped, following a vertical line down the cheek piece of the bridle. Some horses hate their ears being touched, and leaving these will help to keep it warm. There is no point in upsetting the horse unnecessarily so long as the finished effect is neat and tidy. In exceptionally difficult cases your veterinarian may recommend a tranquilizer, but this is rarely necessary if you take the time to gain the horse's confidence.

SHOEING

There's a lot of truth in the old saying, "No foot, no horse." Healthy feet are essential to a horse's well-being. They have to be trimmed at the right angle to keep them balanced and in good condition, and shod correctly for shape and the type of work expected of the horse.

In general, shoeing needs to be done every four to six weeks, but even a horse that goes without shoes still needs the regular attention of a farrier. Many ponies and horses in light work may not require shoes, particularly if they have tough hardy feet. In this case, feet need to be kept trimmed and shaped correctly every four to eight weeks, depending on the climate and their rate of growth. If the shoe is kept on too long the feet will overgrow and cause pressure which will probably lead to lameness.

Shoes may be fitted through hot or cold shoeing. With hot shoeing, it is possible for the farrier to change the shape of the shoe to properly fit the foot. With cold shoeing, the shoe is pre-cast in different sizes designed to fit most feet.

TYPES OF SHOE: FOR WORK AND CORRECTION

There are many different types of shoe, and it is best to discuss your horse's requirements with your farrier. Horses in heavy work may need strong, thick shoes, whereas a racehorse galloping on soft ground is usually shod with light aluminum plates or even plastic shoes for extra speed. Gaited horses and driving horses need special shoes, and this varies according to what is required of them. Even conformational problems can be minimized by special shoeing, as can faulty actions such as swinging a leg. Injuries or disease, such as laminitis (see p.119), can also be helped with remedial shoeing, and close cooperation between veterinarian and farrier is essential in such situations.

Worldwide, most horses are shod with iron or steel metal shoes, either fullered (grooved) or plain. Fullered shoes are lighter and give better grip. A single central toe clip is usual on a front shoe, but this is not used on light racing plates. For hind shoes, there is usually a clip on either side of the toe to hold the shoe in position.

For competitive work, it's a good idea to use studs for extra grip. You can screw these in yourself with a spanner into pre-drilled holes in the heel of the shoe. The size and shape of the studs depend very much on ground conditions and personal preference. Never leave them in for long periods of time, and never use them on roads. They could start problems by causing unaccustomed positioning of the foot, especially if the animal is on hard ground or left in the trailer.

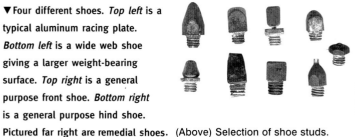

▼ Four different shoes. *Top left* is a typical aluminum racing plate. *Bottom left* is a wide web shoe giving a larger weight-bearing surface. *Top right* is a general purpose front shoe. *Bottom right* is a general purpose hind shoe. Pictured far right are remedial shoes. (Above) Selection of shoe studs.

T-bar   Egg bar

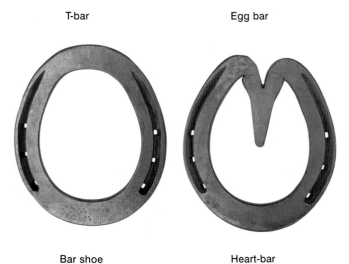

Bar shoe   Heart-bar

HOT SHOEING

1. *The old shoe is removed, if necessary, and any reshaping or trimming carried out.*
2. *The hot shoe that has been shaped to the correct size in the furnace is fitted to the foot. The charring indicates any adjustments required to be made to either the foot or the shoe.*
3. *The shoe is cooled in water, then fitted and nailed in place with correctly angled nails (studs).*
4. *The nail ends are twisted off and bent downward to form the clenches, which effectively keep the shoe in place.*
5. *The foot is finished off with rasping around the clench lines to ensure there are no rough edges.*

If the farrier trims the feet at the correct angle each time it will limit the chances of your horse needing remedial work.

TRIMMING

Q **My mare will not be ridden for three months; do I need to do anything about her feet?**

A Yes. She will need her feet trimmed every six to eight weeks. If she has shoes on, these can either be taken off altogether or just the hind ones may be removed. Talk to your farrier about how she would be best protected. If she is out with company, it is usually safest to keep her hind shoes off to reduce the likelihood of kicking injuries. Front feet are more flared and, being weight-bearing, tend to crack more easily than the hind ones. Keeping the front shoes on will help to protect them.

A paring knife is used to scrape away any excess horn on the sole of the foot before the shoe is put on. It is also used to tidy the frog.

HOW A SHOE IS REMOVED

1. *The clenches (or old nails) are loosened with the use of a hammer and a tool called a buffer.*
2. *Using pincers, the old shoe is levered off.*
3. *Hoof cutters are used to trim the excess horn.*
4. *A rasp is used to level and tidy the foot, now ready for re-shoeing or to be left unshod.*

SUPPLEMENTS

Some horses suffer from brittle or dry hooves, particularly in hot weather, and this can lead to foot problems. It may be necessary to feed a supplement containing amino acids to help promote healthy horn—discuss this with your veterinarian or farrier. Although you can oil the hooves (see Grooming pp.86–89), generally topical applications rarely do much for the foot itself, but they do help the appearance.

EXERCISE

In the wild, a horse roams at will and so is always in a permanent state of fitness. This is not the case with a stabled horse, however, because it is prevented from moving around for long periods of time. Exercise is vital to good health, so it is important to ensure that this element of your horse's well-being is given serious thought.

The type of work expected from your horse will be the deciding factor. If it is doing strenuous work daily on a farm or ranch, it will be fit. If it is only ridden on weekends, it will need some form of exercise during the rest of the week. A horse that is competing regularly, in whatever sporting discipline, will require fitness work on a daily basis (see pp.100–101).

Most horses that are kept for pleasure do not need to be ridden every day, but they do need to let off steam, have a buck or roll, or at least have the opportunity to spend an hour or two out in the paddock eating grass as nature intended.

Riding one horse and leading another can be a useful method of getting two horses exercised at one time. Keep the led horse on the inside, away from traffic.

Lungeing loose allows the horse to have a buck and a kick. If the horse gets too exuberant or needs serious work, put a roller and side reins on for better control.

TYPES OF EXERCISE

Exercise can be carried out in several different ways, depending on your lifestyle and what is expected from the horse:

- Turning out—this will exercise the horse but it won't keep it fit.
- Riding daily—this will ensure that the horse gets the exercise it needs for fitness. It will also keep the horse under control, which can mean less chance of accidents.
- Lungeing—this gives relatively controlled exercise. The method of lungeing will determine the degree of the workout.
- Leading from another horse (ponying)—this enables the busy rider to exercise two horses at once.
- Hot walkers (Horse walker)—this is a useful aid for giving exercise to large numbers of horses in a busy stable.
- Hand walking—a satisfying form of exercise for those who have the time, this helps the handler to keep fit as well as the horse or pony!

CHANGE IN TEMPERAMENT

Q My mare has become stubborn and sluggish out on our daily rides, yet she used to be so cheerful and alert. How can I regain her interest?

A There are a number of possibilities for this change in behavior. First, is she getting enough food? If you are going out for long rides, it could be that you need to increase the amount of food to give her the necessary energy. Second, how does she look? Is she ill or suffering from a virus? Consult your veterinarian if there has been a recent change in her condition. Third, it could be that you are following the same routine too often and that your mare is suffering from a simple case of boredom. Ride her in company and vary your work.

Nothing is more enjoyable or relaxing than a quiet trail ride out in the country with friends. Horses enjoy the company of others—especially when they are being exercised by riding.

WARNING: OVERFRESH HORSE!

Whatever type of exercise is chosen, safety must be the top priority. A stabled horse that is not given adequate exercise can become out of control and dangerous, if allowed. Regulate the amount of food according to the ratio of exercise or work. If the horse starts to become overfresh, it is not having enough exercise to burn off the built-up energy. Some horses require much more exercise than others, depending on their breed and temperament. Sometimes, a spell of a few weeks, or even days, out in a paddock will relax a horse that has become overfresh after being stabled for a long time.

OVERFRESH PONY

Q The pony my child rides has had to be kept in with a heel infection but now looks very overfresh. I do not want to turn him out in the mud. What should I do?

A It is better to be safe than sorry, and if the pony cannot be lunged or ridden by an adult first, it would be best to turn him out for a gallop to let off steam before allowing your child to ride him, or ride him yourself. Safety comes first and the sore heel can be cleaned up properly afterwards.

FITNESS

Like an athlete, a horse needs to be fit if it is going to perform to its best ability—particularly in competitive sports of any kind. And, like an athlete, a horse cannot be expected to go from a life of leisure to one where it has to perform a specific role. A horse has to be prepared in a logical way to bring it up to a fit condition. Only then will it be equipped to cope with the demands being made on it with the minimum degree of stress.

Presuming that all health care needs are attended to—such as worming and vaccinations—basic fitness training is much the same for all horses. Start slowly, and build up the fitness work gradually. When a horse returns to work after a lay-off period, the first month is spent conditioning the horse's muscles, tendons, and ligaments in preparation for the more serious work to come (see "progressive work"). During this time, the horse must be ridden forward well to encourage it to use its muscles and not be allowed to dawdle. Keep to good, consistent ground on roads or tracks, or whatever is available. Only walk and slow-trot on the roads so that your horse is not jarred by the concussion effect. Slippery or deep ground will increase the chance of slides and strains.

PROGRESSIVE WORK

Once the initial slow fitness work is completed, more specific work relevant to what your horse is expected to do can commence, such as arena schooling for dressage, jumping, or pony club events. Again, ensure that any changes are introduced gradually, and that distances, for example, are increased bit by bit. It's important to adjust your horse's feeding routine to reflect the change in the work, bearing in mind the animal's age, type, temperament, and the amount of physical activity.

Controlled galloping up gradual or gentle slopes on good ground is one of the most popular forms of fitness work—the horses really enjoy it.

TRAINING PLAN

As the training for specific roles is established, this must be interspersed with the continuance of fitness work. Generally, most competition trainers alternate three days of fitness work with three days of specific training a week until the horse reaches the required condition. Maintaining this then requires careful balance so that the horse does not become stale from being "overtrained." Generally, this can be prevented by giving the horse a few easy days every now and then, either by turning out or just hacking quietly instead of schooling and working. Remember to adjust the horse's food accordingly during such times.

FITNESS AIDS

Many competition trainers use mechanical aids such as hot walkers, treadmills, and swimming pools to help with their fitness programs. These aids can be enormously beneficial if used sensibly. If you have the opportunity to gain access to such aids, give your horse time to adjust to the unfamiliar. Only if the horse is relaxed mentally and physically will it get the full benefit from them.

TREADMILL Another useful fitness aid, treadmills take up little space. Horses must be warmed up gradually on a treadmill before attempting anything too strenuous at speed or on a slope. They do need to have already done some fitness work before using a treadmill for the first time.

HOT WALKER These are excellent for warming horses up before serious work, for cooling them down afterward, and for maintaining fitness. Many professional trainers like their horses out of their stables at least twice a day, with fitness and schooling done in the morning and exercise on the walker later in the day.

SWIMMING POOL Swimming is excellent to help clear the wind, while giving the legs a rest from jarring. Once again, it is vital to adjust the horse gradually to this different form of exercise. Swimming is strenuous and must never be overdone.

FEEDING

Feeding horses to enable them to perform at their best, and to maintain condition regardless of the environment, requires a careful balance of the right foods. The horse is a herbivore and as such is never happier than when eating grass, which should be its main source of food whenever possible.

Correct feeding generally requires the advice of an experienced professional. However, there are certain rules relative to feeding, which every caring horse person should know. Observation of these will help to minimize any problems.

▲ It is important that the horse is fed according to the work it is doing and treated as an individual. Feed buckets must be kept scrupulously clean. The food used must be of good quality. (Always check that each bag used is within the recommended date of consumption.)

LITTLE AND OFTEN

Horses have very small stomachs. In the wild, they would have spent around 18 hours a day picking and grazing at will, which enabled the food to "trickle" through the gut. If the stomach is overloaded, the food is pushed through too fast to be digested properly, and this can lead to health problems, such as colic (stomach ache), swollen legs, and skin rashes.

OVERFEEDING

It is important not to overfeed your horse or pony. Apart from becoming too fat, the animal may become over-fresh and rank, and start to suffer from health problems because of the nutritional imbalance. Obesity is a prime cause of laminitis, a disease of the foot that causes intense pain. Observe your horse and note whether it is putting on or losing weight, and act to keep it healthy for the type of work it is doing. Remember that while the weight of the horse is the basic determining factor in the quantities of feed required, breeding, temperament, condition, and type of work are important considerations as well.

► Horses out at grass must have adequate fodder and be allowed plenty of space. Always check that the paddock has freely available fresh water. In poor weather, the grass-kept horse may require extra food such as hay or a daily bucket of feed to supplement the grazing.

TURNING OUT

Being a herbivore, the horse's most natural feed is grass. If the horse is not out to pasture, it should be fed hay. The more roughage the horse has the happier it will be. It is this fiber that stimulates the gut to work efficiently.

Grass contains not only roughage but also essential moisture (70–80 percent water). Turn your horse out daily if you can. If you can't, feed succulents such as carrots to make up for it.

If your horse cannot be kept out to pasture you will need to work out how much feed it will need, such as hay and concentrates (which are pure oats, barley, or maize), see the charts on p.104 for general advice.

ROUTINE

Horses are creatures of habit, so work out a routine for feeding at the same time every day. If you are in a stable with others, arrange a time that suits everyone. For horses or ponies out in the field together, take care that you do not get kicked when feeding. Horses can become aggressive at mealtimes, so put some food down quickly in one place then distribute the remainder nearby.

FEEDING A GREEDY HORSE

Q My horse keeps knocking his feed out of his manger.

A Many horses do this, especially greedy ones. Try a feed manger with bars so that he cannot swing his head so much. Add more roughage, including chop, to his feed so that he cannot eat it so quickly.

FRESH WATER

Without water, no animal can survive. Always check that fresh, clean water is freely available. In cold weather it may be necessary to break up ice to ensure that the horse can drink, or you may need to take containers to the paddock. Always clean buckets daily before refilling. If the horse drinks from streams, ensure that the area is safe and the water clean and easy to get to (and not liable to dry up in the summer months).

Water must be freely available to all horses. A water trough such as this one would be better sited under the fence to prevent the horse from knocking itself.

EXERCISE

After feeding, allow at least an hour, preferably two, before you exercise. A full stomach will result in pressure on the lungs, which will interfere with the horse's respiratory system. Food that has not been properly digested will be forced into the intestines early and could cause colic.

MAKING CHANGES

Never change your horse's food suddenly. The digestive system is quite sensitive and bacteria in the gut need time to adapt, as do the enzymes in the digestive juices that help to break down the food. Any dietary changes should be introduced gradually, along with the existing feed, over a period of a week to ten days. Alter the diet only if absolutely necessary. Take care to ensure you always have adequate feed on hand so that sudden changes are not needed.

GENERAL GUIDE TO FEEDING

Below are suggestions for feeding depending on type of horse and work required.

	TYPE OF WORK	MORNING	EVENING	RATIO HAY TO CONCENTRATES
PONY CLUB PONY/ LIGHT RIDING HORSE	Rest	None	None	100% hay/grass
	Light work	1.1lb (0.5kg) 8% mix	1.1lb (0.5kg) pasture nuts	85% hay 15% concentrates
	Medium work	1.1lb (0.5kg) mix + 1.1lb (0.5kg) chaff	1.1lb (0.5kg) mix + 1.1lb (0.5kg) chaff	80% hay 20% concentrates
	Hard work	1.65lb (0.75kg) mix + 1.1lb (0.5kg) chaff	2.2lb (1kg) mix + 1.1lb (0.5kg) chaff	75% hay 25% concentrates
RIDING HORSE/ COMPETITION PONY	Rest	None	None	100% hay/grass
	Light work	2.2lb (1kg) 10–12% mix	2.2lb (1kg) mix + 1.1lb (0.5kg) chaff	85% hay 15% concentrates
	Medium work	2.74lb (1.25kg) mix	2.74lb (1.25kg) mix + 1.1lb (0.5kg) chaff	75% hay 25% concentrates
	Hard work	3.85lb (1.25kg) mix	3.85lb (1.75kg) mix + 1.1lb (0.5kg) chaff	65% hay 35% concentrates
COMPETITION HORSE	Rest	None	2.2lb (1kg) 12% protein mix	100% hay/grass
	Light work	2.2lb (1kg) 14% protein mix	2.2lb (1kg) mix + 1.1lb (0.5kg) chaff	85% hay 15% concentrates
	Medium work	3.3lb (1.5kg) mix	3.3lb (1.5kg) mix + 1.1lb (0.5kg) chaff	75% hay 25% concentrates
	Hard work	3.85lb (1.75kg) mix	3.85lb (1.75kg) mix + 1.1lb (0.5kg) chaff	65% hay 35% concentrates

FEED BY WEIGHT

It is important to establish a system of feeding by weight and not volume to ensure that your horse is getting the correct amount of food for its size and build. It is worth noting what your food actually weighs per scoop by measuring each type in a plastic bag. The following is a rough estimate:

One scoop of chaff/chop	=	1lb (450g)
One scoop of mix	=	2lb (900g)
One scoop of oats	=	2lb (approx. 900g)
One scoop of pellets/nuts	=	3lb (1.3kg)

VITAMINS

This diagram shows which vitamins are beneficial for particular parts of the horse. Vitamins A, B_1, B_2, B_6, D, and E are all essential. If the horse looks out of condition, consult the veterinarian. A vitamin deficiency can be remedied by supplementing the diet with extra vitamins. Most feed mixes will have added vitamins and minerals in the correct amount and balance, they will include most of those listed here and should be adequate to keep your animal in peak condition. It should not be necessary to feed supplements.

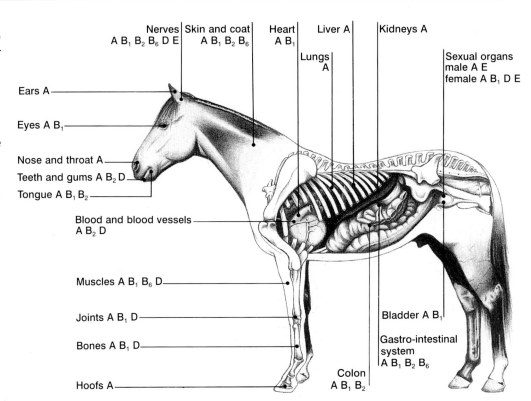

Nerves A B_1 B_2 B_6 D E

Skin and coat A B_1 B_2 B_6

Heart A B_1

Liver A

Kidneys A

Lungs A

Sexual organs male A E female A B_1 D E

Ears A

Eyes A B_1

Nose and throat A

Teeth and gums A B_2 D

Tongue A B_1 B_2

Blood and blood vessels A B_2 D

Muscles A B_1 B_6 D

Joints A B_1 D

Bones A B_1 D

Hoofs A

Bladder A B_1

Gastro-intestinal system A B_1 B_2 B_6

Colon A B_1 B_2

TYPES OF FEED

FIBER FEEDS

Grass This is the natural feed for horses—good young pasture may contain all the required nutrients. Grass contains carbohydrates, proteins, vitamins, and water.

Hay This is dried grass, cut when it is mature. Its feeding value will depend on the area and state of the land from which it is cut. It should be only 15–20 percent moisture.

Haylage This is a form of vacuum-packed grass, dried to about 50 percent moisture. This means that it still retains most of its nutritional value. It must be fed within four days of being opened. It is dust-free and so ideal for horses with a dust allergy.

Chop or chaff A short, chopped mixture of hay, straw (usually barley or oat), and/or alfalfa, this is useful as a hay replacement and to extend other feeds. It is often produced with added herbs, molasses, and extra vitamins and minerals.

Straw As an alternative to poor quality hay, straw is a useful source of fiber (especially for ponies with laminitis, see p.119). Oat or barley straw is best. Wheat straw should not be used as it is not easily digested. In some countries, including the United States, straw is usually only used for bedding.

Alfalfa This is a high protein and fiber feed. It can be fed whole, or in chop or in pellet (cube) form. It is relatively dust-free and so useful for horses with respiratory problems. It is low in energy and so also useful for laminitic ponies.

▲ Mineral feed blocks are very popular and give vital mineral and vitamin supplements.

GRAIN (CEREAL) FEEDS

The energy providers, grains consist of carbohydrate concentrates such as oats, barley, and corn (maize). They are fed whole, rolled, micronized, or extruded. They also appear in proprietary mixes sold as complete feeds, which can be loose or in pellet form. The most commonly used cereals are:

Oats Popular worldwide, oats are high in fiber but low in energy. They are also low in calcium, which can cause a deficiency, but this is generally corrected by feeding alfalfa,

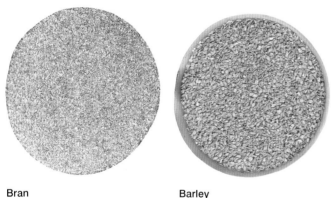

Bran   Barley

Oats

Coarse mix

sugar beet, or a vitamin/mineral supplement. Oats can be fed whole or bruised. Naked oats are higher in energy and oil.

Barley This grain is higher in energy but lower in fiber than oats. It has a hard outer coat, so cannot be fed whole without either soaking or boiling in water for an hour. Generally, it is fed micronized, rolled, or extruded.

Bran The outer coat of the wheat husk, bran is high in phosphorus and fiber. Bran mashes are made by pouring boiling water over the bran and leaving it to soak for half an hour. A good laxative, it also makes an excellent poultice for wounds and swellings. Bran can cause an imbalance in calcium absorption if overused.

Corn Often fed with alfalfa, corn (or maize) is particularly popular in the United States. It is higher in energy than barley and oats but low in protein. It is particularly useful for shy eaters because of the ratio of energy gained to amount fed.

OTHER FEEDS AND SUPPLEMENTS

Sugar beet This is a root from which the sugar is removed and the pulp dried into either pellets or shreds. It is a good source of calcium and fiber. Sugar beet must be soaked in water for 12 hours before being eaten. Dried sugar beet expands when in contact with moisture (to twice its size) and can cause fatal colic attacks if eaten unsoaked. Always mark containers of sugar beet and ensure that everyone knows the dangers.

Oil One of the most effective sources of energy, oil contains no starch or protein and is slow releasing. Most pellets and proprietary mixes contain oils but if feeding straights you can add 4 tablespoons (60ml) of vegetable oil a day to increase energy and add an extra bloom to the coat.

Succulents Carrots, apples, and root vegetables are always appreciated and should be given whenever possible to add interest. Carrots especially should be cut lengthways, as round pieces can become lodged in the throat.

DAILY ROUTINE

Horses are creatures of habit. They like to know when they are to be fed, when they will be going out, and when it's time for bed—and they like it to happen in the same order every day. Whether you keep just one horse or twenty the principle is the same.

Routine is extremely important to a horse's well-being if it is to thrive. Once a routine has been worked out to suit the stable and its particular inhabitants, it is best to stick to it if at all possible. Most barns (yards) run a similar routine of feed and muck out before breakfast, then ride and exercise in the morning, and then tack cleaning (see pp. 140–141). The horses are then groomed in the afternoon, followed by a final check and, if necessary, a feed last thing.

◀ **Horses thrive on plenty of roughage to keep the gut functioning effectively. This is best given in the form of hay for the stabled horse. Always ensure you tie the knot high enough so the horse cannot catch its foot in the net as it empties.**

▼ **Exercise time—this horse is waiting for its rider to take it out for its daily schooling session.**

Of course, for any kind of routine, much will depend on the time available to the owner, and the individual circumstances under which the horse is kept. If a horse is kept stabled at a full-service barn (yard), it is likely that there will be someone around to attend to its needs all day. If the horse is kept on a Do-It-Yourself basis, the owner may be able to visit the stables only twice a day. Then, it may be that the horse is turned out all day to minimize the amount of work required during the week. Only on weekends may it get the full, undivided attention of its owner.

However your horse is kept, try to maintain a regular schedule on which it can rely. Some periods are bound to be busier than others, according to the season. At the same time, you will have to try to work out when you can fit in some of the other necessary stable chores within your schedule. Tack rooms and feed rooms should both be thoroughly cleaned once a week, for example, and every so often the horse's bed should be completely removed and the stable scoured (scrubbed clean) and disinfected before starting afresh with a new one.

TYPICAL DAILY DIARY

7AM *Feed horse (see pp. 102–105) and check over blankets (rugs), or hay up and feed later.*

7:30AM *Muck out, hay up, and refill water buckets.*

8AM *Feed (if not done first thing).*

9:30AM *Tack up (see pp. 143–147) and exercise. Turn out afterwards if possible.*

11:30AM *Clean tack and/or groom horse (see pp. 86–89). Sweep out stable.*

12:30PM *Feed and water.*

3:30PM *Groom horse. Sweep up and prepare bed for night. Hay up and water.*

4–5PM *Put on extra blankets if necessary and feed.*

8–9PM *Last check-over and late feed, if given. Check all is safe and secure. Put on security lights, lock tack room, and shut gates as necessary.*

Picking up droppings and putting them into a receptacle throughout the day will help to keep the stall clean.

Looking after horses is hard work but very rewarding. They are very affectionate creatures, and most respond to all your care and attention with a warm nuzzle and affectionate whinnies. Caring for your own horse and pony every day gives you a chance to really get to know the character that makes it very special.

Keeping the horse cozy is very important to a horse's welfare, otherwise it uses up vital energy just to keep itself warm. This horse is wearing a blanket and jute rug with a roller to keep it in place. The breastplate helps to prevent everything slipping back. (See pp. 90–91.)

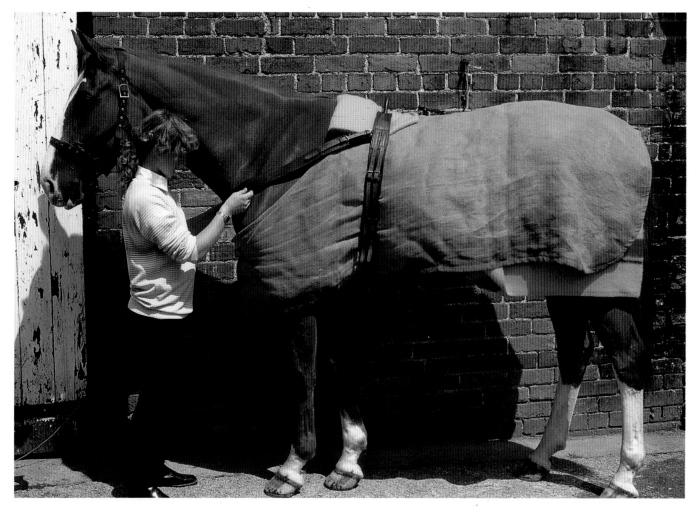

TRANSPORTATION AND LOADING

The transportation of horses and ponies requires a little forethought and planning before setting off on a journey, however short or long. Careful and calm loading and unloading procedures are essential to ensure that the horse or pony is confident and unstressed by being moved.

If the horse or pony is an experienced traveler, there should be little travel trouble as long as the vehicle is driven sensibly. Generally, problems arise only if the horse is swung too fast around corners and finds difficulty in maintaining its balance, or if the brakes are applied too violently. This is why it is so important for first-time travelers to have an easy, happy experience so that confidence is built up from the start. The sooner foals and youngsters get used to traveling, the easier it will be for all concerned. Foals usually travel alongside their mothers and this is the ideal time to start.

▼ Protection on the journey will minimize any abrasions, sores, or damage to the legs brought about by braking suddenly or swerving. (See also p. 110.)

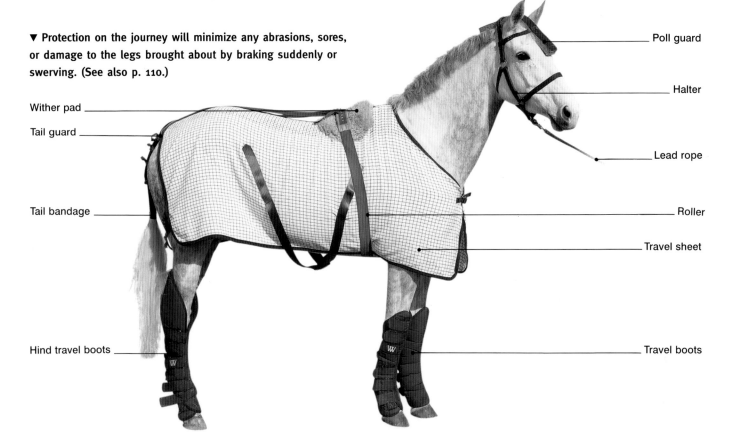

- Wither pad
- Tail guard
- Tail bandage
- Hind travel boots
- Poll guard
- Halter
- Lead rope
- Roller
- Travel sheet
- Travel boots

VEHICLE PREPARATION

Whether a horse van (horse box) or trailer, the vehicle must be in a safe, roadworthy condition—especially with correctly pressured tires for the load. The ramp must be secure and all fixtures—such as restraint bars and tie rings—must be in good working order so that the animal is properly contained. Water buckets and a hay net are a good idea, as is an emergency first-aid kit (see pp. 128–129). Also, the driver must be someone who is sympathetic to the needs of horses and be a careful driver.

Different styles of horse trailer are found across the world. Compare this large goose necked trailer (above right), popular in the United States, with the two-horse trailer (right) which is also popular in Europe.

LOADING POINTERS

Some horses may be frightened of entering a trailer or horse van (horse box) for the first time. To build up confidence, try a few sessions with another horse as a companion or encourage it with food, once inside. A little patience and lots of practice is the key to success.

Be purposeful when loading. If necessary, have some food in your hand and a helper ready both to encourage the horse from behind and to close the door or partition or put restraining straps across once the horse is in. Do not tie the horse up until it is restrained from behind, in case it pulls back or becomes frightened. With a nervous animal, it is helpful to let another horse go in first to give it confidence. Open everything up widely so that it can see where it's to go.

With a horse you know may be difficult to load, it is sensible to take a couple of lunge reins with you as well as some food. The reins will help to keep the horse straight, but you will require two or three people, one to hold and lead the horse, the other two to cope with the reins. Have the food ready to reward the horse once it is loaded.

Always be confident and walk forward toward the trailer or horse van (horse box) in a positive attitude. Keep the horse straight and allow it time to adjust to walking up the ramp.

Make sure you give the horse or pony enough room to turn into its compartment once you reach the top of the ramp. You may need to go on ahead to stand aside to allow it to turn.

SAFETY TIP

Never ride a horse or pony into or out of a horse van (horse box) or trailer!
The horse could panic and rear in the confined space and you could be seriously hurt by hitting the ceiling or sides.

UNLOADING POINTERS

When unloading, untie the horse before opening the partition or breaching strap unless you are bringing the horse out forward. Encourage the horse to move out of the trailer slowly and let it have a look around before getting out. If reversing out, try to keep the horse straight and give it time to adjust to the surroundings. Keep it going straight down the ramp without stepping off sideways, and always maintain control. Don't let the horse drag you out.

Do not hurry the horse down the ramp. It may need a few minutes to adjust to the light and its new surroundings once the ramp has been lowered.

Allow the horse or pony to take one step at a time and come down steadily. The animal may slip or stumble if you rush or do not keep it under control in a calm way.

DURING TRANSPORTATION

Protection when traveling is vital—the most vulnerable areas are the poll, legs, hips, and tail. All should be sensibly protected to ensure that there is minimal damage. In general, horses travel facing backward, forward or on the diagonal (herringbone). They must have sufficient width to brace themselves but not so much that they are swung about. Some horses require more space than others and it is important that this flexibility is available in the partitioning. Some animals become nervous in the dark or when they see the flashing lights of cars and streetlights. This is best overcome by leaving the light on or blacking out any windows.

◀ The horses are generally partitioned for safety in case of accidents when one horse might squash against the other, but sometimes the partition is removed for standing in when stationary or for short journeys. The restraining strap at the back is important to prevent the horses from trying to come out backward. Never undo this strap until they have been untied in front.

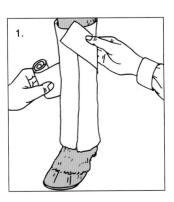

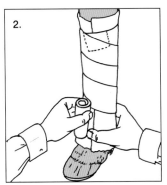

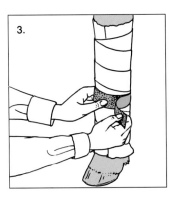

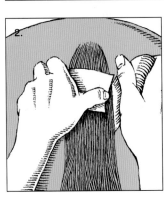

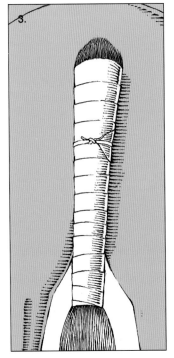

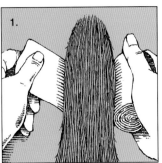

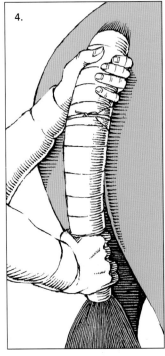

TRAVEL PROTECTION

LEGS
1. Place a bandage over leg wraps or other suitable padding. 2. Continue bandaging down over the fetlock joints or use traveling boots which are specifically designed for this purpose. 3. Secure the end of the bandage with a knot or velcro.

TAIL
1. Gently lift the tail while quietly talking to the horse and fold a bandage around under the tail from left to right. 2. Starting at the top and working down in firm folds. 3. Carry on to the end of the dock, then back up. Secure with the tapes or velcro on the bandage.
4. Bend the dock gently into shape if necessary as shown.

Bandages should not be used, however, on journeys of over four hours as it could cause circulation problems.

DIFFICULT LOADERS

Some horses will not load because they are frightened or unsure—in some cases it's plain stubbornness. Each one will need special treatment, depending on the cause of its reluctance, and all will require a degree of patience. Difficult loaders are usually best handled with a bridle and lunge line to ensure they are controllable. If food does not work, a lunge line held by two assistants, just above the hocks, may encourage a reluctant horse. Lifting each foot in turn and placing it further forward also helps. The secret is to keep the horse going forward straight. Occasionally, a sharp tap with a whip just below the hocks or buttocks works. Remember that loading a horse can be dangerous. Wear suitable gloves, footwear, and a riding helmet in case of injury.

You can encourage a horse into a trailer or box by securing a lunge rein on one side of the trailer and quietly walking the rein around the back of the horse, thus creating a barrier as shown. Maintain a steady pull but release as a reward for every forward step taken. This is best done with two people.

LOADING PROBLEM

Q My horse keeps throwing his head up when we try to load him. Why?

A Some horses will throw their heads up if too great a pull is exerted on the lead rope because they dislike excessive pressure on the poll (see p. 58). Encourage them to go forward with some food held low and out in front, and keep the rope fairly slack. Protect the poll with a poll guard.

The relatively low height of trailers is clearly seen as this horse panics on loading. A bowl of food presented to the horse at ground level may help to keep the head low.

THE HEALTHY HORSE

Owning a horse or pony is a big responsibility. The well-being of your animal is in your hands; you must feed it correctly, ensure the horse is properly exercised, and that it has suitable stabling. The welfare of your animal should be your first thought each day. After all, it is not wild and cannot fend for itself.

This book is intended to give you some of the basic information about caring for a horse or pony which should allow you to make common sense arrangements for the welfare of your animal. One of the most vital skills required of a horse-owner is to know when your animal is healthy and content or is unwell and needs medical treatment.

A HEALTHY HORSE

The bright eye and shiny coat indicate good health. The stage of fitness is gauged on the type of work given.

The horse in good health is a pleasure to look at. It should be bright-eyed and alert, well covered but not too fat (see opposite), eating and drinking normally, and should show no signs of lameness.

Furthermore there should be no signs of discharge from the nose or eyes, and the skin should be loose and supple. The droppings should break evenly when they hit the ground, and the urine should be pale yellow. The temperature, respiration, and pulse rates should be within normal levels (all taken when the horse is quiet and resting).

- *The normal temperature is 100–101 °F (38 °C).*
- *The normal respiration rate is 8–12 breaths per minute.*
- *The normal pulse rate is between 35–45 beats per minute.*

A SICK HORSE

A sick horse or pony may show any or several of the following symptoms:

- *Listless and unresponsive, with head held low.*
- *Not eating or drinking.*
- *Skin appears tight. If you pick up a fold of skin on the neck and release it, the skin does not readily go back into place.*
- *Coat is dull.*
- *The temperature is higher or lower than normal.*
- *The pulse rate is raised, lowered, or irregular.*
- *Breathing is shallow and rapid.*
- *Colic signs—such as restlessness, kicking at the belly, pawing at the ground, getting up and down.*
- *Obvious cuts or swellings to the legs.*
- *Droppings may be very loose, very hard, or absent.*
- *Urine may be red/brown or black (coffee ground) color.*
- *Too thin, with hip and backbones sticking out.*
- *Excessively overweight.*

It is important to know what is normal for your horse or pony. Many have little peculiarities which are normal for them, but may seem odd to someone who does not know the horse.

WHEN TO CALL THE VETERINARIAN

The veterinarian should be called at any time when you suspect that there is something seriously amiss with your horse. As a guide, you should call out a veterinarian in any of these cases:

- **There are serious wounds, especially if they include arterial bleeding (blood spurting out) or if they require stitching. (See pp. 128–129.)**
- **Any signs of colic (see p. 127) which do not settle after half-an-hour, or if the horse shows violent signs—flinging itself to the ground and rolling in obvious pain.**
- **The temperature is high and the horse looks unwell. (Bear in mind that the temperature will always go up after exercise.)**
- **The horse is lame.**

TAKING A HORSE'S TEMPERATURE

To take a horse's temperature, first shake down the mercury in the thermometer or zero rate a digital model. Grease the bulb end with lubricating jelly, and, with an assistant holding the horse's head (if alone, tie the horse up), gently insert this into the horse's rectum. Keep hold of the thermometer so that it does not get drawn into the rectum. Take care to stand to one side when doing this. Remove after one minute, wipe clean, and read.

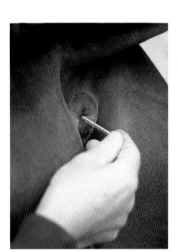

◄ Before inserting the thermometer, always check it is shaken down and grease the end. Stand to the side, raise the tail gently, and talk to the horse.

THE OLDER HORSE OR PONY

Once the horse or pony shows signs of age and stiffness, it should not be expected to work as hard. Discuss the horse's future care with your trainer or veterinarian. Some older horses may enjoy the change of lifestyle; others need further care especially during the winter months when they may need extra feeding and stabling, and perhaps extra blanketing (rugging up) as older horses do not carry so much fat to keep warm. An older horse's teeth need regular rasping (see pp. 114–115 to keep them in good shape. Use your regular grooming sessions to check on the overall condition of the animal. When the time comes that modern medicines no longer give the horse relief from old age or lameness, and if the horse is no longer enjoying life, it is your responsibility to have it humanely euthanized—the least you can do for a faithful friend. It is quick and painless and a kindness to an old, or sick horse.

TAKING A HORSE'S PULSE

To take a horse's pulse, press the facial artery located on the lower jaw against the jaw bone, or the brachial artery located just in front of the elbow (see pp. 58–59). You will feel the pumping sensation. Count the beats for one minute (or 30 seconds and double it). Do not use your thumb as this has a powerful pulse and will confuse any results.

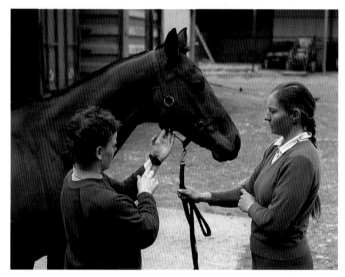

It will take a little practice to take a pulse rate correctly. Don't rush— if you lose the pulse just find the groove in the jaw bone and press the artery again.

TAKING A HORSE'S RESPIRATION

For recording the respiration rate, watch the flanks (see pp. 58–59) and count the inhalation and expiration movement as one breath. You may be able to see this from watching the nostrils if the breathing is fast. Also it is sometimes possible to feel the respiration against the top of your hand if you place this close to the horse's nose.

The condition of the horse or pony can often be determined by the degree of fat and muscle shown over the hindquarters when viewed from behind. This will be affected by feeding, age, kind of work, and general care.
1. Nicely rounded on both sides of backbone.
2. Grossly fat, showing excess fat on either side of the backbone.
3. Poor condition—the muscle is sunken on either side of the backbone and the hip bones are protruding.

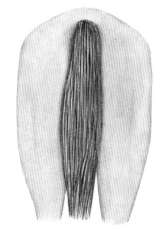

1. Normal

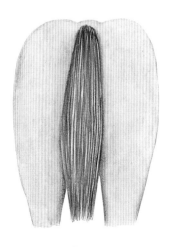

2. Fat

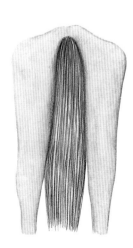

3. Poor condition—thin

TEETH

Dental care is as important for horses as it is for people. A horse that develops problems with its teeth or mouth will not be able to chew and digest its food properly. A bridle and bit may cause extra discomfort, and this will prevent the horse from going forward happily.

The horse's jaw is wider on the top than the bottom. This means that as the horse masticates it tends to wear the teeth down unevenly, causing uncomfortable sharp edges on both the top and bottom molars. These sharp edges can cut the cheeks, and some food, especially grass and hay, may be spat out only half chewed because of the discomfort. You need to ensure that old horses or ponies especially have maximum chewing ability.

A veterinarian or horse dentist should visit twice a year to rasp (float) off any sharp edges, and check that teeth are in good condition and that there are no infections or irritations present. Good horse dentists will use a "gag" to do this effectively. This holds the jaws apart to enable them to work thoroughly without the danger of being nipped. Like a lot of people, some horses don't like the dentist!

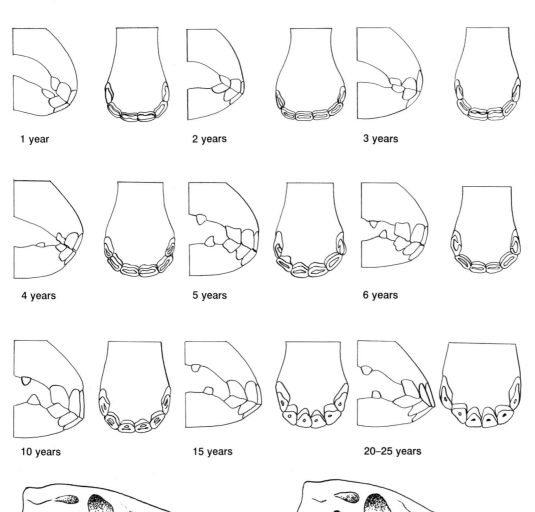

1 year

2 years

3 years

4 years

5 years

6 years

10 years

15 years

20–25 years

Young horse or pony—6–10 years

Middle-aged horse or pony —10–18 years

Old horse or pony —18–25 years

AGEING BY TEETH

The horse can be aged by its teeth fairly accurately up to the age of eight, but thereafter it becomes less easy. However a rough estimate can be made with the shape, degree of wear, and angle of the front teeth, giving the best indication. The horse has replaced its initial milk teeth by the age of five in most cases. In the older horse, the increased angle and more triangular shape give an indication of age. Teeth may be lost around fifteen years onward, or at any time accidentally of course.

CHECKING FOR DAMAGE

Always check your horse's mouth regularly to see for yourself that there are no obvious injuries. It is quite common for the ridden horse to get sores or bruising from the bit or cracked corners to its lips, which will cause discomfort and affect its response to your instructions.

RASPING TEETH

Before inspecting the teeth, the horse dentist will put a special gag into the mouth so that it is possible to put a hand up high into the mouth to feel for rough edges.

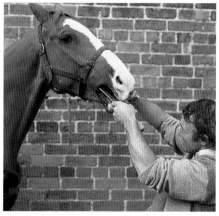

The gag is removed once the worst of the edges are done and the rest are filed with a teeth rasp which is really hard work with a big horse even for a specialist.

READY FOR THE DENTIST

Q I have the horse dentist coming to check my horse's teeth. What should I have ready and what should I expect?

A The dentist will usually bring his or her own set of tools and may arrive complete with bucket and towel. He or she will probably ask for a bucket of warm water into which the dentist may add salt or a mild antiseptic solution. A towel is useful to have at hand. The tools will consist of a variety of rasps and tooth cutters and a special large syringe with which to rinse out the horse's mouth once the rasping is complete.

EATING PROBLEMS

Q My horse finds eating rather difficult and keeps dropping food out of his mouth. Is it because his teeth are uneven?

A This is the classic sign of a horse being unable to close his jaw and teeth evenly and thus allowing the food to fall out. This will affect his condition and general health in time. As the teeth get worn down, it makes it impossible for the horse to chew correctly. Some horses will require their teeth to be filed more often than others, but they should be checked twice a year and will certainly need filing once a year if not more often.

HORSE DENTIST

You need to be feeling very brave to tackle the teeth of something that has four legs to kick you with, a tail to swipe you with, and teeth to bite you! I first try to make friends by talking and soothing any fractious animals before putting in the mouth gag, which prevents the jaws coming together, and enables me to use the rasps to file down the teeth.

Sometimes I spend all day at one big barn (yard) or go visiting several clients in one area. It's an interesting job as I get to know the character of the horses and ponies I treat and often find out that those that are difficult while I'm carrying out work on their teeth are awkward in other ways too. One person even asked me to work on the teeth of a horse they were thinking of buying—it was very cooperative so they bought it!

It can be a dangerous job and I've had several arm injuries when the horses try to fling their heads around to prevent me filing and my arm is right inside. It's amazing how far in the mouth you have to work to reach the back molars. I suppose the reactions of some horses are understandable. I'm not too enthusiastic about dentists either!

By taking hold of the horse's or pony's tongue and moving it aside it will be possible to have an initial look in the mouth and see if there are any sores or bruises. A professional will be needed to look at the teeth properly.

WORMING AND VACCINATIONS

It is essential for good horse-care practice to ensure that your horse or pony is maintained on a regular worming program, and on courses of vaccinations against standard diseases and ailments, such as equine influenza (flu) and tetanus, see pp. 122–129. Failure to carry out such programs and vaccination courses will eventually, and inevitably, lead to your horse or pony becoming susceptible to potentially serious ailments.

Worms are a fact of life for most grazing animals, but especially domesticated horses—which are restricted to feeding repeatedly on the same pasture. All horses carry a certain amount of worms. It is when they become excessive that they cause damage to the digestive system and internal organs. If untreated, the horse could seriously lose condition and even die.

The only way to keep the horse healthy is to maintain a regular worming program. This is best discussed with a veterinarian, as different areas and climates will dictate the frequency required. Most recommend worming every six to ten weeks. A dung sample can be taken to evaluate how serious the problem is if you are unsure of your animal's condition.

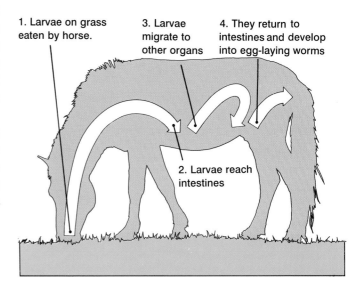

1. Larvae on grass eaten by horse.

2. Larvae reach intestines

3. Larvae migrate to other organs

4. They return to intestines and develop into egg-laying worms

The diagram shows how the horse picks up the larvae from the grass and the larvae's route through the digestive tract.

DEALING WITH WORMS

There are three main worming drugs on the market: benzimidazole, pyrantel, and ivermectin. They are sold under different brand names but all are effective against most of the species of worms that affect horses. They come in powder, granules, liquid, or in paste form—the latter being the most effective to administer because there is little waste.

The main species that invade the horse's system are the small redworm (*Trichonema*) and large redworm (*Strongylus*), roundworm (*Ascaris*), pinworm or seatworm (*Oxyuris*), lungworm (*Dictyocaulus*), bot (*Gasterophilus*), and tapeworm (*Anoplocephala*).

Redworms are the greatest danger, especially the small redworm which can seriously damage the gut. The worms are passed out in the dung and hatch to produce larvae. If the conditions are right—warm and moist—they develop within a week. The horses in the paddock ingest these larvae, which burrow into the gut lining. They emerge six weeks later as egg-laying adults, completing the cycle and ready to continue to do damage. Some can remain in the gut and become fourth stage larvae, against which not all wormers are effective. These emerge later en masse, causing general malaise, colic, and weight loss. A course of benzimidazole should be effective.

Wormers can be easily put in the horse's mouth by means of special paste syringes, as shown.

THE LIFECYCLE OF WORMS

IMPORTANT WORMS INFECTING FOALS AND HORSES
Parasitic worms are a menace to the health and well-being of horses and ponies. Wherever your animals are at grass they will be exposed to infection with a wide range of parasites.

Some types are so small that they can only be seen under a microscope, while others, like the large roundworm, are up to 20 inches (50cm) long. Some species are very damaging, while others are more of a nuisance. It is essential to understand the basic lifecycles to understand how best to control the worms.

	LIFECYCLE		LIFECYCLE
THREADWORMS *(Strongyloides weseri)*	*8–14 days*	*PINWORM or SEATWORM* *(Oxyuris equi)_*	*4–5 months*
LARGE ROUNDWORMS *(Parascaris equorum)*	*10–12 weeks*	*LUNGWORM* *(Dictyocaulus arnfieldi)*	*2–4 months*
SMALL REDWORM *(Cyathostome spp.)*	*5–18 weeks*	*STOMACH REDWORM* *(Trichostrongylus axei)*	*3 weeks*
LARGE REDWORM *(Strongylus spp.)*	*6–11 months*	*LARGE-MOUTHED STOMACH WORM* *(Habronema muscae)*	

Bots are the larvae of gadflies, which worry horses during the hot weather. Gadflies "cement" their eggs onto the horse's coat, often on the legs, which are then licked up. The larvae burrow their way into the mucous membranes of the mouth and tongue, and eventually migrate to the stomach where they attach themselves to the stomach wall until they emerge in the dung to become adult flies.

VACCINATIONS

Most vaccinations are given by intramuscular (into the muscle) or intradermally (into the skin) injections. Usually these should be administered by a veterinarian and a detailed record of what has been given and when a booster will be necessary should be logged into a diary.

TETANUS INOCULATION

All horses and ponies worldwide have to be vaccinated against tetanus. This killer disease is picked up from the soil, and can easily invade open wounds. Foals should be vaccinated at around three months in two doses four to six months apart, followed by a booster one year later. From that time on, horses have boosters every two years.

TRAVELING HORSES' VACCINATIONS

Other vaccinations that should be given depend on the country and any current outbreaks of disease in the local area. You should always check on current requirements before you travel.

Identity or competition passports or vaccination certificates recording the veterinarian's signature, stamp, and date of vaccination have to be carried with the horse—especially when it is competing internationally or being transported abroad.

Competition horses in most disciplines are required to have equine influenza (flu) vaccinations, and these must be given according to the regulations laid down. Currently this requires two primary vaccinations, followed by a six-month booster and then annually thereafter.

Rhinopneumonitis and equine viral arteritis (E.V.A.) vaccinations are given by your veterinarian. It is your responsibility to ensure that your horse is adequately protected according to local recommendations. Both are serious diseases that affect the horse's respiratory and reproductive systems and can cause abortion in breeding stock. The symptoms of a running nose may pass unnoticed, so it is vital that horses are vaccinated.

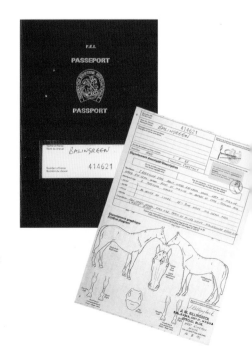

Vaccination certificates will vary according to the country, but all should consist of the written and diagrammatic identification of the horse or pony. Most vaccinations will require annual boosters, so it is important to keep a record and to arrange for these to be given by your veterinarian at the appropriate time.

LEG AND FOOT CARE

Care of the legs and feet is vital if your horse or pony is to stay sound throughout its career. Ignoring what seems like a minor ailment today, could cause greater problems in the future.

There are many factors which contribute toward keeping your horse fit for work. You should always keep your horse shod regularly, and have its feet correctly balanced. Build up fitness work only gradually so that the horse is never put under strain until it is fit to cope with the demand. Never overwork your horse. Overly tired horses are more likely to injure themselves, due to a lack of oxygen reaching the muscles and tendons.

Always heed any warning signs, such as inflammation or heat, and act immediately to ensure they do not become worse. Similarly, treat any cuts or bruises straight away. Call the veterinarian if you are worried or the horse is badly lame.

DETECTING LAMENESS

There are numerous reasons why a horse may go lame, so always check the obvious possibilities first. Sudden lameness may well be caused by a stone lodged in the foot. Check this immediately and remove if necessary. Bruising to the foot is probably the most common cause of all other types of lameness, other than obvious injury.

If further tests are needed to find out the cause of lameness the veterinarian may use hoof pincers to apply pressure to the sole of the suspect foot to test for problems. After lifting the limb to look for possible stiffness or inflammation in the joints the veterinarian may back the horse, or turn it in a tight circle, to check for possible hip or back problems. If the problem is still not apparent then X-ray examinations may be required.

FRONT LEG LAMENESS

Obvious lameness in front is not usually hard to detect. The horse will be reluctant to put weight on the affected leg, and also raises its head up as it goes to touch the ground. To alleviate the pain, it puts extra weight on to the good leg—and lowers its head as it does this.

To check for lameness, get someone to trot the horse, in hand, up and down on a level surface. Keep a loose rein to allow free head movement. If the horse's head stays level, it is sound. If it is lame, its head will nod down with the good front leg, and up as the lame one is put down. How much of a nod will depend on the degree of lameness.

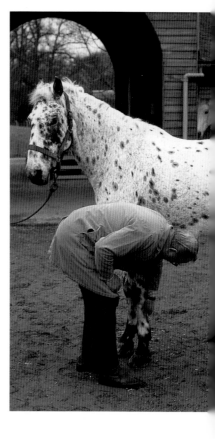

▶ When detecting lameness, the veterinarian will see the horse led in hand after feeling for any heat and swelling on the lame leg. It is important to do both these checks to get a true picture.

HOW TO CHECK FEET FOR PROBLEMS

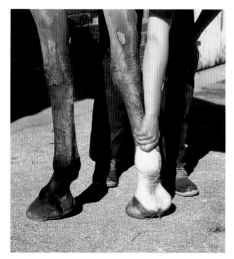

First get an overall impression of the whole leg by feeling down from the top. Look at it from the front and back as well as from the side.

If the problem is in the foot, the hoof may feel warm and a pulse may be felt in the heel by compressing the main foot artery as shown.

Lift the foot up and ensure there is nothing stuck in the foot such as a stone, nail or other sharp object.

HIND LEG LAMENESS

Hind leg lameness is more difficult to detect, especially if only slight. You will need to watch the quarters. The horse will drop on to one side and raise the other, but which one is significant depends on the cause and where the problem is. This is best left to the veterinarian, so long as you have checked for obvious signs such as cracked heels or a stone in the foot. Some older horses will come out stiff behind if they have been cooped up in a stable for 24 hours, but should be fine after five minutes walking.

LAMINITIS

Q My horse is standing as if he wants to get the weight off his front feet and is reluctant to move. Why is this?

A This sounds like the classic symptoms of laminitis, a severe condition causing inflammation of the feet. Because the horse's hoof is hard and cannot expand, the pain caused by the swelling is excruciatingly bad and causes severe distress. The veterinarian should be called. The cause is thought to be dietary and may follow a sudden change in diet or overly rich grass or food. A laxative diet and cooling of the feet by hosing or standing in the river may ease discomfort. Pain killers will be required in severe cases. Fat ponies are particularly prone and should in any case be kept on restricted grazing when the spring grass is at its richest. It is now known, however, that there are several different reasons why horses develop the disease but as yet the causes are not clearly understood.

▼ This horse is clearly in pain and leaning back to ease the weight off its front feet.

CHECKING HOOVES

Q My horse has been lame and when I told the farrier, he took the shoe off as he suspected corns. What are these and what can I do to prevent them?

A Corns are caused by pressure creating bruising under the shoe. The most common area is the heel which may be caused by the shoe being a bit short for the foot, thus putting more pressure in one particular area. It is important that any bruising is cut out so that it does not build up. Some corns go septic, requiring a poultice (see p. 121) to draw out the inflammation before the shoe can be replaced. Sometimes special protective pads or hoof cushions can be used to prevent bruising, or if the horse has very sensitive soles.

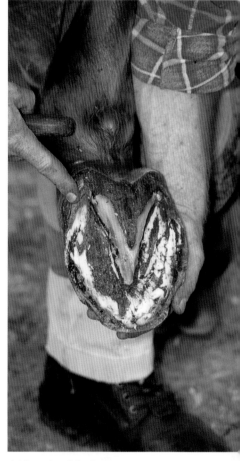

▲ The sole of the foot is particularly vulnerable, especially if the ground has been wet for some time as it tends to soften the feet and make them more prone to bruising and injury. Keeping the feet well trimmed and regularly shod will help toward preventing other injuries.

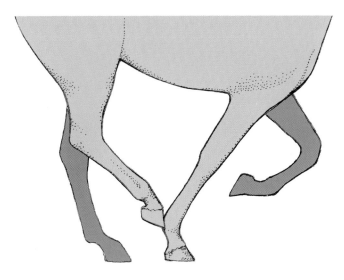

Injuries to the legs are common, especially over-reaching (above) and knocking (below). Remedial shoeing is possible for some problems.

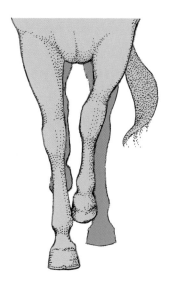

BUMPS AND BRUISES

Sometimes a horse will over reach and give itself a nasty bruise, or sometimes a deep cut on the bulb, of its front heel. This is caused by the back foot over-extending and clipping the front one, and is particularly common when jumping, on deep ground, or when galloping. Some people put on over reach bell boots to protect the heels.

Any bumps or bruises from everyday work are best treated with cold hosing to the area for ten minutes, two or three times a day, to relieve inflammation. After 48 hours of cold treatment, hot poultices or warm dry bandaging are generally the way to create extra circulation to the area to disperse the bruising. The more the animal can move about, the better it will be.

The use of protective boots on the legs will help to minimize knocks to the legs. Bell boots will prevent the risk to the heels from over-reaching.

TREATING SWOLLEN LEGS

Some horses are prone to filled, swollen legs because of over-feeding and under-exercising. It is usually noticeable in the hind legs first, then all four. Check your food/work program and try cutting down the food a little, especially if the horse is in good condition. A bran mash, made with a scoop of bran, a handful of Epsom salts, and boiling water to a tacky consistency (allow it to cool), may help to clear out any excess proteins that have built up in the animal's system. The filling will usually disappear when the horse is exercised. If in doubt, consult the veterinarian.

SORE LEGS

Q I went on a fun ride yesterday and this morning my horse has four filled legs. Is this normal?

A The horse will not usually suffer from this if it has been prepared correctly with a gradual build up to condition its legs and body for the work expected (see *Exercise and Fitness* on pp. 98–101).

You may find that the problem has occurred because you have done more galloping on hard ground than usual which caused some jarring of the legs and this resulted in some filling. Some cold hosing (see p. 129) and quiet walking should help.

TREATING SPLINTS

Horses that are worked on hard ground may develop a condition known as splints. These splints can also be caused by a direct blow, or by too much work with a young horse. They are actually a form of new bone growth, generally located on the inside or outside of the cannon bones, just below the knee or hock. This develops into a small, hard lump, sometimes with heat in that area, and the horse may go lame.

Treatment consists of rest and cold hosing to reduce the inflammation. Rest may be necessary for anything up to six weeks, with anti-inflammatory drugs and DMSO applied to the site. Once the splint has formed and hardened, it rarely causes too much trouble.

◄ Splints may respond to a little ultra-sound treatment to reduce inflammation while forming.

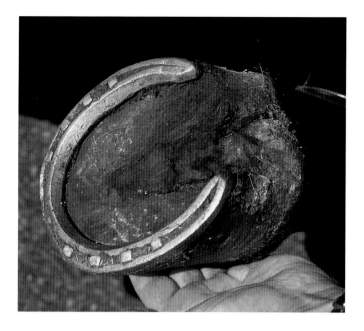

Thrush can be treated with antibiotic spray to dry and harden the area. Ask your farrier to trim any excess frog area.

TREATING CRACKED HEELS AND MUD FEVER

Cracked heels and mud fever are sores that develop in the back of the pastern and heel areas, or anywhere up the legs. They are often caused by damp or muddy conditions, which make the skin soft and sore. Any cracks that develop can quickly become infected if not treated, causing lameness or soreness and swelling.

It is important to clip away excess hair, which tends to hold the moisture and aggravate the problem. A kaolin poultice is effective at cleaning up the area, which can then be treated with an antibiotic or barrier cream to clear up the condition. Keep the area dry and free of dirt. Some animals are more prone than others, especially those with white legs, but early application of barrier creams can help to prevent it.

TREATING FOOT THRUSH

Horses that are kept in poor conditions can develop thrush, an infection of the foot. It is easy enough to detect because the frog of the foot becomes foul-smelling and appears moist. Treatment consists of thorough cleaning of the frog area and spraying with an antibiotic spray to harden it, twice a day. Some horses are more susceptible to the condition than others, but beds should always be kept as clean and dry as possible.

POULTICES

Q How do I apply a kaolin poultice to the bruising on my pony's leg and should it be hot or cold?

A Kaolin, a type of clay, has been used for centuries for bruising and is generally marketed today as a thick paste. The easiest method of application is to spread a thin layer on some brown paper cut to the required size. This can either be applied direct to the leg cold for recent bruising or at blood temperature for treating older bruises or swellings. Cover the poultice with light plastic and padding and bandage for 24 hours. Renew daily until the problem improves (usually from two to five days).

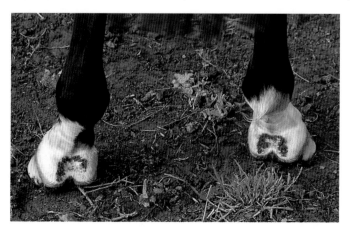

Cracked heels are difficult to keep clean and free of infection, so special care and attention is needed. Regular cleaning care and use of special creams specifically for the condition will help to ensure healing takes place.

COMMON AILMENTS

Your horse relies on you to recognize when it is sick. Illness can happen at any time, and you need to have at least a basic knowledge of the more obvious symptoms. Knowing what to do will help to ensure that the appropriate action is taken. Always call a veterinarian if you have any doubts.

Most everyday problems are fairly minor and can be treated with normal commonsense. The odd little cut or bruise requires much the same treatment of normal hygiene and cooling down (see cold hosing p. 129) that would be needed for any playground tumble. Remember that any treatment given may result in the horse reacting by lifting the injured leg suddenly in such a way that we might say "ouch" to a pin prick or little cut. Have someone hold the horse while treating any wound, or tie it loosely if by yourself so that should it pull back, it can be quickly released.

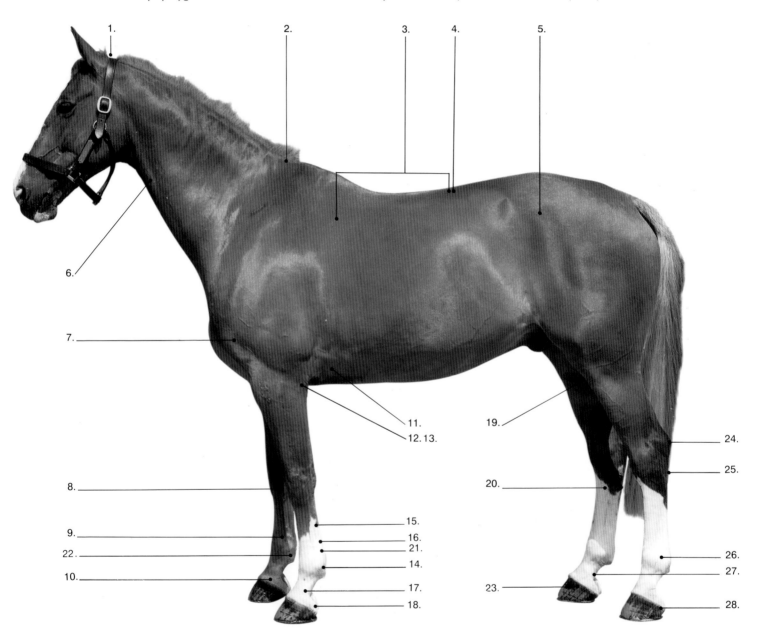

AILMENTS AND INJURIES

You should be able to recognize what is wrong with your horse, so that a veterinarian can give the correct treatment without delay. This diagram indicates some typical problems:

1. Poll evil; 2. Fistulous withers; 3. Sore back (saddle pinch); 4. Sore back (saddle rub); 5. Hip lameness; 6. Whistling; 7. Shoulder lameness; 8. Broken knees; 9. Sore shins; 10. Low ring bone; 11. Girth galls; 12. Capped elbow; 13. Elbow lameness; 14. Brushing injury; 15. Check for ligament strain; 16. Suspensory ligament—check for strain; 17. Side bones; 18. Overreach injury; 19. Hind leg locking; 20. Bone spavin; 21. Bowed tendon; 22. Sesamoiditis; 23. Sand-crack; 24. Capped hock; 25. Curb; 26. Windgalls; 27. Osselet; 28. Contracted heels.

BACK PROBLEMS

Q My horse feels uneven in his gaits. He sinks down when I first get on him and he keeps jumping to the left. He never used to do this, so what is the cause?

A First, look at your saddle (see p. 136). If it is pinching him on his withers, the tree may be too narrow. Is the tree broken? Get a knowledgeable person or the saddler to have a look. A pad may temporarily help if the saddle is too low, but you will have to get it re-stuffed to fit correctly.

Some horses may pull a muscle landing awkwardly over a fence or even put their back or pelvis slightly out of line. These can be dealt with by a horse back specialist.

Young horses may develop minor strains which a week or two in the paddock will cure. Occasionally, it may be that a problem elsewhere, such as in a hock or foot, is causing the horse to move awkwardly and resulting in strain or pressure to certain areas of the back. Gentle pressure from two or three fingers worked systematically down the backbone on either side of the spine for a reaction to pressure may indicate where the problem is.

SKIN PROBLEMS

A variety of skin problems can arise, and may be the result of a reaction to feed or change of diet, irritation by mites, sensitivity to the sun, or a contagious disease. It is always best to treat any suspicious skin rashes or patches with caution, in case they can be transferred from horse to horse or to humans.

RINGWORM
Ringworm is a highly contagious fungal disease. It is easily transmitted by direct contact with an infected horse, infected stables, or equipment, and must be treated with a course of anti-bacterial drugs and creams. Isolation is essential. Isolate the horse, its tack, rugs, and grooming kit from contact with others until the problem is confirmed.

DIET RELATED PROBLEMS
Most skin reactions to feed or change of diet will settle within 24 hours, although severe cases may need an anti-histamine

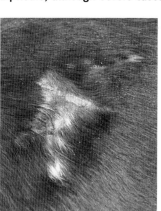

from the veterinarian. Sometimes, a bran mash made with Epsom salts can help. It has a laxative effect, and will help to clear out any excesses from the stomach. Take note of what the horse has eaten. It may be that a change in diet was introduced too suddenly or that the horse had too

Pressure or friction from badly fitting tack causes saddle sores.

Here can be seen the typically rubbed tail and other areas so commonly found with sweet itch: some veterinarians believe tiny mites may be a cause by burrowing under the skin and causing severe irritation.

much protein. Alternatively, the horse could be reacting to a fly bite. Some animals are sun sensitive and may need to be kept in during the day and turned out only at night.

SWEET ITCH
Sweet itch is a condition that occurs only in the summer, and is believed to be caused by an allergic reaction to midges. It causes acute irritation of the mane and tail, leading the animal to rub itself until it produces sores. Apart from proprietary creams, the best remedy is to keep the horse out of the sun and protect the mane and tail as much as possible by ensuring that there is little for the horse to rub itself on. Tail bandages may minimize the damage. Using fly sprays and impregnated tags can help horses that react to fly bites. Sun-block creams can be effective for those sensitive to the sun, particularly on areas of pink skin, such as the nose and white legs.

GIRTH GALLS
Sores found behind the elbow on the girth area are caused by rubbing from the girth (see pp. 136–139) on sensitive skin. These girth galls are particularly common on horses that have just come back to work after a rest, when the skin is soft and the hair often long and dirty. Hard or uncleaned girths can also be a cause. Treat with careful fomentations (topical poultices) and do not ride until the condition has settled. Clean the girth area well before riding and harden the skin with salt water or surgical spirit if the skin is not broken. A girth sleeve and soft well-oiled girths will help to prevent a recurrence.

FLY STRIKE

Q My horse goes absolutely mad when bitten by flies. What can I do about it?

A Flies are a major worry to horses, particularly in hot weather, and some varieties are much more vicious than others. The common horse fly attaches itself to suck blood, and there are others that look rather crablike that drive many horses so crazy they injure themselves.

Fly sprays and impregnated tags that can be attached to the mane will all help. Fringes, for the face, and light fly sheets, which must be adequately secured, are both helpful. Many owners turn their horses out at night and stand them in during the day when the flies are at their worst.

◄ This horse is very well protected against flies, but may still require fly spray around the legs.

CHRONIC OBSTRUCTIVE PULMONARY DISEASE (COPD)

Chronic obstructive pulmonary disease (COPD) is a chronic respiratory illness particularly common among stabled horses, where sensitivity to dust and spores develops into a cough with thick mucus. Left untreated, the horse will gradually deteriorate as the tiny alveoli in the lungs become more damaged.

To treat the condition, provide as much fresh air as possible. Bed the horse on paper or shavings, and soak its hay or feed haylage. Keep the horse out in a paddock as much as you can, and talk to your veterinarian about whether any drugs are necessary. Bronco dilators and expectorants can help to alleviate symptoms in the more serious cases.

EQUINE INFLUENZA

Caused by a virus, equine influenza (flu) is a highly infectious disease and results in a high temperature, cough, and discharge from the nose. The horse may also go off its feed.

The animal must be isolated from other horses and rested. Leading out in hand to graze (so long as this will not increase the risk to others) will help to maintain circulation and prevent the legs from filling. Cut down the energy food intake (grain) but keep up the roughage, such as hay, and make sure there is plenty of fresh water available. Normally, it will take up to two or three weeks for the horse to recover, when a gradual return to work can commence. Regular vaccinations will help to prevent severe cases, even if they do not cover all strains of the virus.

TYING UP

Also known as azoturia, this condition makes the horse's muscles—particularly along the back and quarters—go into spasm. It may start as stiffness behind, then the horse will suddenly slow up as the muscles spasm, start to sweat, and become distressed.

Often, tying up occurs during the breaks at Eventing and Endurance competitions, but it is also common after a day off. It is thought that it may be due to a build-up of protein in the horse's system, making it important to cut down on protein intakes during a day off and to ensure the horse gets some exercise. Electrolytes (salts) may help in hot climates, where dehydration is thought to be a contributing factor.

In severe cases the cramps cause the release of myoglobin into the blood, which results in dark-colored (coffee ground) urine. Watch out for this when the horse passes water. Cease exercise immediately when the condition becomes apparent and keep the horse warm. Take off the saddle or just loosen the girth, if the animal is cold. Arrange transportation home if the horse is very still, as further exercise can do more damage. Once home, rest the horse and give a laxative diet with Epsom salts. Get a veterinarian to take a blood sample, this will determine the severity of the attack by the concentration of muscle enzymes. The test results will then establish the time factor in the horse's return to work, which must be gradual. Discuss a regime of work/food ratio with the veterinarian in order to prevent further attacks.

If your veterinarian suspects a viral infection of some kind it may be necessary to take a blood sample to test in order to administer the precise vaccination or course of antibiotics required.

STRANGLES

Strangles is a severe and highly infectious bacterial disease of the upper respiratory tract that mainly affects the throat area. It causes the formation of large abscesses, which can burst internally or externally and so affect breathing or swallowing. The horse may have a very high temperature, be extremely miserable, and have a thick nasal discharge.

Strict isolation procedures must be implemented immediately. High standards of hygiene are essential if the disease is not to spread. All affected bedding will have to be burned and the whole area thoroughly disinfected. All equipment and clothing will have to be disinfected, as will the hands and feet of any person in contact with the sick animal. Any kit used must be kept only for the affected horse.

Treatment usually takes the form of antibiotics, after the abscesses have burst. A veterinarian will also need to take blood tests and throat swabs to determine when the horse is free of infection. While it is sick, feeding the horse on the floor will make it easier for it to eat. Apply hot fomentations to the throat area regularly and bathe the eyes and nostrils as often as necessary. Birds are known to be a major cause of the disease spreading.

TETANUS

Usually fatal, tetanus is caused by the toxin *Clostridium tetani* present in soil. Puncture wounds are the most likely site for the bacteria to enter the horse's system.

The initial symptoms of the disease are muscle stiffness. Then, the third eyelid can be seen across the eye, jaw movements become restricted, and spasms and paralysis gradually set in. Few recover, which is why vaccination of all horses and ponies is vital. The sick animal should be isolated in a darkened, quiet area and given large doses of penicillin to prevent further absorption of any toxins. A veterinarian may also administer tranquilizers, muscle relaxants, and sedatives.

ARTHRITIS

Q My horse is now about twenty and getting rather stiff and has enlarged areas around some of his joints. Why is this?

A As the horse gets older, it may well develop arthritis in the same way as humans. Talk to your veterinarian, who will probably prescribe some anti-inflammatory drug to relieve any pain or stiffness. You should remember that the condition is there, however, and not over exert your horse, though gentle exercise may help to prevent the condition worsening. The cold weather will often aggravate this, so keep the horse warm and if necessary bandage his legs in very cold weather. There may come a time when pain and discomfort becomes too severe and you need to think seriously whether it would be kinder to put your horse down. Your veterinarian will help to advise you in such cases.

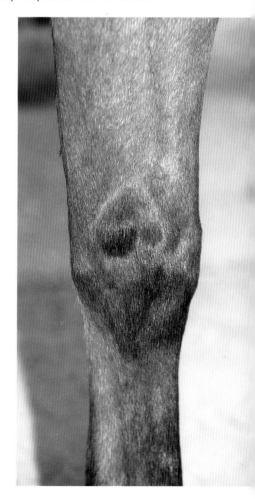

▶ Bony enlargements are typical signs of arthritic changes taking place and causing pain and stiffness.

RECOGNIZING PROBLEMS

As you get to know your horse you will be able to distinguish the difference between simply an off day or the start of an ailment or disease. You may start to worry about your horse getting a patchy coat, or if it starts rolling on the ground sometimes. As explained here, you may be worrying needlessly, but you should ensure you check on your horse regularly in case a symptom shows something serious, such as colic (see right). If you are in any doubt at all, call in a veterinarian.

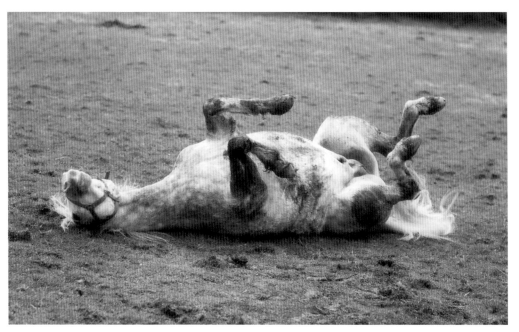

ROLLING ON GROUND

Q I know rolling can be a sign of well-being and pleasure and nature's way of helping to shift the horse's coat. However, as it may also indicate serious pain and colic if associated with sweating, anxious behavior or general discomfort, how will I know when to call the veterinarian?

A If you know your horse or pony, it will be easy to see when it is enjoying itself and when it is ill, but if in any doubt, call your veterinarian for advice and he or she will tell you what to look out for and assess whether a visit is necessary. It is always better to be safe than sorry. Some horses and ponies love to roll and it is very important to get to know when they like to do this—such as after exercise. If so, be sure to take the saddle off immediately or they will go down with that on too if you leave them unattended even for a few seconds!

Rolling: a great luxury for the horse who may use it to stretch, scratch, and play all in one, then very often getting up and galloping off with huge leaps and bucks afterward!

PATCHY COAT

Q It is the end of the winter and my horse is losing its coat. It looks very patchy and comes out in great tufts in places. Is this normal?

A The horse changes its coat twice a year and during the winter generally grows a much thicker coat, although some breeds are much more dense than others. This starts to fall out as the warmer weather comes. Regular use of rubber curry combs (see pp. 86–89) in a circular movement will help to shift the coat during this stage.

Occasionally there are problems with lice (tiny mites that enjoy the thick coats and also suck blood causing general debilitation, itching, and rubbing of the coat). If this develops, seek veterinary advice and get a preparatory powder to sprinkle on the coat for a few days or treat as suggested by your veterinarian. If horses are in a group, it is likely they will all be suffering from this and will all need treating. Wear protective clothing when treating. Weather scald caused by prolonged wet weather on the back may cause loss of hair which will grow over with the summer coat. New Zealand blankets (rugs) in wet weather may avoid this.

This horse looks well enough in itself, but is at the stage when the winter coat is still half in place, thus giving a rather moth-eaten look. A few more weeks and a glossy summer coat will be in place.

COLIC

This term is used to describe a pain in the abdomen. There are several reasons why it might happen, such as a blockage in the digestive system caused by a change in the diet, dehydration, worm infestation, over feeding or kidney problems. It is potentially very serious, and can lead to death.

With colic, the horse will become very restless, often looking around at its tummy and kicking at it. It may start to sweat, and its breathing and pulse rate will increase. If this does not settle after 20 minutes, or if the horse becomes violent or is in obvious pain, call the veterinarian immediately. Discourage the horse from rolling. A short walk may help to prevent further problems developing. Listen for any tummy sounds or noises or if the horse passes any wind. Take note of any urine passed, and check for recent droppings. You will need to pass this information on to the veterinarian.

A TYPICAL DAY FOR A VETERINARIAN

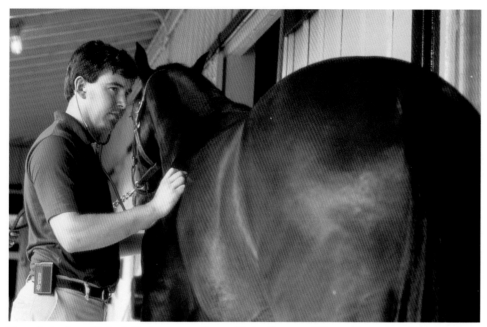

The veterinarian will check the horse over thoroughly in all cases of illness. He or she will usually listen to heart and lungs for any signs of abnormality and for bowel sounds to ensure the gut is working normally.

2.30AM *and fast asleep I get a call out to a bad case of colic as it's my night on call. The horse is in a bad way and requires pain killers and I discovered it had just arrived at the barn (stable) that afternoon after a long journey—a typical reaction to a sudden change of food and environment. Back to bed a couple of hours later, I felt exhausted when the alarm went at 7AM. The colic case was reported to be continuing to do well and I felt better after a quick breakfast.*

8AM–6PM *Clinic time is often fun with owners sometimes reacting in predictable ways—sometimes not. It's difficult to tell people that their much loved horse has a chronic condition and is no longer going to be able to perform a certain role when someone else has convinced them it's only suffering from corns (bruises in the foot). It is very rewarding, however, when difficult problems are finally pinpointed and you are able to see good results.*

Foaling time is a favorite—who can fail to be moved by these independent little creatures' look of amazement and the wobble and flop into an upright position and a final effort to stand then the instinct that takes them unaided to the "milk bar" (or udder).

Meeting so many clients makes the job interesting and, of course, very varied—it's hard work and often very disruptive on one's social life, but I wouldn't change it for anything—I love the animals.

LETHARGIC MARE

Q I bought a mare six months ago and have had a lot of fun with her, but just recently she does not seem to have been as energetic as before and is getting fatter and fatter. I'm careful not to over feed her in case she gets laminitis but she's still getting fat. What should I do?

A Your pony may be getting fat on very little (many ponies do!). This is affecting her energy as she carries the extra weight, but it might be worth getting your veterinarian to check her just in case she is in fact in foal! Many is the time that the neighbor's young colt has popped over the fence at the right moment with both owners being unaware that a little more went on than was at first envisaged. Many a veterinarian has discovered the results of this situation when called to check an "overweight" mare!

FIRST-AID FOR HORSES

Accidents always happen when you least expect them but, if you are prepared, you can minimize the damage caused by an everyday minor injury. In the case of major incidents, such as a road traffic accident, you may also be able to prevent the situation worsening until professional help arrives.

Absolutely essential in any stable is a well-stocked, easily accessible horse first-aid kit. This should contain all the basic ingredients to help you treat a small wound or attend to a bruise or swelling. Use commonsense, stay calm, and assess every situation carefully before attempting first-aid. Then, if you are at all concerned, always contact a veterinarian.

HORSE FIRST-AID KIT

- *Cotton (cotton wool).*
- *Container for bathing wounds.*
- *Kaolin.*
- *Poultices (see p. 121).*
- *Scissors for cutting dressings.*
- *Sterile non-stick dressings.*
- *Salt or antiseptic solution.*
- *Bandages or leg wraps to hold dressings in place and for dry bandaging.*
- *Instant "cold" packs for reducing inflammation.*
- *Antiseptic wound spray and powder.*
- *Thermometer.*
- *Any personal preferences, such as Arnica pills (see p. 132) and ointments for relieving bruising.*

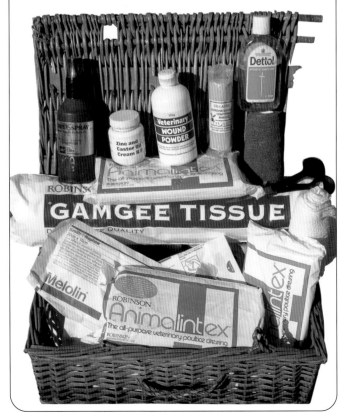

Minor wounds should be thoroughly cleaned with antiseptic or salt water and kept clean.

MINOR WOUNDS

Minor wounds can be cleaned with a saline solution of one teaspoon of salt to 1 pint (½ liter) of boiling water, which has been allowed to cool to comfortably warm, or a mild antiseptic. Check that the wound is really clean, removing all bits of mud, sand, or debris with a cotton pad. Dry the area and apply wound spray or powder. Take particular care to see that there are no hidden puncture wounds, which will need antibiotics and veterinary assessment. If there are foreign bodies stuck in a wound, do not move until professional help is at hand in case of serious hemorrhage.

CHOKING HORSE

Q My horse is very greedy and grabs at his feed, sometimes choking and coughing which is quite alarming. Is their anything I can do?

A Horses that are very greedy will try to bolt down their food. This can be solved by giving them plenty of chaff or chop mixed with their feed thereby making it more difficult to chew quickly.

If possible, small feeds given more often may be better for this type of animal. Feed them on the floor in a feed bucket so that any choking will be done in the most natural position and the hastily eaten feed will be likely to be coughed out.

EMERGENCY!

Whenever a problem or accident happens, remember to think clearly and not to panic! First things first!
• Is it life threatening? Deal accordingly by calling an ambulance or veterinarian as appropriate.
• Prevent further injury to either humans or horses. For example, make sure any unhurt horse or person is moved away from the scene of the accident.

CUTS OR TEARS

With serious cuts or tears, lightly hose the wound or leave it and cover it with a non-stick dressing. Usually the flow of blood will help clean the wound, but bleeding must be stopped if it does not do so by itself after a few minutes. Either a dressing or a clean handkerchief should be placed over the wound and pressure applied. Once bleeding has stopped, another clean dressing can be placed over the wound and a bandage applied until the veterinarian arrives.

SERIOUS CUTS OR ARTERY DAMAGE

Cut arteries are life-threatening, although rare. Call a veterinarian immediately. Apply a firm pad and a bandage, and put another on top if bleeding persists. You will know if it is a cut artery because blood spurts out (veins bleed in a continuous stream). Keep the horse still and quiet. A tourniquet should be applied only if the arterial cut is life-threatening. It should be applied only over the wound or just above, between the heart and the wound. Tourniquets must be loosened every 10 to 15 minutes in case they cause circulation problems.

Keep a clean pad of material pressed firmly onto a serious cut. Remember that even a docile horse may become agitated while being treated because of the pain. You should have the horse tied up.

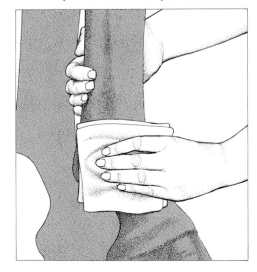

BRUISE OR MINOR SWELLING

A blow to a limb, such as when hitting a jump pole hard, is one of the most common causes of bruises. They may blow up quite quickly or come up gradually. The sooner you can apply ice or a cold pack to the area the better—a packet of frozen peas makes an easy substitute!

You can make an ice pack by crushing ice inside a plastic bag using a hammer or a heavy object. Bandage it lightly over some gauze or toweling to prevent skin scalding. Replace hourly, for two to four hours, then hose with cold water two or three times daily if the bruise is minor. If the bruise is large, increase the number of times you cold hose. Generally, it is the first 24 hours that are most important to reduce swelling and to prevent any further hemorrhage from taking place. Cold hosing can be done for 10 to 20 minutes every two hours, or whenever possible.

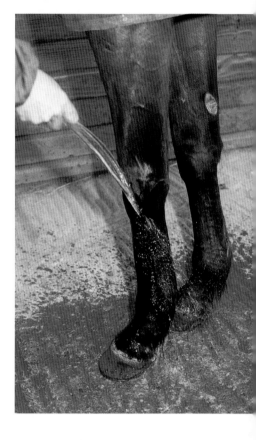

Cold hosing is excellent for bruising and swelling and for helping to clean minor wounds. Keep the flow gentle.

SWOLLEN KNEES

Q My horse hit its knee, which blew up like a football within minutes. How should I treat it?

A Ice to the spot or cold water immediately has an amazing effect on reducing swelling in most cases. Continue to reapply every hour for the first three or four hours, then four or five times a day until the swelling has subsided. The first six hours are the most important and most will have reduced dramatically after twenty-four hours.

PUNCTURE WOUNDS

Q My horse spiked itself on a metal bar. It's only a little hole, but it must be quite deep. Should I call the veterinarian?

A Yes! Small puncture wounds can be quite dangerous and it is much safer to get the veterinarian to ensure the wound is thoroughly cleaned inside. Antibiotics may be prescribed and your veterinarian will want to be satisfied that your horse is covered against tetanus (see p. 117 and 125), so keep your vaccination records up to date.

FIRST-AID FOR PEOPLE

Put horses and people together and there is always bound to be the odd bruise, knock, and fall. No matter how confident you are around horses, they can still be unpredictable. Just as often, the fault is the rider's, with perhaps overconfidence leading to complacency and carelessness.

Aproperly stocked, accessible first-aid kit for people is vital on any stable yard, and of course there needs to be someone who knows how to use it. It is recommended that anyone who is involved with horses should take a course in first-aid. That way, you can assess a situation correctly and cope with a medical emergency until an ambulance arrives.

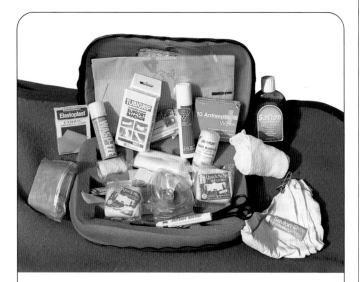

HUMAN FIRST-AID KIT

- *Bandages, including triangular ones to make arm slings for shoulder and arm injuries.*
- *Variety of bandaids (plasters).*
- *Antiseptic solution to clean wounds.*
- *Cotton (cotton wool) and cotton pads.*
- *Sterile dressings for wounds.*
- *Scissors.*
- *Tweezers for drawing out splinters.*
- *Eye bath and solution for eyes.*
- *Thermometer.*

ACCIDENT ACTION PLAN

If an accident occurs, stay calm and assess the situation.

- *Think logically as to how best to help the injured person and cope with any other problems. If another person is available, send them for an ambulance or any other help as required.*
- *Make sure there are no other dangers such as children on ponies unattended, or that loose horses cannot get on to a road and cause more accidents.*
- *Decide on priorities and give emergency first aid. Deal with life-threatening conditions, if there are any, first. An unconscious patient will need to be in a safe position to breathe. Put them in the recovery position first, and make sure that they have a clear airway. Check for any bleeding and deal with any serious blood loss. At the same time, check for any broken bones.*
- *If there is a risk to the back or neck, do **not** move. Support the limbs as appropriate. Keep the person warm and do not leave unattended until medical help arrives.*

Most riding accidents are caused by a fall, and in general there is little harm done except for hurt pride and a few bruises! However, in more serious accidents or falls, which so often look quite innocuous, the injury may be severe. Broken limbs and head and back injuries are the most common, some of which will result in unconsciousness. This will require immediate first aid to place the rider in the recovery position (see p. 130)—always ensuring that before moving the person there is not an injury to the neck. If in doubt wait for professional help.

THE RECOVERY POSITION

To place a person in the recovery position, first ensure there is no neck injury. If in doubt do not move the person. If there is no neck injury then place the person in the recovery position, as shown, on side with nearside arm in halt sign position. Take offside arm across chest and place bend at nearside of face. Hold the hand in position. Lift the offside knee and roll the person toward you. Place the knee and leg in front of other leg for support. Check that the airway is clear, the patient is breathing, and that there is no excessive bleeding.

It is very important to know how to place a casualty in a recovery position should an accident occur.

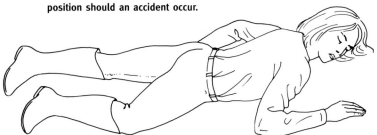

EXTERNAL BLEEDING

To stop external bleeding, in general, pressure is applied and the injury is elevated. By controlling severe bleeding, you help to minimize shock. With slight bleeding, your aim should be to clean the wound thoroughly to reduce the chance of infection.

Severe bleeding should be covered with a clean cotton material pad and firm bandage to help control the blood flow. If bleeding persists, place another bandage on top. Raise the limb slightly if this is appropriate. Arterial bleeding—when the blood spurts out—will need very firm pressure applied. This should be released every ten minutes and then tightened again until bleeding is controlled.

INTERNAL BLEEDING

With suspected internal bleeding, such as that from a fall, keep the person quiet and comfortable. Monitor condition and stay with the person until medical help arrives. As with any accident, make a note of what occurred and keep a record of the treatment given and the person's response. This information should then be passed on to the medical professionals.

IMPORTANT NOTE: You should not attempt either mouth-to-mouth or cardio pulmonary resuscitation without previous training. The information on these pages is intended as reminders. There is no substitute for taking a full, recognized course in first-aid.

MOUTH-TO-MOUTH RESUSCITATION

If there is no breathing, but the casualty has a pulse, mouth-to-mouth resuscitation will be required:

1 Check that mouth is clear of broken teeth or surface dirt.
2 Lift chin and tilt head back to clear the airway.
3 Close the nose by pinching it between the thumb and index finger.
4 Take a good breath in and seal lips around person's mouth.
5 Blow into mouth until chest rises (about two seconds).
6 Remove lips and let chest fall (about four seconds).
7 Continue mouth-to-mouth at a rate of approximately ten inflations per minute until help arrives or the person starts to breathe. Check that the pulse is still beating after every ten ventilations.

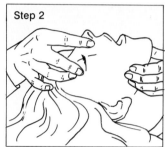
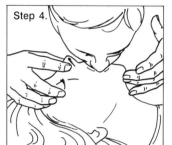
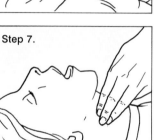

Clearing the airway is the first vital step if the patient is having difficulty breathing. Take a deep breath and seal your mouth over the casualty's. Blow into mouth. Repeat every six seconds.

CARDIO PULMONARY RESUSCITATION (CPR)

If the person is not breathing and there is no pulse, start cardio pulmonary resuscitation (CPR).

1 Find point on the chest where ribs meet breastbone.
2 Place heel of hand on breastbone with other hand interlinked on top.
3 Press down on chest, then release pressure, at a rate of approximately 80 presses per minute. Press smoothly and firmly but not roughly.
4 Combine mouth-to-mouth and CPR together.
5 Give two breaths of artificial ventilations.
6 Give 15 chest compressions.
7 Repeat the sequence with a steady rhythm and no pauses until professional help arrives or the person starts to recover.

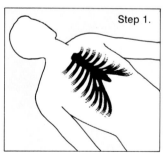
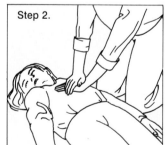

If the heart has stopped or is very faint, there will be no pulse. The patient may be bluish in color and the pupils may be dilated. It is essential to start cardio-pulmonary resuscitation right away.

NATURAL AND HERBAL MEDICINES

Today there is a realization that many of the old remedies of years ago are actually extremely effective. Several so-called "new" discoveries are based on long-known herbs or just forgotten simple therapies. Ice and heat are used in every sports clinic in the world, for example, yet their healing properties were recognized by the Ancient Egyptians! They are the main treatment for any bruise, strain, or sprain.

Herbs are known to have a wide variety of medicinal actions. They can be anti-inflammatory, analgesic (pain relieving), anti-spasmodic, calmative, diuretic, or stimulant. Some animals are more responsive than others to a certain herb, but in most cases there will be some improvement and in many this can be dramatic. These remedies can be very powerful, so it is *always* advisable to seek expert, professional advice on treatment of a horse or pony.

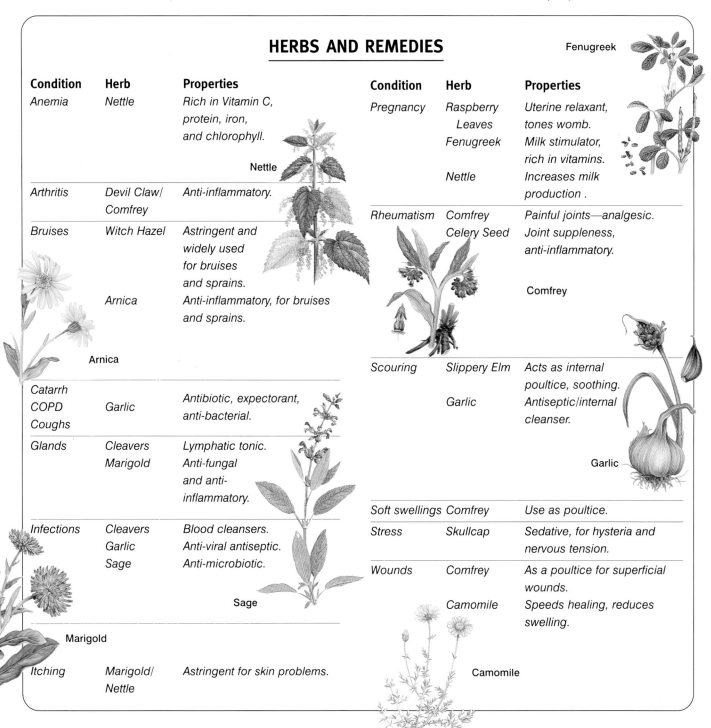

HERBS AND REMEDIES

Condition	Herb	Properties
Anemia	Nettle	Rich in Vitamin C, protein, iron, and chlorophyll.
Arthritis	Devil Claw/ Comfrey	Anti-inflammatory.
Bruises	Witch Hazel	Astringent and widely used for bruises and sprains.
	Arnica	Anti-inflammatory, for bruises and sprains.
Catarrh COPD Coughs	Garlic	Antibiotic, expectorant, anti-bacterial.
Glands	Cleavers Marigold	Lymphatic tonic. Anti-fungal and anti-inflammatory.
Infections	Cleavers Garlic Sage	Blood cleansers. Anti-viral antiseptic. Anti-microbiotic.
Itching	Marigold/ Nettle	Astringent for skin problems.

Nettle

Arnica

Sage

Marigold

Condition	Herb	Properties
Pregnancy	Raspberry Leaves	Uterine relaxant, tones womb.
	Fenugreek	Milk stimulator, rich in vitamins.
	Nettle	Increases milk production .
Rheumatism	Comfrey Celery Seed	Painful joints—analgesic. Joint suppleness, anti-inflammatory.
Scouring	Slippery Elm	Acts as internal poultice, soothing.
	Garlic	Antiseptic/internal cleanser.
Soft swellings	Comfrey	Use as poultice.
Stress	Skullcap	Sedative, for hysteria and nervous tension.
Wounds	Comfrey	As a poultice for superficial wounds.
	Camomile	Speeds healing, reduces swelling.

Fenugreek

Comfrey

Garlic

Camomile

REMEDY APPLICATIONS

Herbs can be mixed with the feed or administered in a number of other ways, according to the desired effect:

Infusion This is rather like making tea. Use approximately 1oz (25g) dried herbs or 3oz (75g) fresh herbs with approximately 9fl oz (250ml) of boiling water and leave to brew for ten minutes. Do not strain.

Poultice Make this with chopped herbs (fresh or dried), moistened with hot water. Apply to the affected part and leave on overnight or hold in place for as long as possible. Leave off during the day and reapply overnight.

Compress This is a liquid-only version of a cold poultice. A cloth is wrung out in the solution and applied to the leg.

Cream You can use herbs to make up your own cream. Melt emulsifying ointment and glycerine in a double saucepan, add dry herbs, and heat all together for three hours. Strain, and stir occasionally until cool. Store in the refrigerator until cold. Then apply as required.

Oil Essential oils are easily available in health food and specialized stores. Add four to five drops, or as advised, to about 1 pint (500ml) of sunflower or grape oil.

MASSAGE

Another natural remedy which has been in practice for at least 3,000 years, and is now becoming popular again, is the art of massage to influence the recovery of damaged tissue. It is also used to prepare the body for exercise and in so doing enhances performance and minimizes injury. Following exercise, massages reduce fatigue and help the body to return to normal condition.

EFFECTS OF MASSAGE

- It helps to promote general health, by clearing the waste from muscles.
- It promotes relaxation.
- It is stimulating.

Different techniques are employed in massage to achieve the various specific effects:

Stroking The stroke follows the direction of major veins. This enhances lymphatic flow and relaxes the horse.

Compression The soft tissues are lightly grasped, picked up, and returned to their original position. This improves the circulation, mobilizes the tissues, and stimulates blood vessels.

Kneading The knuckles and fingers are used as if kneading dough, pressing down and slightly twisting into the muscle. It stimulates deep-seated blood vessels.

Percussion Loosely clenched fists are bounced up and down on the large muscles to increase contraction and relaxation, giving a stimulating effect.

Clapping Cupped hands are used alternately, lifting and dropping the wrist for a stimulating effect.

Friction The skin is moved as one by the use of a single finger in a localized area, to stimulate circulation in that place.

HORSE MASSAGE

Massage routine:

Nearside neck, shoulders, chest, back, quarters, and limbs, then the same on the offside. Ideally, all horses and ponies should have a full body massage before strenuous work or competition. A full massage takes approximately three-quarters of an hour.

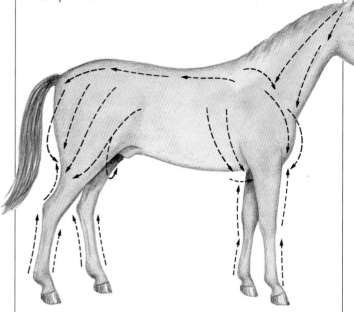

To gain the full benefit, the horse should be kept as warm as possible during treatment. Infrared lamps are ideal.

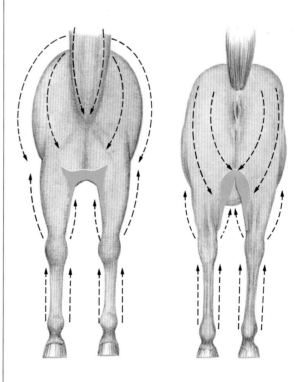

It is essential to know in what direction to massage—basically toward the heart, as the arrows clearly show.

SECTION
3
Equipment and Riding Techniques

TACK AND HORSE EQUIPMENT

Good quality tack and equipment are essential for the safety of you and your horse or pony—always buy the best that you can afford. Treat your tack well and it will repay you with years of faithful service.

Well-maintained, clean and correctly fitting tack will add to the overall appearance of your horse or pony whether you are riding out or in competition, so it is always worth acquiring items that look good and enhance the overall picture of the "horse and rider."

◄ **The saddle, more than any other part of the tack, becomes a very personal item as, after time, it tends to mold to the rider's shape and therefore becomes very comfortable for that rider.**

You should always ensure that the saddle you intend to buy is the correct size for you and is the correct type for the sort of work you intend to use it for, that is—general riding, dressage, or show jumping, for example. A reputable saddler will give you advice on what you require—and how to look after this vital piece of equipment.

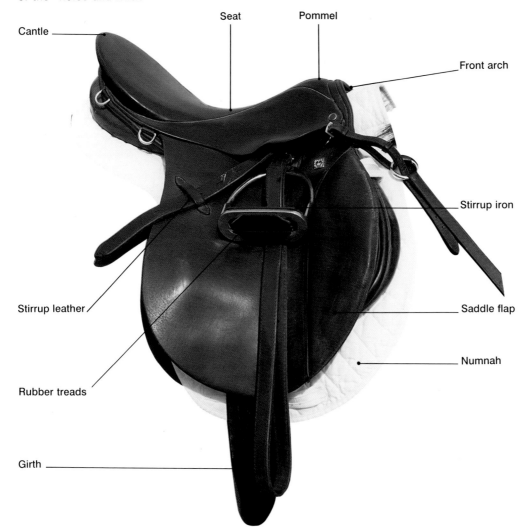

Cantle — Seat — Pommel — Front arch — Stirrup iron — Saddle flap — Numnah — Stirrup leather — Rubber treads — Girth

► **A variety of girths, some with elasticated inserts for extra "give." The two short girths on the left are used with the long girth straps used on some dressage saddles.**

THE SADDLE

A correctly fitted saddle is an absolute essential—get professional advice before making a purchase. An ill-fitting saddle will not only be painful for a horse, but it can also lead to permanent damage. It should also be comfortable for the rider, and suitable for its intended use. A general-purpose saddle is best for everyday riding, whereas dressage and jumping saddles are designed to meet specific requirements. For children, there are different variations of felt or part-felt saddles. These are ideal for beginners because they are flat and not slippery.

The girth is attached to the saddle to keep it in position, and generally is made of leather webbing or string. The stirrup irons and leathers are attached to the saddle via the stirrup bar. The irons must be the right size for the foot, neither too narrow nor too wide (no more than ½in/130mm gap). The various styles available include a safety iron for children, which has a detachable rubber band on the outside. Rubber treads can be used in the base to prevent the boot from slipping through the iron. The leathers should be a suitable size for the rider and adjustable in length, with enough holes to allow flexibility for the long- and short-limbed rider.

Dressage saddle

General purpose riding saddle

Jumping saddle

Stirrup with rubber tread

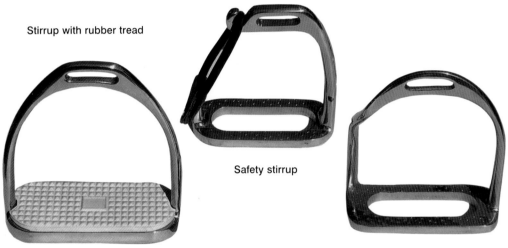

Safety stirrup

Stirrup without tread

(Far left) Rubber treads help to prevent the foot slipping through the stirrup and are highly recommended.

(Center) In the event of a fall the rubber band or strip on a safety stirrup will pull off so that the foot does not get caught and the rider dragged along the ground. This is an ideal type for children.

(Left) The gap in the foot rest of this stirrup without a tread allows the tread on the rider's boot to push through it and keep the foot in place.

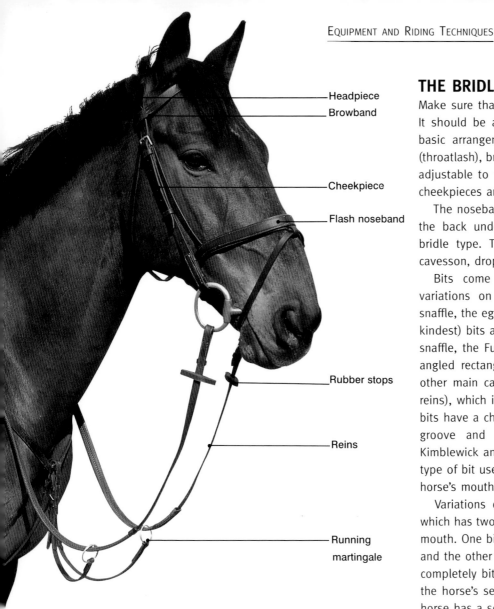

Headpiece
Browband
Cheekpiece
Flash noseband
Rubber stops
Reins
Running martingale

THE BRIDLE

Make sure that you have the right size bridle for your horse. It should be a comfortable fit without being too snug. The basic arrangement consists of a headpiece and throatlatch (throatlash), browband, noseband, two cheekpieces (which are adjustable to fit the length of the head), and reins. The two cheekpieces are attached to the bit as are the reins.

The noseband lies under the headpiece, and is fastened at the back underneath the head, according to the particular bridle type. The most common nosebands in use are the cavesson, drop, flash, and grakle.

Bits come in all kinds of designs, but are basically variations on two main categories. Most common is the snaffle, the eggbutt being one of the simplest (and one of the kindest) bits available. Other variations include the loose-ring snaffle, the Fulmer snaffle, and the Dr. Bristol (which has an angled rectangular plate in the middle, and is severe). The other main category is the curb bit or pelham (with double reins), which is severe in rough or inexperienced hands. Curb bits have a chain attached which is fastened around the chin groove and gives extra control. Variations include the Kimblewick and the Mullen-mouth pelham. Irrespective of the type of bit used, it should always be the correct width for the horse's mouth.

Variations on the bridle itself include the double bridle, which has two sets of reins attached to two bits in the horse's mouth. One bit is a type of small snaffle known as a bridoon, and the other is a curb. A hackamore, on the other hand, is a completely bitless bridle. This relies on pressure on or round the horse's sensitive nose for control, and can be useful if a horse has a sore mouth.

▼ The double-bridle has two bits for extra sensitive riding and is used by experienced riders for lightness of touch and control.

▼ The hackamore is a bitless bridle suitable for horses or ponies with difficult or injured mouths.

WHAT BIT TO USE

Q What is the best bridle to use if you are not very experienced about bits?

A The snaffle bridle is always best but be sure it is the right width for your horse's mouth. A loose ring or eggbutt are the simplest. Remember that a softer bit, such as a rubber or plastic bit, is sometimes more effective than a more severe bit. If the bit hurts your horse's mouth it may not be keen to follow your directions through the rein and will become difficult to control. If in doubt, ask a more knowledgeable person, such as a saddler or your veterinarian, for advice about specific problems. (See pp. 145–146 also.)

A flash noseband with bottom strap fastened below the bit to help prevent the opening of its mouth.

A grakle—a cross-over noseband to prevent the horse from crossing its jaw.

A plain cavesson is most common. It sits just below the cheek bones on the side of jaw.

A drop noseband must be kept high on the nose, but fastened below the bit.

The jaw of the horse evolved over millions of years and developed a gap between the molars and the tushes (front teeth) which has been utilized by humans to fit the bit.

▲ Three snaffles: an eggbutt (top), a loose ring (center) and a double-jointed in a French link (bottom).

▶ Three curb bits with curbchains: a pelham with tongue bar (top), a kimblewick (center), and a half-moon pelham (bottom).

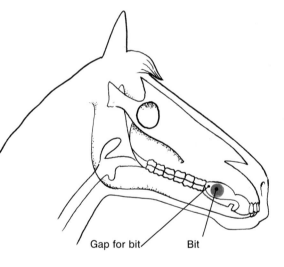

Gap for bit   Bit

THE HALTER (HEADCOLLAR)

Halters are used for tying up or leading, and are a basic form of restraint. Normally made from leather or webbing, they should be comfortable without being too tight (or so loose that the horse escapes!) The noseband should rest about halfway down the head. A halter is a simple device, and can be adjusted to fit just about any sized head.

The halter (headcollar) is used for leading or tying up the horse or pony. You should make sure that it is kept in good repair so that it doesn't snap if the animal gets agitated and pulls up its head.

OTHER EQUIPMENT

Numnah This is a type of pad used under the saddle to soften the contact between saddle and horse, and to protect the leather from the horse's sweat. It is usually made of fleece, cotton, toweling, felt, or synthetic rubber material, and is secured by tapes to the girth straps. Loose pads and sheepskins are also used.

Neckstrap This useful strap is placed around the horse's neck for beginners, to give added security and to prevent the rider from pulling on the animal's mouth. Often it is also used on youngsters, or whenever the rider requires something secure to hold on to.

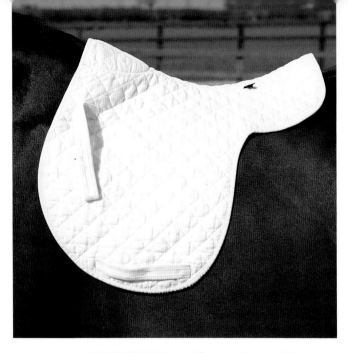

▲ The numnah or saddlepad is used under the saddle for extra comfort. It should be washed regularly to prevent rashes.

◀ (Left) The running martingale helps with control and steering of the horse. There must always be "stops" fitted as shown.

◀ (Far left) The leather breastplate or breastgirth prevents the saddle from slipping back.

Martingale This device is used to prevent the horse from putting its head up too high and out of the angle of control. It gives greater control and steerage. There are two main types: the "standing" martingale, which is attached only to the cavesson or flash noseband and the "running" martingale, through which the reins run. It is essential to have "stops" with a running martingale to prevent the rings from catching on the billets of the reins.

Breastplate Also known as a breastgirth, a breastplate is designed to prevent the saddle from sliding back—perhaps because the horse is lean and fit, or just because of its conformation. Generally, it is used in racing or competition work.

Crupper Usually a leather loop, a crupper is used to prevent the saddle from sliding forward, particularly with small, fat ponies who often have insufficient withers to keep it in position. It is attached under the pony's tail to the back of the saddle, to which it is necessary to have a "D" ring added.

▶ The crupper does not cause the horse or pony any discomfort but is sometimes necessary to secure the saddle. The red bow denotes that the horse or pony is liable to kick out, so keep other animals and people away.

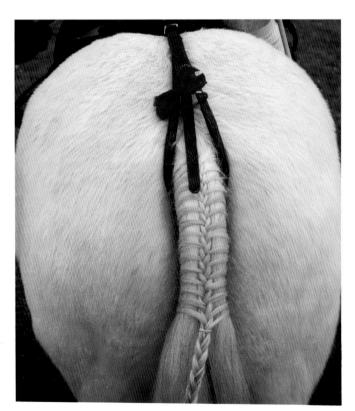

CLEANING THE TACK

All tack should be cleaned after use. Cleaning it also a good way of keeping a check on wear and tear, and whether anything is about to break. Keep tack in good condition and it should last for years.

The safety aspect is most important and cannot be over-emphasized. Never leave anything that is starting to unstitch or break, but put it out for repair. Such problems are most noticeable at tack cleaning time.

METAL WORK

Metal work should be cleaned with a damp cloth and dried. For showy occasions, the rings of the bit (not the mouthpiece), stirrup irons, and any silver or metal wear can be buffed up with metal polish for an extra shine.

CARE OF THE BIT

Make a habit of rinsing the bit immediately so that it is quick and easy to clean later. Dip it in a water bucket or under a faucet as soon as it is taken off the horse.

It is always best to clean metalwork immediately after use before any dirt or mud dries and hardens.

LEATHER

All leather should be wiped over with a damp cloth and then soaped with a saddle soap. Occasionally, or if hard, the leather should be oiled to keep it supple. Do not over-oil saddle flaps as these need to be kept firm. If grease tends to build up on the leather, especially on the saddle or reins, rub the area gently with a little horse hair or a slightly abrasive cloth to remove it.

Always hang bridles and saddles up after use. Never drop the saddle. This could break the "tree" (the frame inside), rendering the saddle dangerous and useless. Carry the saddle by placing the front arch into the crook of your elbow. If possible, place the saddle over a rail or door at all times when it's not in the tack room or in use.

CARE OF OTHER MATERIALS

String girths should be washed regularly—except for the fleecy type which should be brushed to get dry mud and hairs out.
A *webbing collar or halter* should be washed once a week with a good detergent.
Numnahs should be washed regularly. Remember to check all stitching on all equipment to ensure it is safe.

The bridle is being cleaned from a tack hook, which is used in tackrooms especially for hanging and cleaning tack. It can then be stored with other equipment until next required. Keeping an orderly, well-organized tack room is very important.

CLEANING THE SADDLE

Start with a wipe over with a damp sponge to clear any surface dirt, then use a well soaped sponge of saddle soap to keep the leather supple. Hard leather can be oiled periodically with special oil available from saddlers. Do not over oil the saddle flaps as they will wear quickly. Stirrup irons can be washed or wiped clean.

Put the saddle on a good support. Then the saddle's top and underside should be wiped all over with a moist cloth or sponge.

The same areas, as well as the girth straps, should then be soaped well with a damp cloth and saddle soap—but don't make the leather too wet.

Remember to notice any stitching that is starting to come loose at any time so that it can be repaired at the saddler.

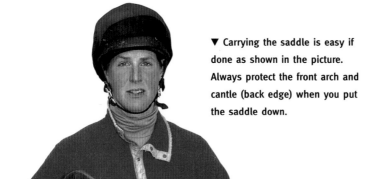

▼ Carrying the saddle is easy if done as shown in the picture. Always protect the front arch and cantle (back edge) when you put the saddle down.

SADDLE CARE

If you have to place the saddle on the ground, there are three ways you can do it safely:

1. Stand it on its front arch with the girth tucked up to protect the pommel.
2. Lean it against the wall with the girth coming up under the arch and over the cantle to prevent scratching.
3. Place it on the ground with the flaps out.

MAINTENANCE AND REPAIRS

Metal work should be washed regularly and carefully dried. If left damp it may rust. *Leather* should be wiped with a damp sponge or cloth and saddle soap. Repairs to leathers or any part of the bridle or saddle should be carried out by a professional saddler. For safety reasons you should not attempt "patching repairs."

▶ Always check tack before use to ensure it does not require restitching or repairing in any way.

TACKING UP

Fitting your horse or pony in the equipment required for a ride or a particular job, such as a dressage event, soon becomes second nature, but fitting the equipment correctly is essential for your safety and the animal's comfort and so must always be a task carried out with care and attention.

It is worth going to a professional barn or yard to see what tack and equipment is really necessary before investing in too many gimmicks. Watch the people working there as they "tack-up" to learn how to use all tack correctly.

Prepare to tack up by tying up the horse and, if necessary, brush off any mud before you start. Prepare the saddle with the girths attached on the offside, and the stirrups run up, as shown below, so that they do not bang on the horse's sides.

THE SADDLE

From the near left side, place the saddle over the horse's withers and gently slide it back into position just behind the shoulder blades. Never pull the saddle forward as this will ruffle the coat underneath and could cause saddle rubs. If a numneah is being used, generally this is secured to the saddle first. Loose pads or sheepskins are placed in position on the horse's back and the saddle fitted on top. Always pull numnahs and pads up into the front arch of the saddle before tightening the girths, to ensure there is no pressure on the withers. There should be a clear channel between the saddle and the horse's back and at least two fingers depth between the front arch of the saddle and the withers.

Drop the girth gently down the far right side and ensure it is hanging straight before bending down and taking it up to the girth straps on the nearside. Do not tighten too much at this stage to allow the horse time to get used to the feel. Check both sides to ensure that all is secure.

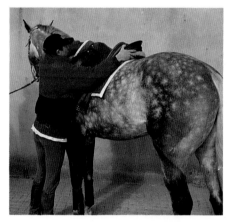

This rider is using a saddle pad which is placed on the horse with the saddle centrally fitted on top.

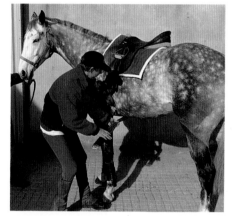

The girths are slipped over the far side of the horse and taken up under the belly for fastening on the near side.

Make sure the skin is smooth and not puckered up between the girth and saddle flap when tightening.

Check that all is secure by looking at tack on both sides of the horse.

▲ With some horses, the skin may be pinched a little. In this case both front legs (fore legs) can be gently pulled forward as shown to release any loose folds of skin.

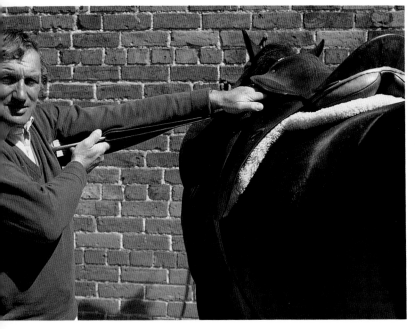

ADJUSTING THE LEATHERS

Q How should I adjust my leathers if I am mounted?

A Keep your foot in the stirrup and take the reins in one hand. Take hold of the stirrup leather near the buckle and ease the leather up or down until you feel you are at the length required. Repeat on the other side in the same way, taking care to ensure you have adjusted both sides evenly. Leathers are generally shorted two to three holes for jumping and galloping.

Before mounting, the stirrup length can be measured from tip of fingers into the armpit for a general estimation.

CHECKING FIT OF SADDLE

Q How do I know if the saddle is the right fit for my horse?

A It is best to get an experienced person to check this to ensure the tree is not too narrow or wide for the horse and that it fits just behind the horse's shoulders. There should be at least two to three fingers width between the top arch of the saddle and the horse's withers and clear channel down the top of the spine which is essential if damage is not to be caused to the spine.

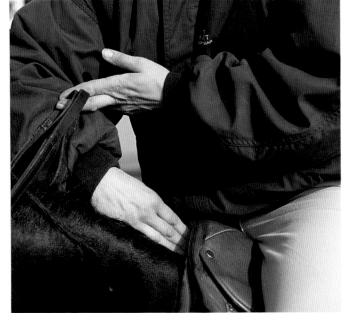

▲ Checking an adequate gap between wither and top of saddle is best done with the rider's weight in the saddle. It may look sufficient before mounting.

◄ The girths can be tightened by taking the reins in one hand, raising the saddle flap and then feeding the girth straps into a higher hole. Take care when doing this with a young, excitable horse in case it moves and you fall.

THE BRIDLE

Take the bridle—which should have the throat latch and noseband undone—in the left hand and go to the near left side of the horse. Place the reins over the horse's head and, facing toward it, unfasten the halter, keeping hold of the horse by the reins. With the right hand holding the bridle, slip the bit toward its mouth. With the left hand, slip your fingers gently between the lips at the side, where there is a gap between its teeth, to ask it to open its mouth. Slide the bridle up and slip one ear at a time through the headpiece. Straighten the browband. Then, fasten the throat latch (throatlash)—it should be loose enough to allow you to slip four fingers underneath it. Secure the noseband, allowing at least a finger's breadth for freedom of the jaw. Check that the bridle is correctly positioned between the cheekbones and lips so as not to cause soreness. Check that your girth is tight enough before setting off for your ride.

The reins are placed over the horse's head and the bridle raised up over the front of the head.

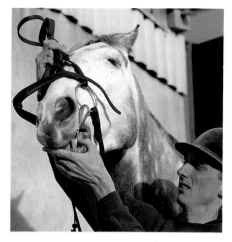

Once the bit is level with the horse's mouth, ease a finger into the side to open.

Slip the head piece over each ear individually and straighten the headpiece.

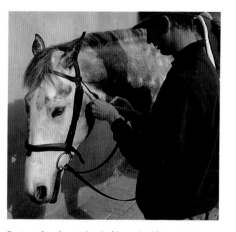

Fasten the throat latch (throatlash), ensuring there is room for the width of one hand between this and the jawbone.

The noseband is then fastened, allowing room for freedom of the jaw. Take care it does not press against the cheekbone.

SECONDHAND EQUIPMENT

Q Should I use or buy secondhand equipment? The local saddlers have a big secondhand department.

A The use of secondhand equipment or saddlery will always depend on the quality and state of the items. Have everything carefully checked by the saddler or a professional. If a saddle is involved, be sure the tree is not broken. If tack has been well cared for, it should last for many more years. However, check all buckles and fastenings for excessive wear and tear. You may be lucky in many cases, but care is recommended nevertheless when purchasing secondhand equipment.

CHOOSING A BRIDLE

When choosing a bridle for your horse or pony try to choose one that complements the look and lifestyle of your animal. A big, strong hunter type requires a tough looking bridle with wide leather straps. A rather petite, fine looking horse would look best in a more refined type of bridle with narrow leathers. Always check that there is room for adjustment, both upward and downward, so that if you use a different bit with bigger or smaller rings it is possible to alter the bridle appropriately.

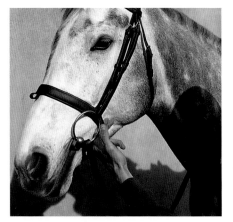

You should be able to fit two fingers underneath the noseband.

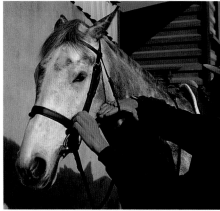

The hand is placed where shown when checking the throatlatch (throatlash).

THE BIT TOO HIGH

Q My horse looks as if he's smiling when his bridle is on but someone told me the bit is too high. How do you tell when it's too high?

A The bit should rest comfortably in the horse's mouth allowing for just one crease at the corners of the mouth. It is very important that the bit is the right width for the horse's mouth. Too narrow and it will pinch the corners— too wide and it will not hang comfortably and may encourage the horse to put his tongue over, which can be very uncomfortable. Every horse will be a little different and you may need to experiment with bits and the height at which they will feel most comfortable for the horse.

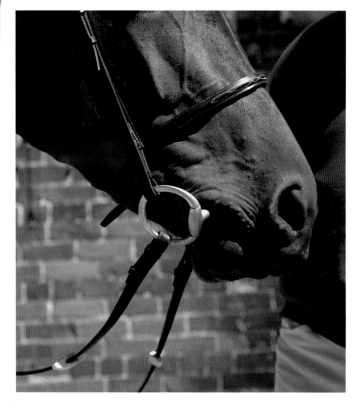

THE BIT TOO LOW

Q My horse keeps tossing his head and lolls his tongue out at the side and sometimes won't go forward like this. What should I do?

A This may be caused by the bit being too low on the mouth and is a typical reaction to the discomfort when the horse puts his tongue over the bit. Ask a professional to advise you on the correct height and whether your horse is using a suitable bit for what you require of him.

UNTACKING

Of course, the same sort of care should be taken in untacking as in tacking up. Both you and your horse will soon become familiar with these daily routine tasks. Make sure you are able to keep the horse controlled by having the halter at hand unless untacking inside the stall or paddock.

THE SADDLE

Before you do anything, take the reins over the horse's head and slip them through your left hand so that you have proper control of the animal. Then, run the stirrup irons up the leathers. Undo the girth without letting it bang onto the horse's legs. Lift the front of the saddle at the pommel and slide it toward you, catching the girth with your right hand and placing it over the seat.

RESTLESS HORSE WHEN UNTACKING

Q My horse keeps moving round when I try to untack her. How should I control her?

A Some horses are excitable after a ride—or over eager for their next meal and can't wait to be untacked. If this is the case, it is best to untack in the stable or after securing the horse with the halter. If you can't do either of these then try to hold her straight up against a wall or fence and then untack.

Always be sure to lift the saddle high enough to clear the back once the girths are undone.

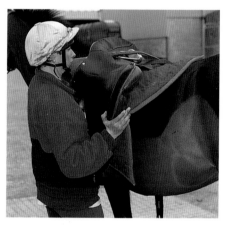

Slide the saddle toward you quickly and place it over your arm ready for carrying.

Take the girth and place it over the center of the saddle before taking the saddle to the tack room or place it safely over the door.

THE BRIDLE

With the reins still over the horse's head, undo the noseband, throatlatch (throatlash), and curb chain (if used). With your left hand on and just above the nose, ease the bridle off over one ear, then the other, keeping hold of the headpiece. Gently lower the bridle so that the bit can slip out of the horse's mouth easily. Never rush this or the bit may catch the horse's teeth and cause discomfort. If the horse is to be tied up instead of released, place a halter (headcollar) around the neck before taking the bridle off. Then, this can be put straight on without risking losing the horse.

Check that everything necessary has been undone before easing it off over one ear at a time.

With some horses it is best to keep your hand above their nose to help prevent them throwing their head up as the bit is released from the mouth.

THE RIDER'S EQUIPMENT

Safety is the all-important factor when deciding on what equipment to acquire. Prioritize what you absolutely need and what you can afford, particularly if taking up riding for the first time. Fashionable jodhpurs won't make you a better rider, but a safety helmet could save your life.

Although it is always nice to be well turned out, riding clothes and equipment can be expensive. Some saddlery stores sell good secondhand clothing but the one thing never to buy secondhand is a riding helmet (hat).

HEADWEAR

The head is the most vulnerable part of the body, and everyone should wear a safety helmet (hat) when riding. This should be light and conform to current safety standards, and the chin strap must be secured at all times when mounted. Countless lives have been saved by the safety helmet.

FOOTWEAR

Another consideration is the type of footwear. Some form of heel (about 2in [5cm]) is essential to prevent the foot slipping through the stirrup iron. The jodhpur boot is ideal, as it is comfortable, practical, and safe. Long leather riding boots are expensive and need to be looked after properly but do give protection against chafing. A cheaper alternative is rubber riding boots.

LEGWEAR

A safety helmet and boots will suffice to start with, along with jeans or pants until you get more ambitious. Some people can get rubbed on the insides of the legs because of chafing against the stirrup leathers. If this is the case, use pantihose (tights) or equi pants, or invest in some jodhpurs especially designed with extra padding. Leather chaps also prevent this problem. You can get them full length or just half chaps, which protect the upper leg only. Usually, Western riders have a wonderfully exotic choice.

SPECIALIST CLOTHING

The more serious rider will need to acquire extra bits of equipment, depending on where their interests lie (see Competitions and Riding Sports). Breeches and hunting boots are required for competition work, for example. The traditional long black boots are used for dressage, show jumping, eventing, and showing. Some sports have a slightly different shaped boot. In polo, players wear a special, more protective boot, which is usually tan-colored.

Endurance riders need footwear they can run and ride in, and many prefer some form of trainer with good cushioning for this work. Comfort is vital, and careful consideration needs to be given to every aspect of the clothing, from the socks up.

Vaulters need pantihose (tights) and/or leggings and leotards or pantsuits. For racing, lightweight breeches, boots, and silks are worn. Each specialist sport has its own specific requirements, with particular regard to safety aspects. Once you are serious enough to need specialist equipment, get an experienced friend to accompany you to a good riding wear store to obtain your outfit. To look professional, always go for quieter colors such as brown, blue, or black. Bright colors are generally only used for special occasions such as parades.

PROTECTIVE WEAR

Q Should I use a back protector when riding in competition?

A A back protector is an excellent safety precaution in case of a fall, and in many cases are compulsory for the jumping phases for such activities as eventing, pony club and racing. They are generally styled like a padded waistcoat with extra protection round the shoulders and down the spine. They are hot and can cause dehydration so only wear when necessary in hot weather and be sure to drink plenty of water.

This rider is wearing a traditional hunt cap instead of the correct helmet with safety harness (see opposite).

GENERAL RIDING BASICS

- *Helmet (hat) with safety harness*
- *Breeches/jodhpurs*
- *Boots*
- *Waterproof jacket*
- *Gloves—non-slip variety*

COMPETITIONS/SHOWS/HUNTING

- *Helmet (hat) with safety harness*
- *Jacket*
- *Shirt*
- *Tie or stock and pin*
- *Breeches/jodhpurs*
- *Jodhpur/hunting boots*
- *Gloves—non-slip variety*
- *Whip (check rules on length)*
- *Spurs (check rules on type and length)*
- *Cross-country colors*

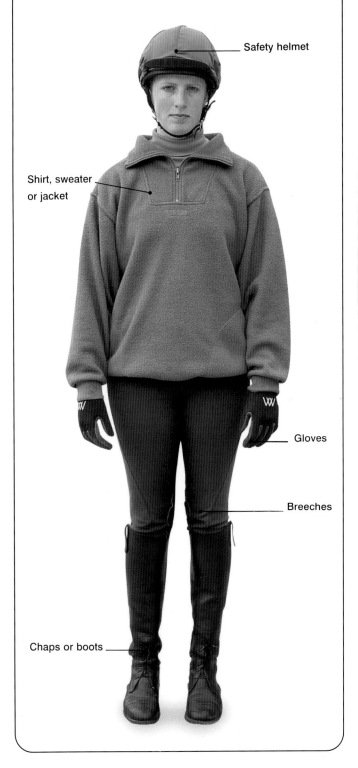

Safety helmet

Shirt, sweater or jacket

Gloves

Breeches

Chaps or boots

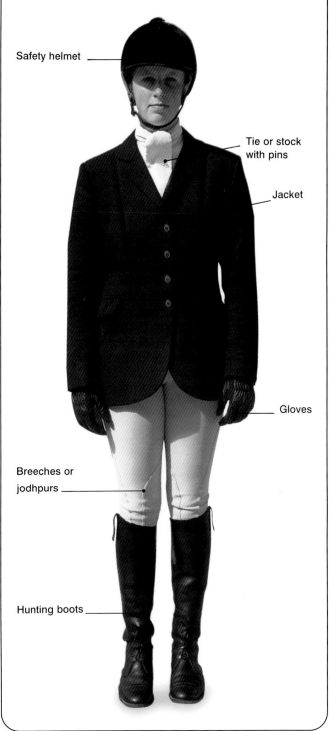

Safety helmet

Tie or stock with pins

Jacket

Gloves

Breeches or jodhpurs

Hunting boots

RIDER FITNESS

Riding is strenuous whether you are just out hacking or riding in one of the world's top events or races. The perpetual movement of the horse requires a response from every muscle in your body, and your own personal fitness will determine how much enjoyment you get from the sport.

If you are not an outdoor person in everyday life, you should think of fitness training for yourself. You need to be able to increase your overall ability to cope with the extra activity.

GENERAL FITNESS

One of the best ways is to go to a gym or fitness center. Work out a program specifically tailored to riding with one of the fitness trainers, remembering that you will be stretching your legs and pushing with them in a position they will not normally be accustomed to. Stretching exercises are useful for any form of serious exertion, but particularly for riding. All the major joints are used, so any stiffness in any of them will affect your progress. Shoulders, elbows, hips, knees, and ankles are affected particularly, not to mention the wrists and fingers when holding the reins.

Any amount of walking to increase your breathing capacity will be beneficial, and sport of all kinds will help to increase your overall feeling of fitness. Regular jogging, bicycling, and swimming are all useful as long as they are not overdone. Every person is different. What will be helpful to one may not be so helpful to another, but riding itself is the best form of exercise to ensure that you become fully tuned to the horse and its movement.

FITNESS EXERCISES ON THE HORSE

Once the rider is proficient enough, there are numerous exercises that can be done on the horse. Never do them for too long at any one time. Always have a professional or an experienced person with you, and only do them on a quiet, suitable horse or pony. Start slowly and build up gradually as fitness improves.

WORTH GETTING FIT?

Q Why is it so necessary to be fit when the horse is doing the work?

A Riding is, in fact, a very physical form of exercise requiring the ability to breathe correctly whilst maintaining balance and coordination. The rider also has to be able to move "with" the horse in such a way that he or she does not hinder it at any time. In the trot, the rhythm is most important and the rider must rise up and down in the saddle to follow the horse's movement. This is quite demanding on untrained muscles. Stretching and warm-up exercises before a riding session are also a good idea.

WHY EXERCISE ON HORSEBACK?

Q How important are exercises on horseback?

A There are few substitutes for practicing the type of exercises on horseback shown opposite, as they help tremendously with balance, confidence and suppleness. These should only ever be done with an experienced person to hold your mount.

▼ Push-ups build strength in the upper body and so are a very useful form of exercise if you have a strong horse to cope with. Full push-ups are very strenuous and should only be attempted if you are fit. Build up to full push-ups only after you have perfected the technique under the supervision of your fitness trainer.

You *must* consult your doctor before starting *any* exercise routine if you have had any health problems.

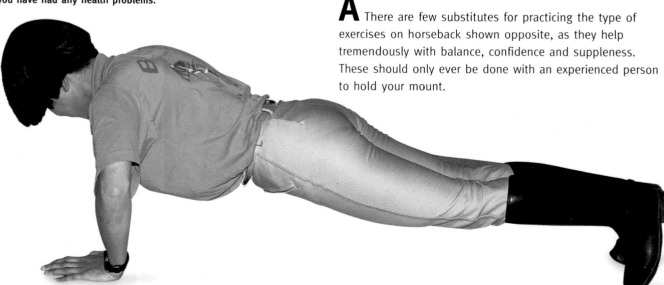

EXERCISES ON HORSEBACK

These exercises are useful to help achieve suppleness and balance:

The horse should be held still by an assistant when doing the following exercises.

- Raise the shoulders as high as possible and then drop them down again. Raise again. Repeat 5–10 times.
- Raise the arms up to shoulder height. Rotate them forward and backward in controlled circular movements, 5–10 times.
- Raise arms above the head, then touch your shoulders. Hold them out to the side, then touch your shoulders. Hold them out to the front, then touch your shoulders. Relax. Repeat 3–10 times.
- Bend forward and touch your right toe with your left hand. Sit up again, then bend over and touch your left toe with your right hand. Repeat 3–5 times, both sides.
- Pull one ankle back up to your hip and release. Repeat on other side. Repeat 3–5 times, both sides.

▲ Performing various arm exercises will help with stiffness and balance. Someone should hold the horse still to prevent an accident.

▶ Shifting your weight forward or backward while on the lunge is useful to help an experienced rider keep supple and practice balance. It should only ever be attempted while stationary by less experienced riders.

The most useful of all riding exercises: the sitting trot without stirrups.

- Rotate ankles in clockwise and counterclockwise direction. Repeat 5–10 times.
- Raise both arms to shoulder height. Swing clockwise as far as is comfortable, then counterclockwise. Repeat 3–5 times.
- Allow head to fall forward into the chest and slowly roll it to the side, to the back, then around to the front again. Repeat in the other direction. Take this slowly. Repeat 5 times.

Consult your doctor before you start any exercise routine— especially if you have had any neck, back or joint injuries.

The exercises pictured on this page are used to improve balance, leg control—and confidence. You should have someone present to hold either the lunge rein or bridle as required. The sitting trot without stirrups (left) should be practiced while on a lunge if you are not experienced. An experienced rider on a quiet horse or pony may do without a lunge but should still be supervised by an assistant.

MOUNTING AND DISMOUNTING

For the beginner, the first important achievement is getting on and off the horse correctly. It may seem like a difficult and daunting task at the start, but it is not difficult once, with practice, the technique has been mastered. The aim is to mount and dismount in a fluid movement that does not pull at the horse's back or alarm the horse in any way.

Mounting: there are two main methods of getting on—one from the ground and the other via a mounting block of some sort, which involves less pulling on the horse's back. Alternatively, you can also get a leg up from a helper or, if you are experienced and athletic, you can vault onto the horse, cowboy style!

Before mounting, always check that your girth is tight and that your stirrups have been pulled down on both sides. Choose a suitable area to mount and ensure the reins are in place over the horse's neck. Always mount from the nearside (left side) of the horse.

MOUNTING: FROM THE GROUND

Whatever form of mounting you decide on it is essential that you feel confident that you can do it unaided before you start to ride alone. Keep practicing from the ground and from a mounting block so that both methods have been mastered and that you are proficient enough to manage alone.

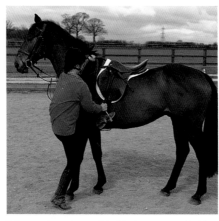

Take up the reins and hold them at a suitable length to keep the horse controlled without forcing it backward. Face to the rear and take hold of the outside of the stirrup, raise the left foot, and put it into the iron.

With your right hand now resting on the seat of the saddle, swivel toward the horse and push your weight down into the stirrup.

Jump upward until you are standing with your weight in the left stirrup.

Swing your right leg over the quarters and ease yourself into the saddle gently.

Place your right foot into the stirrup and adjust yourself centrally in the saddle.

GETTING A "LEG UP"

One of the easiest ways of mounting a horse is by being given a "leg up" from a helper. This, however, requires a certain degree of athleticism from the rider who must spring upward when the helper indicates into the saddle. Mounting this way, as with a mounting block, helps to prevent pulling on the horse's back.

Having a leg up is a most effective way of mounting if there are enough people to do this.

It should not be necessary to have someone at the head if the rider takes up the reins to control the horse first.

EASY MOUNTS

Q Are some horses easier than others to get on?

A The most important aspect is that the horse stands still during this crucial stage. The height of the horse can make a big difference as well as your own ability to stretch up to reach the stirrup if mounting from the ground. If possible, use a mounting block of some description to make the process easier if the horse is rather large. If the horse moves a lot you will need a helper until you and your horse have come to an arrangement! Practice making the animal stand to command until it learns to respond.

HOW NOT TO MOUNT FROM THE GROUND

It is easy to see how athletic the rider has to be to mount from the ground. This rider is making it very difficult by trying to face toward the horse instead of away from it.

MOUNTING FROM THE GROUND

Q It worries me that I may damage the horse's back when I try to mount from the ground. Is it a problem?

A If you find mounting from the ground very difficult and have to pull and heave at the saddle, you could cause a strain to the horse's back and a twist to the saddle tree in some cases. Again, a mounting block is much the best answer, however these are not always going to be available so it is essential that you do master this important technique.

GIRTH CHECKS BEFORE MOUNTING

Q My horse humps her back when I first get on and does not like her girth tightened. How should I deal with this?

A This is a sign that your horse is filling her lungs with air to make her rib cage bigger so that the girth will be loose when she breathes out again. One of the best ways to deal with this is to tack the horse up early to allow her time to grow accustomed to the saddle. Tighten the girth in stages, one hole at a time until the saddle is secured.

MOUNTING: USING A MOUNTING BLOCK

The mounting block is an invaluable aid for all riders but a necessity for those who have trouble raising their leg high enough to put a foot in a stirrup from the ground. Blocks enable the rider to mount with relative comfort without having the difficulty of pulling and heaving up from the ground into the saddle. Mounting blocks consist of some form of solid platform of around 18–24 in (45–60 cm) high alongside which it is possible for a horse to stand. The closer the horse can stand to this the easier and safer it will be to mount.

Take the horse alongside the mounting block. Step onto the block and take up the reins. Place your left foot into the stirrup.

Swing the right leg over the horse's back and ease down into the saddle.

Once settled, move the horse straight forward until clear of the block before turning.

VAULTING ON

Q I've seen children who have been riding a long time vaulting onto their ponies. How do they do it?

A You need to be very athletic to do this and the horse or pony needs to be used to the movement. Grab a bit of mane or the front of the saddle and do a double jump on your feet before swinging up into the saddle. A vaulting mount is ideal for the young but a bit of a struggle for the older rider.

DISMOUNTING

Like all basic movements it is most important to practice to get the hang of this vital part of riding. Once you are used to what is required, it will soon become easy as you become accustomed to the distance to the ground and how to keep your balance and flex your knees.

DISMOUNTING A LARGE HORSE

Q I find it difficult to keep my balance on landing when getting off my rather large horse. How can I correct my dismount?

A The important thing to remember when getting off is to bend the knees when you land. This helps you to stay forward close to your horse as you slide down off the saddle. Keep your hand on the saddle when dismounting so that you have a bit more security. If you have a suitable mounting block, you can train your horse to stand beside this and dismount onto this which stops you having to drop too far to the ground off a tall horse.

First, come to a halt and take the reins into your left hand. Take both feet out of the stirrups and swing forward.

Put your right hand onto either the knee roll or the saddle. Swing your right leg over.

Make sure you clear the horse's rump as a bang with your foot may make the horse take a jump forward.

Land on both feet on the ground facing the horse. Remember to land with flexed knees to prevent jarring. Take the reins over the horse's head and run up the stirrup irons on both sides.

FALLING OFF

Q What happens when you fall off—are there any precautions to take that can make it less painful?

A The secret when falling is to try to stay relaxed and roll away from the horse as quickly as possible. Whether this is always an option entirely depends on the circumstances. Tuck your head in before you hit the ground and always ensure your safety harness is properly fastened whenever you are mounted. Back protectors obviously decrease the risk of back injuries and serious bruises. There is an old saying that "you can't ride until you've fallen 100 times!"

HOW NOT TO MOUNT FROM A BLOCK
◄ This rider is making the mistake of trying to get on to the horse when it is not close enough to the mounting block laying himself open to a slip off the block and the possibility of frightening the horse. Practice leading the horse up close to mounting areas and standing it there until it understands its role.

RESTLESS HORSE WHEN DISMOUNTING

Q My horse keeps moving around when I try to dismount which is rather frightening. How do I make sure she keeps still for me?

A You must teach the horse to stand still to command by practicing each day. Walk your horse forward, halt her then relax, making her stand for a few minutes using your voice command only. Like humans, some horses are a little impatient—so pat her to reassure her you do want her to stay still. When you want to dismount, be sure you are not pulling the horse round with too tight a rein. Remember to take both feet out of the stirrups and prepare to dismount as instructed on this page. Ensure that you are on a non-slippery surface so that the horse feels secure. It is also a good idea to dismount in an enclosed area rather than a wide open field as this gives the horse less incentive to want to move around.

RIDER POSITION

Once mounted, it is important to find the right position in the saddle and one that is comfortable for you. The rider's position is called the "seat." This will not only affect your balance and comfort, but also that of the horse or pony.

To a certain extent, your position will be determined by the saddle and whether it is a suitable size and shape for you. Your own physique will also make some difference—a short person in a large jumping saddle will find it as awkward as a large person placed on a small-sized dressage saddle. Generally, a medium-sized, general purpose saddle is best for the beginner.

A GOOD "SEAT"

The overall aim must be to sit as still as possible on the horse and, to achieve this, the rider has to be in good balance at all times. This is called "having a good or independent seat." The rider should be relaxed yet able to stay with the horse's movement. The shoulder, hip, and heel should remain on a perpendicular line, with the weight evenly distributed between the rider's two seat bones.

HEAD POSITION

The head must remain looking upright and straight ahead. If it tips forward, the balance will shift with it. The shoulders must be relaxed but upright and the back straight, but not stiff.

LEG AND FOOT POSITIONS

The upper legs must be flat against the saddle with relaxed knees, the lower legs gently resting against the horse's sides. The hip, knee, and ankle joints must be relaxed to allow the rider to sit down well into the saddle.

The balls of the feet should rest lightly in the stirrup irons, with the weight going into the heels. This will keep the heels lower than the toes, which should face forward and upward.

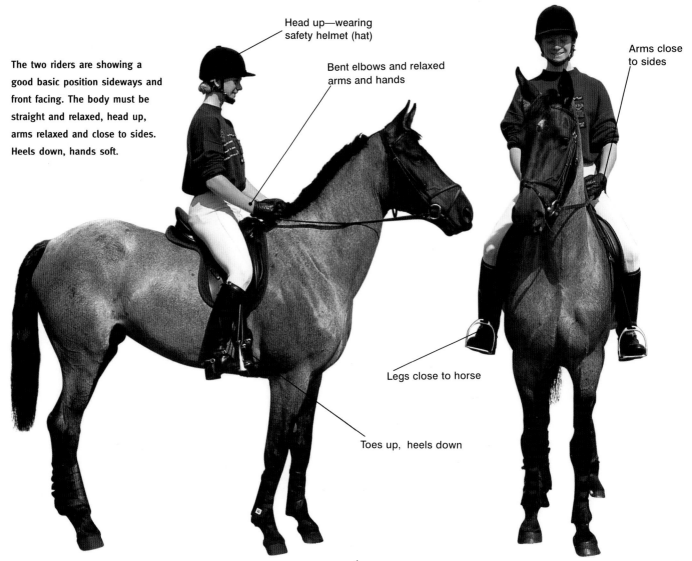

The two riders are showing a good basic position sideways and front facing. The body must be straight and relaxed, head up, arms relaxed and close to sides. Heels down, hands soft.

Head up—wearing safety helmet (hat)

Bent elbows and relaxed arms and hands

Arms close to sides

Legs close to horse

Toes up, heels down

CORRECT LEG POSITION

Q Some people say my leg is too far forward, but it feels comfortable. How do I tell what is correct?

A The leg will be less effective if it is too far forward and the straight vertical line from shoulder through hip to heel is lost. This means you slip to the back of the saddle putting all your weight too far back for the horse to be able to balance itself. A straighter cut saddle may help this problem.

CORRECT HEEL POSITION

Q I feel I need to cling on with my heels but I'm supposed to keep my toes up—how do I do both?

A It is important to push all the weight down into your heel to enable you to give effective leg aids. Raising the heel tends to make you rise up out of the saddle.

ARM AND HAND POSITIONS

How you hold your arms and hands and, therefore, how you hold the reins is very important. The reins, via the bit, are the principal means of controlling the horse, apart from the leg and seat movements and the horse will be sensitive to every move of the arms or hands.

▼ The arms should hang down in a relaxed attitude, softly bent at the elbows with the hands resting just above the withers. The fingers should remain loosely rounded inward with the thumbs uppermost.

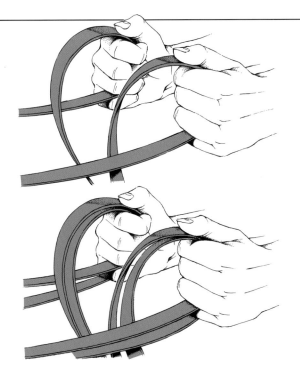

▲ The hands hold the reins between the fourth and little fingers, allowing the reins to come up through the palms between the thumbs and first fingers. The contact should be light and relaxed. A well-schooled horse or pony will respond to the movements of the fingers and wrist. The top diagram shows how to hold single reins, the bottom one illustrates how to hold double reins.

CONTROL AND THE AIDS

To be able to control and influence the horse's direction and speed, it is important for the rider to understand the accepted way of making this possible—by using control methods and the aids that have evolved over the centuries. To ride well you must ensure you are giving the instructions clearly, simply, and in time, so that your horse or pony feels confident too.

The "aids" are the means by which the rider tells the horse what to do. They consist of the effective use of the rider's hands, legs, and seat—known as the natural aids. The voice can also be added to this. The whip and spurs are known as artificial aids.

NATURAL AIDS

The hands The rider's hands are not only used for controlling and turning the horse but also to create balance. At all times the rider needs to be aware that the horse has a metal bar through its mouth, and that the mouth is extremely sensitive. The lightest touch will produce a response from a well-schooled horse and the rider should relax the rein a little before asking for another response, when necessary. An inexperienced rider will tend to use the hands to balance with at first, which is a disaster for the poor horse. The legs and seat are responsible for the rider's balance.

The rider must be sympathetic and gentle to the horse or pony. Try to keep an even feel on the reins, using the fingers and wrists and lightly to help keep the balance, control, and relaxation of the horse's jaw so that it responds willingly. Rarely should the rider need to use the arms to pull the horse back. The hands should remain fairly passive and quiet, being used only to give and to feel what is happening, and to influence the degree of control required.

To turn the horse, a little more contact is exerted on the side you wish to turn toward and the opposite leg is used to control the body of the horse as it changes direction. The outside rein is used to support the horse and maintain the balance while the inside one establishes the bend.

The legs The rider's legs help to create forward movement, to guide, and to control the balance of the horse. Used gently in nudges or little vibratory kicks, the horse will respond by going forward, reining backward, or by going sideways in response to leg pressure. A constant kick will either result in a "dead-sided" animal, immune to the stimuli caused by excessive use of the aid, or one that is so over-responsive it will take off and become out of control.

The legs are applied just behind the girth and must hang loosely at the horse's sides. The rider must not be tempted to tighten upward, which has the effect of drawing the weight up out of the saddle and may cause tension in both rider and horse. The legs are used evenly on both sides for general forward movement.

On turns and circles, the inside leg pressure prevents the horse from falling in on the circle while the outside one maintains the bend and forward movement. The leg can be used to push the horse away from the way of going, such as in lateral work. In the half pass, for instance, the left leg can push the horse across to the right. This can be useful when you are opening a gate and you do not want to dismount.

USING THE CONTROLS

▶ This photograph shows how to make use of the hands, legs and seat.

The back is straight and the head up helping with good balance.

A firm deep seat in the saddle.

A strong leg with low heel.

The hands are loose, relaxed, and independent creating good balance.

The horse is accepting the rider's hand instructions through the reins and is responding by being on the bit.

To create speed, the legs are used strongly (depending on the horse's response). In reining back the use of the leg and a restraining hand cause the animal to step backward.

For balance and to create extra impulsion, the legs are used in conjunction with the seat and hand. In top-level dressage movements, such as *passage* and *piaffe*, the balance is created through an effective leg. The better schooled the horse, the more responsive it will be, but this will only come about if the rider's instructions are subtle, direct, and not overdone.

The seat Once the basics of balance and position have been mastered, the seat is the most influential aid. Straightness in the saddle is essential and it is important to be aware of feeling yourself sitting straight with your weight evenly distributed on both seat bones. It is possible to create extra energy by sitting heavier in the saddle. Then, the seat influences the balance of the horse through greater or less impulsion caused by the horse's hind quarters coming more underneath it. However, this can have the effect of "hollowing" the horse if the rider is not skilled enough to keep a relaxed back (to absorb the extra energy created) and apply the correct leg aids. To start with, it is better to work on straightness in the saddle and maintaining balance rather than become over-absorbed in how much weight to keep in your seat. It all falls into place with experience and time.

The development of your horse will also have a bearing on weight distribution. A young horse not yet fully matured or strong in its back will not be able to cope physically with a rider with too deep a seat.

The voice This can be a useful extra natural aid, especially for horses that respond well to the voice. It is fun to teach horses to answer simple commands such as whoa, trot, canter, and halt, and often takes only a week or two of patient training (using repetition and reward).

Here the horse is on its *forehand* and the rider is leaning too far back in an effort to keep the horse's head up. Correcting the leg position would help to create better balance.

STARTING CORRECTLY

To ride forward Nudge or gently kick the horse, at the same time softening the hands. This will allow the horse the freedom to move forward. You should then follow the horse's movement with your own body.

Walk: At walk allow yourself to lean slightly forward as the horse moves and relax your back to his movement.

Trot: In a trot you will need to rise up and down in time to the horse's movement taking the weight through your heel.

Canter: In canter, go forward with the horse and keep your hands low and still. Circle round gradually if it feels a bit fast.

HOW NOT TO STOP
This rider is hauling at the horse's mouth with the hands and using no leg pressure—a disastrous method of trying to stop.

STOPPING CORRECTLY

To stop or reduce your speed Give a gentle pull on the reins, say "whoa" or "ho," then release the pressure. Keep doing this until you stop. As your skill improves, you can start to use your seat and legs to gain a much more subtle reduction in speed. By then you will start to have a slightly more refined use of the hands rather than pulling back.

The rider sits up and prepares to slow down using a deep seat and use of the legs to create a good balance. The hands on the reins register a slight pull which will restrict forward movement from the horse.

The horse shortens its stride in response to the previous instructions. As shown here, the horse should come to a smooth, relaxed stationary position (a halt) because the rider's movements are smooth and relaxed.

Once stationary, the rider relaxes the hands to enable the horse to relax in a halt. The horse should be allowed to remain still for a few seconds before moving forward to perform the next movement.

TURNING TECHNIQUE

To turn the horse, the rider must take a more positive feel on the rein on the side to which the horse is to turn. Then a slight pull to the inside rein indicates direction and a strong pressure from the outside leg prevents the horse's quarters swinging outward. Both legs should keep the horse moving forward, maintaining the rhythm.

This rider is turning the horse's head off the forward track by turning the horse's right shoulder in toward the direction of the turn. Pressure is also applied by the legs to control the horse's turn.

REINING BACK

Reining back is a training exercise to help improve balance and coordination for both rider and horse. Before asking your mount to perform a reining back motion, bring it to a halt first. Ask for the rein back by restricting the forward movement with the gentle but firm use of the hands on the reins and use of the leg. Once the horse realizes it cannot go forward it will start to step back. Keep all the instructions through the natural aids slow and quiet.

Here, the rider is applying the leg and has lightened the seat before beginning to restrict the forward movement by applying gentle pressure on the rein.

It is important to ask for only one or two steps to begin with, then reward the horse with a pat on the neck or an encouraging word and then move forward.

CHANGING DIAGONALS

When the rider is in a rising trot, he or she is thrown upward by the movement of the horse's left leg or right leg as it moves forward in each stride. The rider sits for one stride—up again, then sits. This is known as riding on the left or right diagonal. To ensure the horse is not strained by always pushing the rider's weight upward with the same diagonal pair of legs (see diagram on right), it is important to change diagonals whenever there is a change in direction.

When changing to the right diagonal, watch the horse's right shoulder go forward as you rise out of the saddle. If you are sitting at this point, miss one stride by sitting and then rise again with the horse's right shoulder moving forward. When going to the left diagonal, rise upward as the horse's left shoulder moves forward.

In trot, the off fore and near hind legs move together first (above left) and then the near fore and off hind leg move together (above right). This is called "moving alternate diagonals."

Lungeing the horse on the circle is a good way to see which diagonal the rider is rising to. Then you can instruct the rider when to change diagonal.

ARTIFICIAL AIDS

The artificial aids are extremely useful if used properly. They come in several different sizes and shapes and are designed for different uses.

The whip This is used to reinforce the leg aids and to increase responsiveness. The long schooling or dressage whip is used by bringing the hand away a little from the neck and just tapping the horse behind the rider's leg or, to create extra activity, down the animal's hind leg. The crop is useful for tapping down the shoulder to keep the horse straight. The rider can also take the hand off the rein and use the whip behind the saddle to create more forward movement. Never keep your hand on the rein while using the whip behind the saddle, as this has the effect of catching the horse in the mouth at the same time. On the occasion when a horse needs a reprimand for deliberate disobedience, this needs to be done immediately after the incident has occurred. Even half a minute later the horse will be unable to understand why it is being punished. With inexperienced riders, it is usually the horse's inability to understand muddled instructions that cause the problem. Therefore the rider must try again to indicate his or her wishes to the horse. *Never ever use the whip in anger on a horse.*

To change a short whip from one hand to the other, first take both reins and whip in one hand. Pull the whip upward through the palm with the other hand until free. For a long whip, this is quietly swung in a 180° arc in front of the rider's face with a turn of the wrist. The opposite hand then takes the whip and brings it back into position.

There are two main types of riding whip. The short jumping or cutting whip (top) and the long dressage whip (bottom).

Whips are generally held close to the top end. In competition, the jumping whip should not be longer than 30 in (75 cm). Note the correct angle to hold this type of whip is shown in the photograph.

The dressage whip is very flexible because of its length and needs very sensitive handling. It should be used to accentuate the rider's leg aids. Dressage whips come in various lengths depending on the requirements.

CHANGING WHIP

Horses may need encouragement to move forward by feeling a light touch of the whip. For instance, if it were shying to the left away from a spook fence then you would tap the right side.

While riding, you will need to change your whip from hand to hand occasionally. It takes some practice to make the change smoothly and you must remember to talk to your horse and reassure it when you perform this movement.

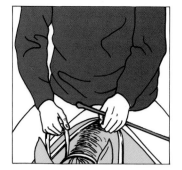

It is usual to ride with a whip on the nearside (left side), held in a light grip and only touching the horse when you are asking for a particular action or requiring more forward movement.

To change the whip hand, take the top with the opposite hand and draw it through the hand holding the whip, as shown, in a smooth action.

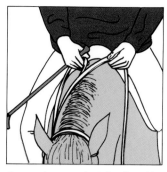

Ensure that you don't let the whip tap your horse while you transfer it into your other hand as this may frighten the animal.

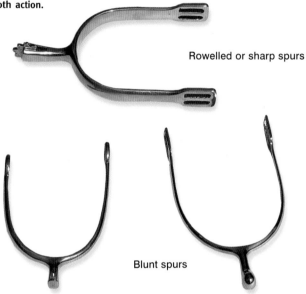

Rowelled or sharp spurs

Blunt spurs

Spurs These increase the horse's feel and responsiveness to the leg. They should only be used by experienced riders who have acquired an independent seat and are capable of full control of the leg.

Usually, spurs are placed along the back seam of a boot with the curved shank pointing upward and downward. The buckle must be fastened on the outside so as not to chafe the horse's sides. To use, the rider's toe is turned out slightly to bring the spur in contact with the horse's side, then released again. It should not be used incessantly, just brought into action when a little more response is required.

THE USE OF SPURS

Q When should I start to use spurs and what are their uses?

A Spurs are an artificial aid which have been used for centuries to improve the effect of the rider's legs. When used sensibly, they increase the forward impulsion of the horse. Assist with the bend in the body, especially in lateral work and with the general overall balance. Once the rider has an independent seat and is proficient in all school movements, they can be used periodically for greater effect. They should never be used on a very sensitive horse or by a rough or inexperienced rider.

This horse is resisting away from where the rider wishes to go. Strong legs with spurs may help if this is a persistent problem but it should never be necessary to "dig in hard" with spurs.

THE PACES

The horse has four basic paces or gaits: walk, trot, canter, and gallop—the latter being an extended canter. There are variations within these paces, depending on the degree of training, which demonstrate collection or extension. Some horses have unusual gaits, such as pacing, the running walk, the "amble," and the "rack," but in most cases these are specific to the breed.

The schooling of the horse or pony and its responsiveness to the rider's aids will make all the difference to how it is able to perform paces. For the rider, the comfort of the gait is important. In competition work, the quality of the pace will determine the horse's degree of success, to a certain extent.

THE WALK

The walk, the slowest gait, is a four-time walk with the animal picking up each leg independently of the other. It should be a forward marching movement in which the horse is allowed the necessary amount of hand freedom to be able to move its head and neck slightly as each leg is used to propel it forward. The four beats should be even and regular at all times and there should be no stiffness. In dressage work, there are four different walks recognized: the collected, medium, extended, and free walk.

The rider must sit still and square on the horse, allowing the movement underneath to express itself. The rider's body must follow forward with the movement and the hands should be able to move with the horse's head. When riding on a loose rein, such as when trail riding or out hacking, sit upright and keep the reins from slipping down the neck. Left to its own devices, the horse is extremely adept at picking its way through the roughest terrain and will often foresee boggy conditions undetectable to the human eye.

It is possible to see how the legs move forward in the walk in the following four movement sequence of this gait: off hind, off fore, near hind, near fore.

THE TROT

The trot is a two-time gait on alternate diagonal legs (near hind and off fore and vice versa) with a moment of suspension in between. It should be free and active with regular steps. The quality of the trot depends on the horse's natural movement, but with correct schooling even a moderate animal can be made to improve dramatically. There are four trots recognized in dressage: collected, working, medium, and extended.

The rider can rise or post (sit) to the trot. Most riders prefer the sitting trot once the up-down rhythm has been mastered, but young horses may find it hard on their backs if a rider sits for a long time. In the rising trot, the rider rises out of the saddle as the horse goes from one diagonal pair of legs and sits as it changes to the other, in an up-down, up-down rhythm. The weight must be pushed down into the stirrups. You have to adjust your balance a little as you maintain the forward momentum on the upward rise and must not get left behind the movement as you sink back down. To start with, it is easier to find your balance by tending to go too far forward than too far back.

The trot is a two sequence gait where the rider is thrown upwards as the horse transfers its weight from one diagonal pair of legs to the other—the off fore and near hind point forward.

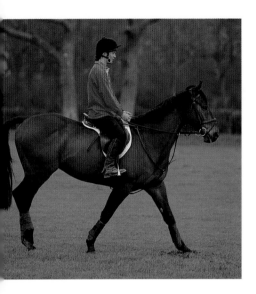

The horse will stretch its neck slightly as each stride is taken and the rider's hand should move with this so that there is no restriction.

Some horses will glide across the ground, while others will appear rather stilted; it all depends on whether they have a short or long stride.

By this stage, it is easy to see the horse is now stretching forward the opposite front leg to the one it started with and has completed the sequence.

In this picture, the rider is out of the saddle in rising trot and the horse is bringing up the front leg towards its highest point.

Now both opposite front and back legs are at maximum height and are about to shift the weight onto the opposite diagonal pair. The rider is right up out of the saddle.

The sequence completed and it is possible to see the horse now has its near fore and off hind pointing forward. The rider is sitting in readiness for the next stride.

THE CANTER

The canter is a three-time gait. The foot falls follow one another in this sequence: left hind, left fore leg and right hind together, then right fore leg. This is followed by a moment of suspension, with all four feet in the air, before the next stride begins.

The canter can be an extremely comfortable pace, whether just loping along or performing in a dressage arena. It is the most important pace to perfect for jumping, as the quality of the strides determines the way the horse will be able to approach the fence. From a controlled, even canter, the horse is able to jump out of its stride. If this is erratic or there is a change in tempo or speed, this will seriously affect the animal's ability to approach the fence in the good, even rhythm so essential in the jumping horse.

Generally, the child's pony, western, and trail animals are expected to do any cantering on a fairly loose rein with little guidance from the rider. These horses may need to adjust their balance without obvious interference from the rider or, in some cases, because of interference from the rider—such as when an inexperienced child loses its balance and nearly falls off.

The three sequence gait of the canter is demonstrated here where only the off hind is on the ground taking the entire weight of the horse.

THE GALLOP

The fourth pace, the gallop, is an extended canter. The speed very much depends on what the horse is doing. The racehorse in a sprint race is traveling at around 25 mph (38 kph), whereas it may only be going 15 mph (22 kph) in a four-mile (8 km) chase.

For endurance work the horse may be traveling slowly at a steady 6–8 miles (9–13 km) an hour, or, in certain races much more over shorter distances at the gallop. Galloping around steeplechase or cross-country courses is particularly exciting and in the Maryland Hunt Cup in the United States, the solid timber fences provide an even more thrilling occasion.

The balance of the rider at speed is helped by use of a shorter stirrup, hence the reason jockeys ride so short. This provides them with extra leverage to be able to hold a pulling horse at speed. They can brace their legs forward, in most cases providing an effective means of staying under control.

In the gallop, the horse really lengthens and lowers its frame, reaching forward in ground-devouring strides. Some horses have a lovely fluid way of galloping which takes far less out of them than those with a short, choppy, jarring stride. The reins should be short and the rider must maintain an even feel on the reins. Any pulling or shifting of weight could seriously unbalance the horse. It is important to ensure you have a suitable bit to enable you to maintain control when galloping.

The gallop is a speeded-up version of the canter. This makes the four movement sequence much more difficult to see when all the weight is on the off foreleg.

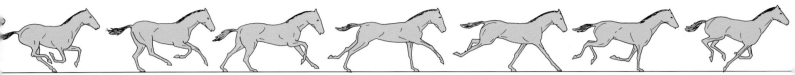

The balance has gone forward and the two hind legs and near fore are taking the weight at this stage. The off fore is now free of the ground.

The weight is now on the near fore as the other three legs are lifted forward to come into position for the next stride to take place.

The stride completed, the horse is now back in the same position as it was at the start. The rider's hands have eased forward slightly with each stride taken.

The moment of suspension when all four legs are just off the ground. You can just see the legs prepare for the landing onto three legs.

At this stage, the horse is on three legs, stretching forward again ready to propel itself into taking the next stride. The rider is leaning forward over the horse's front legs.

The horse is back into the next stride and in the same position as in the first picture for the sequence to start all over again.

PREPARING TO JUMP

The horse is a natural jumper. In the wild it can be seen leaping over bushes, ditches, and puddles, and careering down drops or scrambling up mountain trails with great ease. When ridden, it has to adjust its balance to cope with the weight of the rider.

The way your horse is introduced to jumping may influence its attitude for life. The young horse needs to be physically fit and mature enough before being asked to do anything strenuous too soon. The rider needs to be confident and sufficiently experienced to cope with what is required, and to have a basic knowledge of how the horse jumps and how to respond. Both horse and rider out trail riding or hacking will have encountered small jumps of a natural type and jumped them unwittingly. This is the ideal way to learn gradually, making a conscious effort to observe any small obstacle worth jumping and go for it.

The canter is the most important gait for jumping and practice at riding in the forward jumping seat is vital so that the change in balance can be mastered. The horse must go forward willingly with rhythm and balance. This energy is created by the rider's legs pushing the horse into the hands, which control the speed and power necessary for the horse to make a good, "round" jump.

With a forward going horse, it is easy to achieve a good canter. The lazy horse has to be stoked up and asked to go faster than necessary to create a sufficiently forward approach for it to remain in canter until over the fence.

POLE WORK

A useful start to jumping is by the use of poles. These can be placed on the ground at random distances and the horse first trotted and then cantered over them. Practice your approach by coming in toward them absolutely straight. Later, practice approaching off a turn for example, or on a large circle. Change the direction of the pole, all the time aiming for a steady rhythm. A series of three or four poles placed approximately 3 yards (3 meters) apart for horses (2½ yards [2.5 meters] for ponies) will help to create the "jump" feeling, as the horse should make the effort to jump over each pole in the canter if they are evenly spaced. That way, the rider will be able to recognize the feeling of what it is like to "go with the movement of the horse." The rider must swing slightly forward as the horse lifts off over the pole and then sit up as it lands, following the animal's movement.

Polework in training will teach the horse to look where it is going and to think what it is doing.

It will also teach it to adjust its stride and get used to colored poles which it will soon have to jump. Once happy, move on to single small fences.

The small single fence in the background is the next stage. A low double of two fences with one or two strides in between can then be introduced.

Many people lunge their horses over raised poles such as these to increase balance and concentration.

This young horse appears very happy and has introduced some variety into its everyday training.

The raised poles have been placed on a slight circle and must always be spaced to suit your horse's stride length.

THE FLYING LEAD CHANGE

One of the most useful exercises, the flying lead change, can be practiced at the same time as pole work. This is the method of changing from one leading leg in the canter to the other. Once mastered, it becomes easy to do it with a half halt or rebalancing of the horse, and then shifting the weight and rein contact to the opposite side during the moment of suspension when all four feet are off the ground. Often this is taught over a pole initially. Timing is paramount as the horse can only change when its front legs are off the ground and the hind leg of the side you are changing onto is coming forward.

Canter on a circle on the inside lead and diagonally "jump" across the pole, changing your hand aid to the opposite side as you are in the air. Shift your weight toward the leading leg as you go onto a circle in the opposite direction, making a figure eight. Use of your outside leg will help to put the horse onto the lead.

One method of teaching flying changes is to change direction during the moment the horse is in the air over a pole. Keep practicing until you feel confident about the technique.

PHASES OF A JUMP

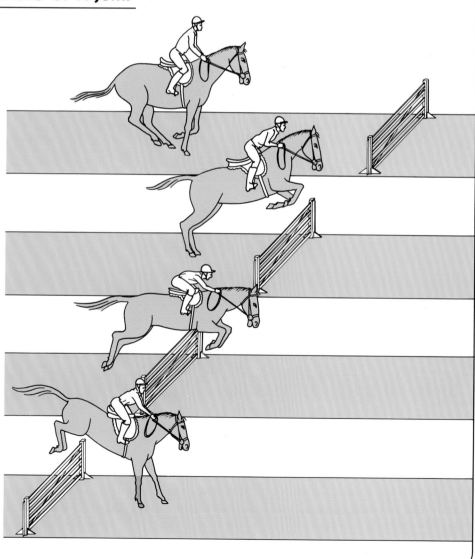

There are four basic phases to how the horse jumps the fence. *The approach* must be balanced with the horse maintaining a good consistent pace into the fence.

The take off requires the horse to bring its hocks well up underneath if it is to spring upward over a fence of any height. The rider can ensure that the horse arrives at the right spot by regulating the stride into the fence.

The moment of suspension over the fence requires absolute freedom from the rider to enable the horse to round its back over the top of the fence and prepare for the landing without interference.

The landing is a time during which the horse requires the rider to be in a good upright position and balanced so that he or she does not lean too far forwards and thereby push the horse onto its forehand. He or she must sit up and settle the horse into a steady rhythm before the next fence.

JUMPING

Only by hours of training will it be possible to build up the rapport between horse and rider that is so essential for that all important clear round at a competition. Jumping should be practiced two or three times a week, with different exercises to ensure horse and rider are fully prepared for all eventualities.

Single fences are easy to jump. Always use a straight approach and ride at the middle of the fence. Ride away straight afterward so that you are teaching yourself and the horse to be prepared to jump another. If you are in a class with other horses and riders, never jump a fence and let the horse run back to the group, as this will let the horse develop bad follow through on the jump and encourage the horse to disobey commands.

The earlier you can start to ride and jump, the quicker you will be able to master the art! Most children are totally fearless and love the sensation of jumping.

GRIDS

An excellent training exercise is to set up a series of poles and fences in a sequence or grid. The distances between them must be suitable for the size and standard of the individual horse. It is unwise to have a horse and pony using the same grid, as the pony will have a much shorter stride. Build up the number of poles and fences gradually, as it can be confusing to see a line of poles if you are unprepared. Leave the horse to do the jumping, and think of approaching with enough impulsion to maintain the rhythm necessary. Sit up over the poles to help balance the horse and go with the horse over the fences. Cross poles, verticals, bounces, and spreads can be used in grids, in between poles on the ground.

GRID WORK

The young horse may benefit from having done some grid work on the lunge or been ridden at an early stage in its career.

Grids consist of jumps and poles at varying distances. Make sure you start gradually as it may prove very intimidating for the horse to see too many poles at one time.

Try to vary the exercises so that your horse becomes adept at doing several different types of strides on the lunge or ridden.

DOUBLES

Doubles consist of two fences in line with one another, called an "in and out," or two strides in between. It is important to approach with enough impulsion to maintain the rhythm so that the horse can jump, land, recover, take one (or two) strides, and jump the second fence. Too big or too fast a jump over the first element will result in a problem at the second. Approaching with too little impulsion will also cause a problem, as the horse will land short over the first fence and find it difficult to make up the ground to jump the second—and so may stop.

The quality of the canter is so important that it requires daily practice to enable horse and rider to master the act of balance and rhythm at this pace. Keep the horse's head up and use sufficient leg with every stride to ensure the hind legs come well underneath it. Only by doing this will you be able to keep the even stride and tempo necessary to approach and jump the fences.

The canter becomes more and more vital as you move up the jumping ladder, particularly when approaching combinations.

TRIPLE COMBINATIONS

Triples (trebles) consist of three fences in a line, with one or two strides between each. The triple is the same principle as the double but with an extra element. The rider must think of riding forward all the way through, and maintain propulsion and balance over each fence.

JUMPING A COURSE

Practice putting three or four fences together. Maintain a good rhythm to jump them in sequence. Gradually increase the number of fences, incorporating changes of direction. Keep the fences small to start with but vary the types of jump—verticals, spreads, gates, and walls. Make yourself remember a set route. Once confident over small fences, increase the size gradually.

Don't ask your horse to jump anything that is too big for it at any stage of its training or you will get a refusal.

WESTERN RIDING

Western riding is epitomized by old movie images of cowboys galloping across the prairies, performing lightning turns and stops with breathtaking dexterity. Developed by early pioneers out of need, this unique style of riding has become a sport in its own right.

All western training is done through response from the horse to rein pressure on the neck or other rider aids.

The history of this style of riding can be traced as far back as the 16th century, when even the notion of using horses as transportation was unheard of in the Americas. Credit for introducing this concept is attributed to Spanish pioneer Hernando Cortés and his conquistadores, who brought horses and a type of deep-seated saddle which would form the basis of many adaptations over the years.

Indeed, the design of the saddle is integral to the gradual development of western riding as a style of its own. It had to be comfortable and secure enough for ranch hands to spend days at a time in the saddle, and make it easy to sit a difficult horse. Cowboys also had to be able to "work" cattle from the saddle, hence the pommel became lengthened into a horn for roping. Two girths—known as cinches—fastened at the front and the back of the saddle, which was held firmly in place over several blankets. This arrangement not only kept the heavy saddle rock steady, but also distributed the weight evenly so that it was comfortable for the horse. The saddle became the trademark of the cowboy and a source of pride, hence the existence of so many wonderful, elaborate designs.

TRAINING

Today, the working cattle horse remains an essential part of many American ranches, but it is in the show ring that western riding has become popular worldwide. To perform well, the horse has to be trained to respond to the rider in a calm, obedient manner so that horse and rider work together in complete harmony. Any horse can be trained in the western manner, and you don't necessarily need to use the special tack (although the western equipment does undoubtedly lend a certain authenticity).

Much of the early training of the horse starts on the ground, such as asking always for square halts. Responding to a hand against its side or shoulder, and moving away from this pressure, is a start to the horse performing turns on the haunches and forehand. Responding to pressure on the chest is the start of the rein back. All this is taught with the use of the voice and with great patience.

Some western horses are trained in a round pen to start with, many trainers following the principles of Monty Roberts, the horse whisperer (see pp. 68–69). This amazing man learned to communicate with horses by understanding their body language and studying their habits and now promotes what he calls the "join up" method. In part thanks to his influence, patience and understanding have taken over from the often harsh methods employed in earlier times.

Maintaining the harmony between horse and rider is an essential part of all training.

172

WESTERN SADDLE

The saddle The most important single item for the western rider is the saddle. Its large bearing area ensures the weight is spread evenly over the horse's back, and a pad underneath allows for long-term comfort. The stirrups must be broad and flat with a fender (wide stirrup leather) of the right length for the longer leg position, used soaked to ensure they hang at a comfortable angle for the rider. A straight fender can be uncomfortable because it twists the rider's foot inward. The cinch (girth) is tied in a knot to the ring on the saddle. Some saddles have one, others two, depending on the design and use. Many saddles have beautifully embossed leatherwork, especially those used for western pleasure classes.

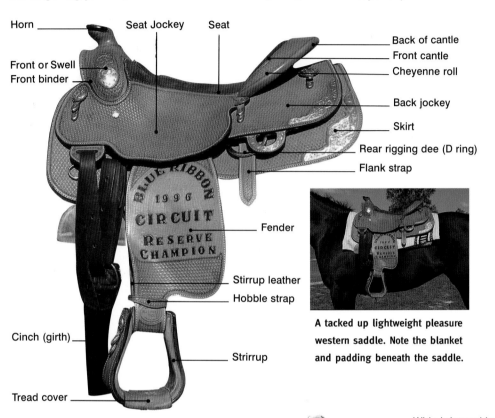

Horn
Seat Jockey
Seat
Back of cantle
Front cantle
Front or Swell
Front binder
Cheyenne roll
Back jockey
Skirt
Rear rigging dee (D ring)
Flank strap
Fender
Stirrup leather
Hobble strap
Cinch (girth)
Strirrup
Tread cover

A tacked up lightweight pleasure western saddle. Note the blanket and padding beneath the saddle.

▲ Western saddles have a large bearing surface and come in a variety of designs. Padding under the saddles helps to disperse the weight of these relatively heavy saddles.

◄ The typical western outfit with plentiful leg protection to ease the long hours spent in the saddle.

▼ The typical broad stirrups are comfortable and less slippery than the metal types used for English-style riding. Note the western boot and roweled curved spurs used for western work.

WESTERN CLOTHES

Aside from helping to look the part, western clothes are designed for comfort and practicality. It is essential to be correctly dressed for this type of riding. A wide-brimmed hat is designed to provide protection from the sun, and the leather chaps worn on top of jeans prevent rubbing or soreness. Leather boots with high heels ensure the foot remains comfortably in the stirrups. The long-sleeved shirt, again, offers protection from the sun, although special, all-in-one suits are becoming popular in showing classes.

Wide-brimmed hat
Vest/Waistcoat
Chaps
Cowboy boots

WESTERN TACK

The bosal is a bitless bridle.

Slit eared bridle.

The bosal This is a simple thick noseband made of rawhide, finished with a knot at the back of the jaw. It is attached to a plain headstall with reins. Usually, this is the first type of bridle the horse uses. It is bitless and its action works by the give-and-take action from the rider's hands.

The bridle The bridle comes in three main types: slip eared, with a sliding piece attached to the headpiece; one eared which has a slit in the leather to allow the ear through; and slit eared which has a slit in the leather band for the ears to go through.

There is no noseband and the bridle is designed for ease of putting on and comfort. Reins may be either split (Texan style) or closed (Californian), where they also combine as a whip hanging down over the thigh. Usually, the bit is of a curb design, so extreme lightness of the hand is essential. In early training, often a conventional bridle and snaffle bit are used until the horse is ready for more advanced work.

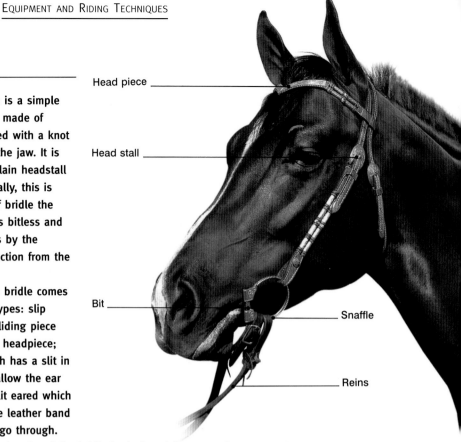

Head piece

Head stall

Bit

Snaffle

Reins

A slip eared bridle has a sliding headpiece. This one has a colored browband accentuating the nobleness of this lovely head.

▲ The Texan style of holding reins is similar to the English style (shown on p. 157).

◀ This well-dressed rider is using the Californian style of reins, the end of which can be used as a whip.

PUTTING ON A WESTERN SADDLE

Putting on a western saddle is very similar to any other saddle but it is quite heavy even though new designs are becoming lighter. First tie the horse up and keep it still before following the instructions on this page. If you are tacking up a tall horse you may need to use quite a swing to get the saddle up onto the horse's back. Make sure the blankets and padding are straight and centrally placed under the saddle before tightening the cinch (girth).

The saddle is tightened by several loops through the cinch and this keeps the saddle secure.

It is worth looking closely at the saddle to ensure you have discovered where each part is located before first tacking up.

Having placed the padding in position first, the saddle can then be put in position on top and the cinch (girth) dropped down on the far side.

The saddles themselves are often beautifully embossed, particularly those awarded as trophies for winning a particular class or parade for western riding.

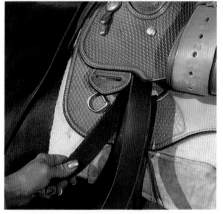

Once the cinch is fully tightened, the end is tucked through the top tie holder and the fender (stirrup leather) is dropped back into position ready for mounting.

For extra security you could make sure the end is looped again and tucked in.

Here the tie strap is being given a final tightening pull before being secured through the tie holder.

The fender on this new saddle carries the information of a much valued win. Note the silver edging common on such saddles.

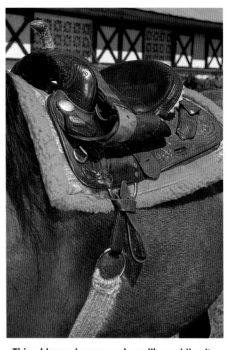

This older and more workmanlike saddle sits on a colored pad. The cinch has been secured with a shorter tie. The ring on the cinch is smooth and rounded, but care must be taken to ensure the horse does not get chafed due to puckering of the skin. A soft sheepskin cover or pad can be placed over the ring if necessary to make the horse comfortable.

WESTERN SADDLE

Q Why are western saddles so heavy and why do they have so much padding?

A Western saddles were designed to carry a person for very long journeys and very long hours and so needed to be comfortable for the rider as well as the horse. They also needed to be as functional as possible. The large amount of padding traditionally of blankets helped to disperse the weight of the rider over a large area of the horse's back. Modern saddles are made of much lighter materials and so padding is less profuse. The blankets were often used as bedding for the rider at night on those long journeys.

WESTERN BRIDLES

All three types of western bridle are simple to put on and which you choose is a matter of personal preference. The most important thing about putting on any bridle is to be gentle and don't pull at your horse's mouth or ears too much.

Western bridles are extremely easy to slip on. First draw the bridle up the front of the head until the bit is resting just below the teeth—most horses will open their mouths.

Insert fingers, if necessary, between lips at the side to encourage the horse to open its mouth, and slip the ears through the headpiece one at a time. Straighten browband if necessary.

The throatlatch (throatlash) should be tightened but left loose enough to allow a hand's width between it and the jaw. Keep the reins over your arm so they are not trodden on.

MOUNTING

Getting on is little different to normal English style except that you must remember that the western saddle is higher, so you will need to swing your leg up that little bit further before settling into the saddle. The position in the saddle is practically the same except that a slightly longer leg is adopted. However, it is essential to have some degree of flexion in the knee and ankle to ensure adequate balance, and to enable you to rise up out of the saddle when getting on and off. The hands are positioned above the horn and the reins may be held Texas or Californian style. Some people find it easier to mount by facing in the same direction as the horse, stepping upward with the left leg in the stirrup, the right hand on the horn, and the left hand holding the reins up near the withers.

To mount a western saddle, first face forward on the nearside looking at the horse's head and take hold of the reins with your left hand and the horn with your right.

Pull yourself forward and push up with your left foot in the stirrup. Swing your right leg up over the saddle, keeping your balance by holding the horn lightly.

Once you have settled into the saddle, place the right foot into the stirrup and take the reins in one or both hands, depending on how you intend to ride.

DISMOUNTING

Dismounting is done in much the same way as the English method but taking one leg at a time. Take your right foot out of the stirrup and, while keeping a firm hold on the reins (with your hand resting in front of the withers), swing the right leg up as you lean forward. Bring it high enough over to the left side to clear the saddle. Step down by the horse's side and take your left foot out of the stirrup.

Take your right foot out of the stirrup and place your right hand on the horn. Swing forward slightly from the hips and keep the horse still with an adequate contact on the reins.

Swing the right leg back and over the horse's back, then step down onto the ground onto your right foot while still maintaining a hand on the horn.

Take your left foot out of the stirrup and release your hold on the horn. The reins can then be slipped over the horse's head for leading away.

RIDING WESTERN STYLE

As with all riding, sitting straight in the saddle and evenly distributing your weight down into the heel play important parts. The leg should hang comfortably down but still must enable you to rise up out of the saddle.

The Californian—or closed—method of holding the reins involves both reins coming up through the palm of one hand and out between the thumb and first finger. The ends, known as the romal, lie under the opposite free hand and are used as a whip. In the Texan—or split—method, the reins are held between the thumb and first finger of one hand and pass down through the palm. The reins are not joined and hang loosely across the thigh. To start with, it is best to ride with both hands until you feel you have found your own balance in the saddle. Once this is achieved, practice riding western style with one hand. The horse is trained to neck rein, which involves moving away from the feel of the rein on its neck and the leg on its side. The feel need only be light for the horse to respond. In fact, all western riding involves lightness, so the rider must indicate wishes to the horse with the most delicate touch. The rider must cease the aid as soon as the horse responds.

RESPONSE TO NECK REINING

Neck reining requires the horse to respond to pressure on the neck. It does this by turning away from the area of pressure which should be light and done with a loose rather than tight rein. A well trained horse will react to the slightest pressure instantly. The rider must stay straight in the saddle but use the inside leg on the girth and the outside one behind the girth when moving in either direction.

RIDING POSITION

It is easy to pick up bad habits. Straightness in the saddle is essential for good western riding. If riding one-handed, the reins are held in the left hand and the right hand should remain on the right thigh.

Keep the body straight and only move the hand across the neck.

Keep your rein hand comfortably just above or in front of the horn, but never so high that it causes you to lean forward.

WALK AND JOG (OR TROT)

Practice at the walk—halting, turning by neck reining, and reining back. At the trot (called the jog because it is a slower pace), the horse must remain in a consistent rhythm and be smooth, with easy, accurate transitions. It will need to cope with various obstacles and opening gates, so practice these as well as going over and around poles. Putting on a coat while the horse remains still is another exercise where obedience and trust are required.

Many hours are spent teaching the various movements to keep the horse calm and relaxed in between different exercises. This one is stretching down and relaxing after a work session. Note the rider's balanced position with a straight line between her shoulders from the hips to the heels.

LOPE (CANTER)

The lope or canter is again a slower pace, very smooth and controlled, and extremely comfortable. The horse needs to be beautifully balanced to perform this correctly and the rider must be supple in the hips to be able to move easily in time to the animal's movements.

MORE ADVANCED WORK

Advanced training includes such exercises as lead changes (flying lead changes), spins (western pirouettes), sliding stops, and rollbacks (turns on the haunches). Most of these are fast but smooth versions of dressage movements, mostly influenced by the rider's body weight and seat rather than many hand or leg aids. The spin is spectacular to watch, with the horse turning in a series of 360° turns.

The sliding stop is purely a show movement. It requires the horse to have special shoes to achieve the right effect and protective boots to prevent injury to the fore legs. The horse learns to halt from a gallop, tucking its hind legs well underneath it, with its back rounded and neck arched, as it slides anything up to nearly 30 feet (9 meters) to a stop.

This horse is being taught to do the rein back, one of the most important of all training exercises. The horse must respond to the lightest touch on the reins.

179

SECTION
4
Competitions and Riding Sports

DRESSAGE

For many people, there is no sight to compare with the grace and beauty of a horse performing dressage. The precision required of the paces in a dressage performance can only be attained by years of practice by both horse and rider. At the highest level, it is a form of equestrian ballet, and the ultimate partnership between horse and rider.

Dressage is the word used to describe the complete training of the ridden horse on the flat. There are several different levels, from novice up to advanced, progressive stages taking the horse up to Olympic standard. This is the most advanced level, which comprises Grand Prix tests.

Training the horse is a fascinating subject in itself, and both horse and rider need to learn the basics correctly to be able to perform the movements required in the set tests. These are performed from memory in the dressage arena, which may be either a small area, 66 × 131 feet (20 × 40 meters), or the larger 66 × 197 feet (20 × 60 meters). The judges sit at the end opposite the central entrance. In more advanced tests there may be up to three judges along the short side and two at the mid-way sides.

The judges are looking for the quality of the paces demonstrated, as well as correct execution of the movements asked. Circles must be round (not lozenge-shaped or oblong) and the horse must go forward willingly without resistance. Any signs of stiffness or tension are marked down.

There are tests designed for all standards, ages ranging from Pony Club level to seniors. Most nations organize the sport under their own national federation rules, with grading systems usually based on points awarded for wins and placings at each level. All international dressage is run under the rules of the F.E.I. (Fédération Equestre Internationale) and riders can be entered for these only by their own national federations by qualifying in national events.

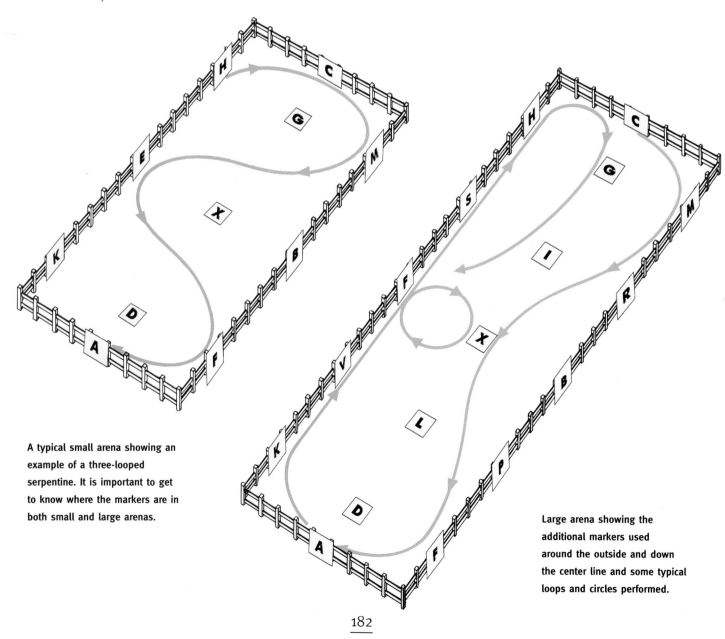

A typical small arena showing an example of a three-looped serpentine. It is important to get to know where the markers are in both small and large arenas.

Large arena showing the additional markers used around the outside and down the center line and some typical loops and circles performed.

DRESS AND TACK FOR DRESSAGE

Various restrictions apply to the type of equipment that can be used in dressage. At novice levels, only snaffles are permitted, with cavesson, drop, or flash nosebands. At higher levels, a double bridle must be used. Boots or bandages are not allowed. Riders are expected to use a straight-cut dressage saddle, which allows the longer leg required to give more subtle aids to the horse. Long dressage whips are usually allowed under national rules up to a certain level. Gloves and spurs are compulsory in all F.E.I. tests, and most national ones too.

At novice levels, blue or black jackets are worn with hunting tie (stock) or tie pin and black hunting boots. In Britain, many children and adults wear tweed coats at this level. For advanced tests, tail coats and top hats are required. Double bridles are compulsory for F.E.I. tests at this level. Most riders wear white saddlepads and the horses are braided (plaited) English style or with white tape. Flashy colors are frowned upon. Read the sport's rule book before entering any competitions. Many rules change annually and it is the competitor's responsibility to know these.

Hat

Stock or collar and tie

Jacket

Gloves

Breeches

Boots

Riders in traditional dress for novice or junior competition (on the left) and for advanced work on the right. A plain blue jacket or black jacket is also correct for novice classes.

TRAINING

It takes years to get to the top—to build up the horse's muscles to be able to perform the very strenuous movements required at advanced levels. At the lower levels, however, results can be achieved relatively quickly, and it won't be long before you can start to compete.

The most crucial element in performing dressage well lies in ensuring that the horse is "on the bit." What this means is that the horse must respond to the driving leg aids and yield up into the rider's hands without stiffness or any resistance. It requires obedience and suppleness on the part of the horse, and consequently is a long-term training job. The horse must respond by arching its neck and shortening its frame as its hind legs take up more of the balance and energy. The use of the rider's hands, legs, and seat will then determine how well the horse will perform.

DRESSAGE EXERCISES

Responsiveness to the aids is essential to all training. The horse must be trained to halt and move forward willingly and immediately when asked. The turns through the corners must be forward and without stiffness. Practice riding into the corners. If necessary, place a barrel there so that the horse moves around without falling in onto the inside shoulder.

Leg yielding **This can be started almost immediately. It requires the horse to move forward and sideways away from the rider's leg. It is generally performed going away from the long side of the arena. The horse's head is either straight or slightly inclined away from the direction in which it is traveling. Practice frequently on either rein in walk and trot. Start with just a few steps at a time, pushing the horse away from the inside leg. Do not confuse the horse by using the inside leg at the same time.**

The half halt **The most useful and essential of training exercises, half halt is literally what it says. It is used to rebalance and concentrate the horse's mind before asking for any change in pace or transition from one movement to another. The rider prepares to halt by sitting up and applying the rein aid, then immediately uses the leg to push the horse forward again. This creates more energy from the horse's quarters and**

This rider is training in *passage*. Note the protective bandages used when schooling to help prevent injury in this strenuous art. It takes months of patient work and the building up of sufficient muscle to perform such movements successfully.

makes it easier to change pace or direction, as the animal will be in better balance and not on the forehand.

Lateral work Although leg yielding is the first step toward lateral work, it is not until the horse is working in a more collected manner that further exercises can be performed. These include *renvers* and *travers*, which encourage the horse to be loose and supple through the back. The half pass is the most advanced lateral movement. It requires the horse to travel forward and sideways bent toward the direction of travel. It can be performed in the trot and canter and is perhaps one of the most esthetically pleasing movements to watch.

Collection and extension These become more intense as the horse progresses up the grades. Training must be geared toward developing the paces so that the horse can lengthen its frame and shorten again without tension. As it becomes more advanced, you will be able to see the change from the long and low outline of the novice to the supremely proud and shorter frame of the fully trained advanced horse.

Counter canter A useful exercise, counter canter involves the horse cantering on the outside lead. It requires balance and collection, with the rider making a conscious effort to keep the body weight over the leading leg so as not to unbalance the horse and force it to change legs. Start by doing gradual loops off the track and then returning.

Flying lead changes Doing a flying lead change at the canter from one diagonal onto the other takes time and patience, as in dressage it is done with the horse in a slower, more rounded outline. The rider sits upright, indicating with the right leg for the horse to change to the left diagonal and so on. Once single changes have been mastered, work starts on sequence changes every six, five, four, three, and two strides, until the ultimate is reached when the horse can change on every stride.

The most advanced movements of *piaffe* (trotting on the spot) and *passage* (elevated trot) take years to perfect and require a high degree of collection and training.

THE COMPETITIONS

Dressage competitions start at preliminary level, although these may have different names and vary slightly in different countries. There are competitions for children, juniors, young riders, and novices, but in general these are geared to the

Olympic rider Robert Dover performs a spectacular extended trot on his gray horse Metallic. The elevation and rhythm of the steps play an important part.

horse's level rather than that of the rider. Points are awarded for wins and places in competitions. The novice horse is expected to demonstrate simple movements, willingly, and show forwardness, straightness, and obedience.

The art of presentation plays a big part in dressage. The ability of horse and rider to enter the arena looking professional and confident can greatly influence the marks. If the horse is moving correctly, with a loose swinging rhythm, and the rider is sitting nicely with his or her head up, the overall impression will be favorable. An idle horse slopping around the arena with a hunched-up rider looking down will never achieve more than mediocre marks.

At novice level, the horse is expected to perform simple movements in all paces. Some lengthening of the stride will be required, and the horse may be asked to rein back or do half pirouettes.

At medium level, horses are required to show more collected paces within the gaits. The judges are looking at the quality of the movements and the ability of riders to communicate their wishes to their horses, which must respond willingly. Movements at this standard will include counter canter, half pass, and single flying lead changes.

At advanced level, horses need to be capable of flying lead changes in sequence, advanced counter-canter loops, pirouettes, *piaffe*, and *passage*—the ultimate in dressage training. The three highest stages at this level are the F.E.I. Prix St. Georges test, Intermediate I and II, and the Grand Prix. These involve all the movements expected of the dressage horse and are enthralling to watch. Yet another discipline, the Kür, involves dressage to music, which gives an added dimension to the sport. It is rather like watching an equestrian ballet, the horse appearing to dance to the music.

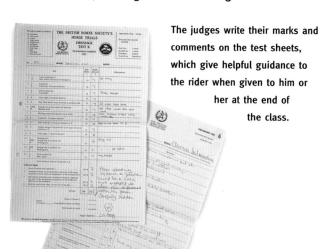

The judges write their marks and comments on the test sheets, which give helpful guidance to the rider when given to him or her at the end of the class.

THE CANTER PIROUETTE

The degree of balance and collection required must be maintained throughout the movement to enable the horse to remain on one spot during this very advanced movement.

The hind legs must stay almost still while the front legs are raised as the horse starts its turn completely on the spot away from Marker A.

The rider maintains the bend to the right and uses his legs to continue the turn step by step, keeping his body upright, but following the movement of the horse.

The horse's hind legs have been taking tiny steps as it completes its turn. Notice how firmly the rider's outside leg is pressing on the horse.

Almost there. The horse is taking the last step back onto the track. The power and strength required for this very collected movement can be seen in the muscles of the hind quarters.

Back on the track and straight again the horse's movement is completed and it is ready to perform whatever the rider asks of it next.

DRESSAGE EXERCISES

Q When should a rider start to learn dressage?

A The sooner the better! Younger riders are much more receptive and more relaxed about training. The earlier they can get competitive experience the easier they will find it when performing in front of the judge which, for some, is an intimidating experience. There are numerous juvenile activities which include dressage and other forms of riding, but the Pony Club has a popular dressage series.

◄ Starting early. This junior rider on her Welsh Section B pony is competing in Pony Club dressage.

SHOW JUMPING

Show jumping is a sport that can be enjoyed by all ages and at all levels of experience and expertise. From the inspirational heights of the Olympics down to the local schooling show, anyone can enjoy the thrill of a clear round.

The type of course that show jumping competitors have to jump is determined by the various levels of competition standard. Each course is specifically designed in terms of height and technicality, according to the level expected of horse or pony and rider in that event. As well as general competitions, there are many specialist events that focus on particular aspects of the sport. For example, the puissance events are specifically designed to test a horse's ability to jump exceedingly high fences. There are also speed classes, and Grand Prix and Derby-type competitions for horses with the exceptional scope needed to jump big courses.

The national governing body controls the sport and makes the rules relating to the specific classes. At international level these are run under Fédération Equestre Internationale (F.E.I.) rules. At the lower levels many shows run unaffiliated classes where neither horse nor rider need register with their national show jumping organization. There are generally three to four

In international competitions, the riders wear their national flag on the horse's saddle cloth. The jumps are not only huge but very imaginative and colorful. Both horse and rider demonstrate their confidence and experience over this parallel.

different grades, which the horse moves up into as experience and points or money earnings accumulate.

TRAINING

To train a horse for show jumping, start with pole work and single fences. Then you can work on grids to loosen and strengthen the horse. The canter must develop so that it is possible to shorten and lengthen the stride with ease, without losing balance, rhythm, or impulsion. Placing a pole in front of the grid will ensure you arrive at the right spot to jump the fence correctly. A pole can also be placed in front of single fences if you have a horse with a tendency to rush—9–10 feet (2.75–3.1 meters) in front is about right. A pole set a similar distance after the fence can further help to slow up a horse who goes too fast, and will also have the effect of encouraging it to arch well over the fence.

Practice doubles and triple combinations (trebles) so that the horse is confident at seeing two or three fences in a line. The mass of poles and fillers can look daunting to a youngster—the more it can see and do early in its training, the better.

Learning the ropes. This horse and rider are practicing over a variety of colored fences.

TYPES OF FENCES

Fences come in all shapes and sizes, but most fall into basic types. Each type is designed to test the horse in a different way, so not all methods of approach are the same.

Verticals As the name implies, these fences are built vertically from the ground without a spread. Examples are the wall and brush and rail. When approaching a vertical fence, accuracy on take-off is vital. Taking off too close or too far away will make it difficult for the horse to clear the fence properly. This means that a collected, balanced stride is necessary to ensure that the exact take-off spot is found. If the horse takes off too far away, it is likely to flatten and hit the fence on the way down. Too close will make it difficult to get up in the air in time to avoid hitting the fence on the way up—unless the horse is really balanced and has its hind legs underneath it sufficiently.

Spreads Fences, such as the triple bar, consist of width as well as height. They are easier for the horse to jump, as the width encourages the horse to take off in an arc shape. At the highest point over the center of the fence, the horse should be rounded over the jump with its knees and fore legs well folded up, the head and neck stretched forward and out, and the withers just a shade higher than the rest of the body.

The approach to spreads should be in a forward but controlled bouncy canter with the hind legs well underneath. It is important to get fairly close in to the obstacle with enough pace and impulsion to spring over it. Standing off spread fences often makes them impossibly wide. Practice over small fences before trying a larger one. The more obedient and controlled the horse is on the flat, the easier it will be to work with it in jumping.

There are numerous different types of fences to be found within a complete course. Walls, bushes, gates, triples (trebles), parallels, and so on some of which are shown. The horse will jump a more solid and imposing looking fence better than one made of flimsy materials.

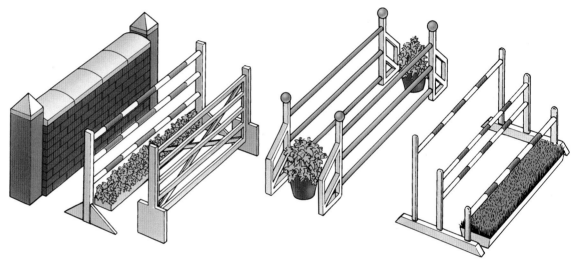

Spook fences Some fences can be quite frightening to horses, so it is worth practicing over all sorts of different designs. Fences with ditches underneath, very garish fillers, even a sheet draped over a pole—all will accustom a horse to the different sights which it will be expected to jump unquestioningly.

Doubles To jump doubles (in and outs or combinations), it is important to get a good first jump in so that the stride is then set for a clean exit. By standing off at the first element, you will find it difficult to make up ground for the second and the horse may stop. By going in too fast, you will land too tightly for the horse to put in a proper stride before taking off for the second element (and so may knock it down).

Most doubles have one or two strides in between the fences. They may consist of a spread fence in to a spread out, two verticals, a vertical to a spread, or vice versa. Speed, balance, and impulsion into the fence are the important factors.

Triple combinations (Trebles) These consist of three fences over a related distance, usually with one or two strides between each. They are similar to doubles, but they demand even more accuracy and obedience. If you are not right at the first element, it is imperative to give the horse every bit of freedom and impulsion from the legs to get itself through.

A big spread fence with artistic wings. The horse must be familiar with all types of fencing and decorations.

Water This is often found on the more advanced courses, and it is important to ensure your horse has been trained over water when schooling before meeting it in the ring. Practice jumping with a pole over the top of the water so that the horse learns that it is expected to clear the obstacle and not go in it! A jump with plastic sheeting can be used, but make sure the landing side does not have anything which could injure the horse.

WALKING THE COURSE

In a competition, the only way to familiarize yourself with the obstacles and distances between each one is to walk the course on foot. The show organizers usually allocate time before a class for this purpose. Try to walk the lines to your fences as if you were riding them—remembering to use as much of the ring as possible to get a good line into the jumps.

Assess the course as a whole at the end of your walk, and be sure to remember the problem areas—which combinations have short or long strides and where you need to be sure to ride strongly out of a corner or turn to meet the next fence with enough impulsion. Note the start and finish, and don't forget to listen to the start bell so that you know what sound it makes before starting your round.

RIDING YOUR ROUND

How you can ride your course will depend on several factors—in particular your horse, its stage of training, and what you are hoping to achieve on that given day. The ultimate aim is always to achieve a clear round, as this helps to build up confidence and gives an indication of whether you and the horse are sufficiently in tune to work together.

Stage fright is common, but try to ride in the ring as you would at home. Keep the horse in a well-balanced canter and approach the fences with enough controlled impulsion to be able to jump them with ease. Ride the course as you planned when you walked it. Try to be positive in your approach and not transmit any anxiety to the horse.

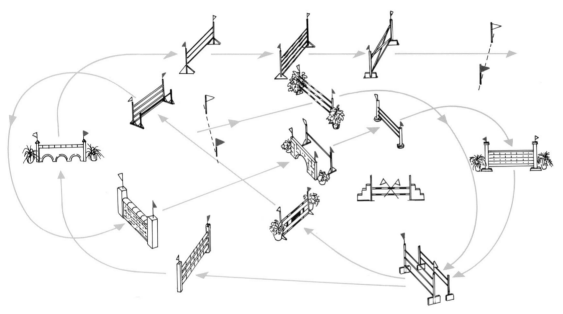

Course plans are always available in the collecting ring area for riders. These allow them to determine their route and timing, as well as the rules governing the judging of the class. Remember to check where your start and finish are and how you intend to approach the start. Look carefully at your turns and walk the distances between. Plan your striding within combination fences.

JUMPING STAGES

The approach to the fence is vital. The rider must judge what is required and influence the speed and impulsion required for the type and size of fence to be jumped.

The take-off requires the horse to bring its hind legs sufficiently far forward to enable it to spring upward high enough to clear the fence.

For the horse to get the upward spring it requires, it must be unhindered by the weight of the rider. The rider's weight should be forward to allow the horse to take as much rein as it needs.

IF THINGS GO WRONG

Try not to panic if everything does not go according to plan. If you have a refusal, give your horse every chance by going back far enough from the fence to re-establish a good canter. Sit up and use your legs more effectively to get over the fence. It is vital to restore confidence immediately if anything unexpected happens, so forget what your style is like and just think and act with determination to complete the round.

Should you demolish part of the fence, the bell will sound and the clock will be stopped. Once the fence has been rebuilt, the bell will sound again and you can re-start at that fence and complete your round. Do not do a circle after the bell has rung as this will be counted as a disobedience or refusal. Keep your horse moving during any holdup so that it is mentally ready to go back to jumping the moment required.

If you have a stop in the middle of a combination, you must go back and jump it from the beginning. Never dismount before you leave the ring, even if you have gone through the finish flags. Make sure you know the rules inside out so that you are aware of what to do or not to do in all situations.

This rider is demonstrating some of the classic faults: looking down, resting the hands on the neck and allowing the lower leg to slide back. She is also too far forward which could result in a fall if the horse decided to stop suddenly. A rider's position can make a huge difference to the success of a round, and it is important to remain upright as you keep your horse moving forward in front of the leg.

THE JUMP-OFF

In most events, a jump-off will take place for all those who have achieved a clear round (except in those classes confined to young horses or where clear rounds qualify for certain classes). This may be over a shorter and higher course, or over one where speed will be the deciding factor. A draw determines the order of jumping. If you make it through to the jump-off, you will need to decide how to ride the course and what route you will take. This may involve some tight turns if you intend to go out to win. If you are on a young horse, you may decide to take a longer route and go for a steady, clear round.

To win by going at speed, you must ride forward through every stride yet keep your horse balanced. Do not let yourself down by pulling at the horse—which will cost you time—but keep it balanced with your legs and use of your body. Sit up on the approaches and be mentally turning toward the next fence as soon as you are in the air over the one before. Be alert, be positive, be effective until you are through the finish.

Most neat jumpers love the challenge and rise to the occasion when jumping at speed. However, a few cannot cope with the pressure and are best when not pushed in jump-offs. If this is the case, go for safe clears and quick turns—often such horses do well if they are taught to be quick and balanced on turning.

The horse must have complete freedom as it tucks up its fore leg hocks and knees to clear the height and spread over the fence. The rider pushes her hands forward.

The descent starts and the hind legs flick up to ensure the back pole is not knocked. The rider's legs go forward to brace for the landing and his body starts to move into an upright position.

The strain on the front legs is plain to see in the vital stage of landing, so the rider must sit up as shown to help the horse balance itself for the next stride.

EVENTING

Eventing is one of the toughest challenges for horse and rider. It involves dressage, cross country, and showjumping—three disciplines which together demand the ultimate in fitness, stamina, agility, and obedience.

At the highest level of the sport, the three-day event is the ultimate aim. Then, the various disciplines are split over three days. Dressage is performed on the first day, although if there are a lot of competitors—such as in Britain and Europe—the tests may take place over two days. The second day is known as the speed and endurance day and is designed to test the horse's fitness and training. It is divided into four separate phases: A, B, C, and D. Phases A and C are the roads and tracks. Phase B is the steeplechase, designed to test the horse at speed around a set course of chase fences (which vary in distance according to the standard of the class). Phase D, the cross-country event, takes place after a ten-minute compulsory halt when the horses are checked over by an inspection panel to ensure their fitness to continue.

On the last day, a single round of showjumping to prove the stamina and fitness of the horse—following the demands of the previous day—completes the competition. Penalties are incurred for faults at obstacles and for exceeding time limits. These are added to the dressage score to give a final total. The horse and rider with the lowest score is the winner.

A successful cross-country rider requires superb balance and "stickability" when meeting the unexpected!

PENALTIES FOR EVENTING COMPETITIONS

SHOW JUMPING	PENALTIES	CROSS COUNTRY	PENALTIES
Knocking down an obstacle	5 penalties	First refusal, run-out, circle of horse at obstacle	20 penalties
First disobedience (refusal, etc.) of horse	10 penalties	Second refusal, run-out, circle of horse at same obstacle	40 penalties
Second disobedience in whole test	20 penalties	Third refusal, run-out, circle of horse at same obstacle	Elimination
Third disobedience in whole test	Elimination	Fifth cumulative refusal	Elimination
Fall of horse or rider	30 penalties	Fall of horse and/or rider at obstacle	60 penalties
Error of course not rectified	Elimination	Second penalized fall of horse and/or rider	Elimination
Omission of obstacle or boundary flag	Elimination	Error of course not rectified	Elimination
Retaking of obstacle in wrong order	Elimination	Omission of obstacle or boundary flag	Elimination
For every commenced period of 4 seconds in excess of Time Allowed	1 penalty	Retaking of obstacle already jumped	Elimination
Exceeding Time Limit (which is twice the Time Allowed)	Elimination	Jumping of obstacle in wrong order	Elimination
		For every commenced period of 3 seconds in excess of Optimum Time	1 penalty
DRESSAGE		Exceeding the Time Limit (which is twice the Optimum Time)	Elimination
1st error of course	2 penalties		
2nd error of course	4 penalties		
3rd error of course	8 penalties		
4th error of course	Elimination		

CLASSES

Eventing (also known as horse trials) has different standards of class catering to novice or preliminary horses, intermediate, and advanced. In some countries there is also a "pre-novice" or training class, which is an ideal introduction to the sport for the less experienced rider. All these classes are known as one-day events, even though they often take place over a weekend or two to three days.

The one-day event is the training ground for a three-day event. The horse will need to gain sufficient experience at each stage to move up the grades to advanced level. Usually, this is achieved by winning points for placings at the events. While a horse may be able to compete in several one-day events throughout the year, it could only be expected to do two (or at the very most three) three-day events over a 12-month period because of the tough nature of the sport. Generally it will take two to three months' training to prepare a horse for a one-day event depending on how fit it is. Three-day eventers take at least four weeks longer.

THREE-DAY EVENTS

At international level, the three-day event is categorized by a star system. One star is considered suitable for novice/ preliminary level and juniors. Two stars means it is suitable for intermediate and young riders. Three stars is advanced. Four stars is the highest level, and generally is used only in certain competitions, such as the World Championships. Britain's Badminton and Burghley are the only international three-day events in the world to be given this status. There are annual championships for pony riders, juniors, and young riders, as well as seniors, plus the Olympic Games and World Championships taking place on a four-year cycle.

The earlier you can start the better. There are numerous Pony Club events to begin acquiring cross-country skills, as well as pony and junior eventing levels.

GETTING FIT

Before doing any serious training, it is vital for the event horse to have had a thorough and conscientious build-up to prepare it for the demands of the sport. A four- to six-week period should be spent on "legging up" or conditioning the horse's muscles before it is asked to do anything more serious and strenuous.

Galloping Galloping is done once or twice a week depending on your horse after the initial fitness work has been completed. This will help to develop its breathing capacity by exercising the lungs regularly. Many people use interval training as a method of conditioning the horse. This is a regulated formula of work and rest periods built up over several weeks. You might start with a three-minute canter × three, interspersed with three-minute walking periods. Gradually increase the canter sessions and decrease the walking. This helps to stimulate heart and lungs to cope with increased demands as the horse adapts to the extra work.

◄ Galloping is an essential part of fitness and competitive training. Practice your position and balance without sitting too heavily.

Jump training When it comes to jumping, the horse needs to be athletic and well balanced to cope with the different types of fences met, both on the cross-country and show jumping (stadium) courses. Not only does it need regular schooling sessions to teach it to be agile and foot-perfect over poles and fences at home, but also over a variety of cross-country fences. Seniors have to carry a minimum weight of 165lb (75kg) on the speed and endurance phase, so practice riding with weights if needed. Galloping will need to be done once or twice a week, to help develop the horse's breathing capacity. Remember, too, that you will need to be able to gallop and jump at speed, while maintaining balance and control.

The inexperienced event horse needs to become accustomed to all types of jumps. This branch adds a rustic look to this single rail.

Many horses who become idle on their own work much better in company. It is also nice to have company during the slow laborious fitness work essential for the proper conditioning of the event horse.

Training for the roads and tracks The endurance element of the three-day event should not be underestimated and distance rides three to four times a week should be started four to six weeks before the competition. These should include long hacks, preferably up and down hills on safe, suitable tracks if available. Increase the distance gradually and teach the horse to trot and canter on a loose rein so that it takes as little as possible out of itself. This is the secret if your horse is likely to over-exert itself. Your own attitude of mind will be influential so practice calmness and correct breathing so that there is as little as possible to worry about. If trotting for any length of time remember to change diagonals so that there is no prospect of straining the horse by sitting for too long on the one side.

The speed for roads and tracks is 220 mpm, which works out at just over 1 km at 4 minutes per mile (km).

Training for steeplechase If aiming for a three-day event remember to have a few practices on how to gallop and jump at speed remaining in balance yet maintaining a good feel in the hand. The ideal way to ensure you are doing this right is to go with your trainer and practice going up a line of full-sized steeplechase fences. The speeds required vary with the standard of class from 640–690 mpm.

Protection when training The varied ground and different training requirements mean that the event horse must have adequate protection on its legs. Use well-fitting boots that do not rub or correctly fitted bandages. Over-reach boots are a wise precaution when galloping or cross country schooling, or at all times if the horse is prone to over-reaching. A small cut or bruise at the beginning of the season may develop into something a lot worse, with maddening consequences. Don't forget studs, which are vital in hard, wet, or slippery conditions to give a better grip.

Practicing your test During the last couple of weeks before the first competition, make sure you and your horse are confident about all the movements required in the dressage test. Do not practice the whole thing more than a couple of times or your horse may start to anticipate the movements. Ride certain parts to ensure you have mastered any difficult areas and ensure the whole test is committed to memory. Many a competition has been lost by riders forgetting their tests.

If the horse has never been in a dressage arena, it is a good idea to ride in one before the day. Practice coming down the center line, required at the beginning and end of the test, and any of the more technical movements.

THE ONE-DAY EVENT

Preparing for the big day takes a lot of organizing. All details of the standards of competition will be found in the Rule Book of the Sport. Follow these carefully and enter as stated. Check through all your tack and kit and ensure you have everything ready, and that you can find it as and when required. Check that the truck is full of fuel, tires checked and that the oil and water have been looked at before the horse is loaded.

ON ARRIVAL

Allow yourself plenty of time to prepare everything. Collect your number, find out where dressage and showjumping take place and where the cross-country start is located. Find out at the secretary's tent if there are any changes to the course plan and look at this to see if there are any flags to take note of on the course. Red flags are on your right, white ones on your left. You will be eliminated if you miss any on the course. They are usually there either for your safety or to ensure the distance is correct for the class.

EQUIPMENT REQUIRED

Tack—bridles, saddle, girths, breastplate, weight cloth, martingales, and any extras.
Traveling kit and blankets for the day—coolers, blankets, waterproofs (according to weather).
Water—enough to drink and wash down. Hay and feed.
Buckets and wash-down kit.
Stud box and tap, spanner, cleaning nails, variety of studs.
Grooming kit, including hoof pick, scissors, and braiding kit.
Leg protection—bell boots, competition boots, and bandages.
First-aid boxes—fully stocked, both for horse and human.
Fly spray and halter.
Rider's clothes for all three phases—dressage, stadium (showjumping), cross country, and a change. Hat and helmet, boots, spurs, whips, and gloves.

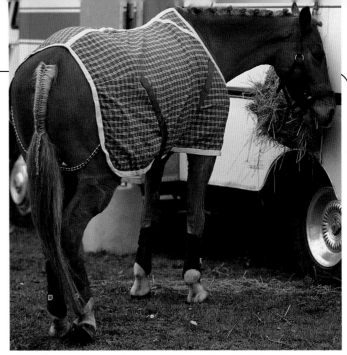

The event horse often has a long day and will appreciate its hay net.

WALKING THE COURSE

If you have not already walked the cross-country course the day before, plan when you are going to do this and allow enough time—it always takes longer than you think. Walk the showjumping course as soon as you arrive or during a break in the class. Always look at the start and finish carefully and your line into the first fence and to the finish from the last. Concentrate on your line into fences if they are approached from a turn and how you are going to get from one fence to the next.

On the cross country think about the ground and how this will affect your horse. Very hard ground will often cause the horse to shorten its stride. The horse will gain ground going down hill. If it is deep going the horse will have to make extra effort to clear the height and will tire more easily, as it will on a very hilly course.

Try to go the most direct route from one fence to another—mentally think that as soon as you land from one fence you start to focus on the next.

Remember to think of balancing your horse before multiple fences in particular, but still maintain a good forward rhythm throughout. Think of riding positively around the entire course and try to visualize how you will ride each fence.

If possible walk your course twice so that you are thoroughly familiar with it and always have an alternative plan ready to use should anything go wrong such as at a corner or other fence when accuracy is vital. Do not waste time, get on and jump the alternative option, and then practice at home before the next outing.

DRESSAGE

Get ready and warm up so that the horse is settled and relaxed before you are due to enter the arena. Some horses need far more work than others. Keep them quietly occupied with lots of circles and transitions. When your time comes trot round past the judges and wait for the start bell or horn (know which is yours) before entering the arena.

Badminton winner David O'Connor completes his test at the Olympic Games with a final salute to the judges. The horse must remain stationary and steady to obtain good marks for this movement.

SHOW JUMPING

In one-day events the show jumping may come before or after the cross-country depending on the country, but always give the horse time to warm up well and then give it a couple of jumps over an upright and spread before going into the arena. Start straight after the bell has sounded and give your horse the best chance by approaching each fence straight and positively.

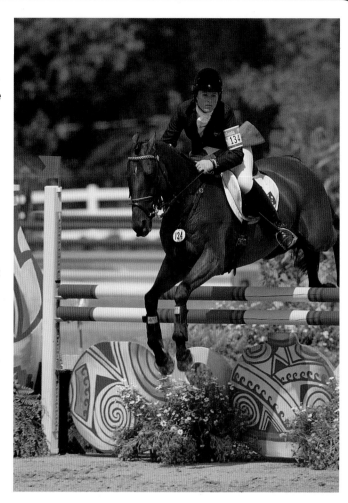

Wendy Schaeffer on Sunburst in Atlanta in the final phase was just one example of the toughness shown by many event riders in this rugged sport.

Only six weeks before, she had badly broken her leg but was determined to compete and went to great lengths to be judged fit enough to ride. Her dashing round was one of the event's highlights and a great inspiration to fellow competitors at the Olympic Games.

CROSS COUNTRY

If you do not already know your dressage score it is worth finding out before going into the cross-country phase as this may make a difference on how you ride. A poor dressage and show jumping performance may make you decide to just go round the course for a gentle school, or you may want to use it as a chance to jump all the more difficult routes or to go for a safe clear to qualify for something. A good dressage and show jumping score may, however, mean you intend to make the most of this situation and achieve a good time and perhaps a place or a win.

Get yourself ready with the necessary protective helmet and back protector and make sure your horse is well prepared with boots, or with bandages and studs if used. Warm it up and get it motivated and in a "go" mood before entering the start box.

Practicing cross-country riding by yourself is fun but not for the fainthearted! This big hedge to practice over is typical of the type of fence found in most parts of the world.

Helmet—it is compulsory to wear a crash helmet while riding in an eventing competition at all levels. (The helmet may be covered in the rider's colors—sometimes called "silks.")

Body protector—this is a padded garment worn like a vest (waistcoat).

Long-sleeved cotton shirt or jersey.

Jodhpurs

Long boots

Dressed for cross-country, this rider is wearing a safety helmet and back protector vest (waistcoat). Her number bib would be worn over this. Most countries now require that you strap a medical card with nersonal det ils o your arm.

Ride straight, be positive, and maintain a rhythm toward, over, and away from your fences. Pull up gradually and walk the horse until it has stopped blowing, loosen girths and noseband as soon as practical.

Once back at the truck, quickly remove boots or bandages, studs, and tack, and wash the horse down well. Keep it walking until it is relaxed and offer the horse quarter buckets of water every ten minutes until it is satisfied. Make it comfortable and give it a small feed or hay before going to see how your score looks on the board.

THE THREE-DAY EVENT

This is every eventer's dream. However, it often takes four or even five days (if two days of dressage are required to cope with numbers) to complete in most cases. Before the event starts horses have to pass a fitness inspection in front of the judges and veterinarians. There is a briefing and official tour of the roads and tracks and steeplechase course for competitors, who are then free to walk the cross-country course.

This usually causes a lot of excitement and comment with everyone comparing notes and asking the experienced riders their advice on how to tackle the various obstacles. Once the dressage phase has been done many riders give their horses

JUMPING FENCES WITH ALTERNATIVE ROUTES

Many fences, especially at the more advanced levels are designed to give riders alternative routes to choose from. Some have a quicker but more demanding option, while others may be slower, but safer. The decision to jump one in preference to the other often rests on which route best suits a rider's particular horse. It is up to the rider to choose the best. The fences shown give typical examples of how certain obstacles could be tackled and the different striding required at each.

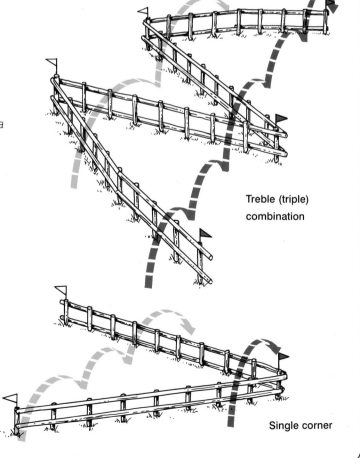

Treble (triple) combination

Double combination

Single corner

The dashing style of Kerry Milliken shows what cross-country riding is all about. However few horses will land safely in water if approaching it too fast. It is important to build up confidence in early stages.

a good short, sharp gallop or "pipe opener" the day before the cross country to clear their wind.

On cross-country day the equipment required during the ten-minute compulsory halt, before the cross-country phase, is placed in "the box," the confined area where the horses are checked over, refreshed, and attended to before setting off on Phase D, the cross country. They return to this area at the end for a further check and wash down before returning to the horse van (horsebox) or stall.

Riders have to weigh out and in at the end in this area and may not leave "the box" until allowed to do so by the steward in charge.

On the last day the horses must first pass the final horse inspection, which is designed to ensure they are still fit to compete after the demands of the previous day. Inevitably a little stiff in some cases the horses should be given a gentle hack and then five or ten minutes loosening work before being presented for inspection.

The show jumping takes place around a single course of jumps relative to the standard of competition. The final score from all three days determines the result, and for those who complete the contest there is that wonderful sense of achievement at having completed what is probably the most demanding of all equestrian sports in all-round riding and training of the horse.

The "trot up" is one of the most nerve-racking moments for the event rider. There are three occasions when the horses must pass an inspection for fitness before the event begins, during the 10-minute halt and on the last day before the show jumping. Any failure results in elimination from the competition. It is essential to keep the horse in a good rhythm and to ensure it keeps its head straight in front of the panel so that it takes even steps.

ENDURANCE RIDING

Throughout history, there have been legendary tales of outstanding feats of endurance on horseback. Endurance riding as a sport is relatively new, but still relies on fitness, stamina, and determination to succeed from both the rider and the horse.

Today, thanks to the pioneering work of American Wendell T. Robie, endurance riding is an internationally renowned sport. It takes supreme horsemanship, dedicated fitness programs, and attention to detail, although the sport can be as relaxed or intense as the rider wishes.

In its simplest form, as pleasure trail rides, a lone rider or a group sets off with map, compass, and possibly overnight equipment to explore the countryside with no time limit. With competitive endurance rides, on the other hand, the pre-designated route must be completed within a set time. These competitive rides may be held over one to three days and, as well as completing it within the set time, competitors must incur minimum penalties at the veterinary checks along the route to gain the top awards. It is the overall soundness and condition of the horse at the end that is the vital factor. Generally, endurance rides start at around 20–25 miles (32–40km) at the lower levels, and work up to a gruelling 75–100 miles (120–160km) distance.

The condition in which your horse is presented at each veterinarian check will determine how successful you are, so a good backup team is essential for watering and cooling the horse at every opportunity.

RULES AND FITNESS

To compete at the highest level, it is essential that both horse and rider are extremely well prepared. The effects of dehydration and the importance of teaching the horse to drink; the essential straightness in the saddle and equal distribution of the rider's weight; the use of suitable tack and clothing for such long distances—none of these elements can be overemphasized. Also crucial is the fitness and feeding program, as is the right type of horse for the job. It needs to be tough, wiry, well balanced, and basically sound, with good overall conformation. Obviously the legs and feet need to be correct and in good condition, with a nice broad chest above.

THE HORSE

Arabs have proved their superiority in the sport. In the United States' great endurance race, the Tevis Cup, purebred Arabs won 22 times in the first 30 years! Other breeds that have excelled include Appaloosas, Trakehners, Selle Françaises, Standardbreds, American Saddlebreds, Welsh Cobs, Akhal-Tékés, Andalusians, and Thoroughbreds.

AROUND THE WORLD

Endurance riding is extremely popular in the United States, Australia, South Africa, the Middle East, and many European countries. In the United Arab Emirates, endurance races are held across the desert sands in the searing heat. These races require special, highly tuned horses to cope with the extreme conditions—Arab horses are especially good at these events.

Internationally, the sport is governed by the Fédération Equestre Internationale (F.E.I.), but each nation has its own governing body. Apart from the Tevis Cup in the U.S., there are the Golden Horseshoe and Summer Solstice rides in Britain, and the Quilty across the Blue Mountains of New South Wales in Australia. In South Africa, the National Endurance Ride covers 130 miles (209km) and is spread over three days.

It is a bonus to ride along the beach when there is a little sea breeze. Note the relaxed attitude and cool headgear of the riders.

The rider must be as fit as the horse if he or she is to be of any use to it. Comfortable running shoes are a must if you are to be able to move quickly on the ground as you rest the horse's back occasionally.

FLAT RACING

It takes breeding, training, and a lot of luck to produce a champion for the "Sport of Kings." This worldwide spectator sport supports a massive gambling industry, and fortunes have been lost and won on the nose of a galloping racehorse.

Early racing prints show the jockeys with very long stirrups, a style quite unlike the short stirrups today.

Horse racing in its present form started in England during the 17th century. The first permanent racecourse was built at Newmarket thanks to King James I (who reigned, 1603–25), and has remained the center of English racing ever since. However, it was his grandson, Charles II (who reigned 1660–85), who became known as "the Father of the British Turf" because of his contribution to the establishment of the sport. He rode in races himself and set up many of the rules and regulations on which the sport is based today.

Most of Britain's monarchs were enthusiastic racers, and this helped to popularize the sport (which today is a vast industry). This interest helped in the development of the Thoroughbred—the finest and fastest breed in the world. Every Thoroughbred racehorse can trace its ancestry back to the three Arabian stallions imported to Britain in the 1800s—the Darley Arabian, the Byerley Turk, and the Godolphin Barb.

There are literally thousands of horses that have excelled on the racecourse over the years, with owners from all walks of life, ranging from prime ministers to diamond dealers. This wonderful sport brings together a unique group of people of such varied backgrounds through a common love of the horse.

These Australian jockeys at Kineton Videoring look as determined as any to keep their mounts up to the mark.

THE SUPERSTARS

As in all sports, it is the stars that capture the hearts of the public—and racing is no exception. However, the top flat racehorse remains under the spotlight for only a relatively short time, usually two years, before being retired to stud. This means that the public gets to know only those that are exceptional or have achieved memorable feats of greatness.

There are so many racehorse stars, it is difficult to pick out a few. One brilliant performer was the "Horse of the Century," Secretariat, who broke the track record in each of the Belmont Stakes, Preakness, and the Kentucky Derby (which are the United States' Triple Crown), winning the Belmont by a staggering 31 lengths in 1973. Most countries have a Triple Crown of Classic races as the most prestigious in the racing calendar. In Britain, there is the Derby, 2000 Guineas, and St. Leger for colts, and the Oaks and 1000 Guineas for fillies. The Prix de Jockey Club at Chantilly, the Prix de Diane, and the Prix de l'Arc de Triomphe are the French Classics.

Mill Reef, already an outstanding English Derby and Prix de l'Arc de Triomphe winner suffered a serious leg injury just before meeting his arch rival, Brigadier Gerard, to decide the greater of these two fine horses, on the course. It was not to be however, but he became an outstanding sire.

Cigar became the sporting legend of the United States in the 1990s, with 19 wins earning $9 million (£6 million). His grand, devouring stride and mental determination to win was obvious to all who watched him, and never better illustrated than when just nosing ahead of Soul of the Moths in the Dubai World Cup in 1996. This performance put him in the same league as another great American superstar of the 20th century—Citation.

OTHER FAMOUS RACES

France The Prix de Jockey Club at Chantilly (the French Derby), and the Prix de Diane (the fillies classic) and the Prix de l'Arc de Triomphe (the European Championship) are the most famous of the French Classics.
Australia One of the most famous flat races in the southern hemisphere is the Melbourne Cup.

THE RACES

Races are run for two-, three-, and four-year-olds, as well as older horses. Generally, the "Classics," the most prestigious races, are for colts and fillies of three years. Other races are open to geldings and older horses. Most races are sprints up to 8 furlongs (1 mile/1.6 km), middle distance (1–2 miles/1.6–3.2 km), or longer distances (2 miles/3.2 km plus). There are weight handicaps for horses in some races and a system of weight for age in others. This is dictated by the Jockey Club, which has a system of allotting weights according to a "scale of weights" formula (taking into account the horse's age and sex as well as distance and the stage of the racing season). Group Races and Pattern races are included in a special international series of events catering to the same standards. There is a formula in the weight allowances based on the theory "every extra 1 lb/450 g on the horse's back is the equivalent of a fifth of a second or half a length in time or distance."

THE SALES

Most racehorses are bought and sold at prestigious sales around the world. Every year, owners and trainers collect at venues such as Keeneland in Kentucky, and the Newmarket Sales in Britain, for serious bidding on young bloodstock. Preparation and training for the sales takes place months in advance so that the youngsters are confident and well behaved on the day, before coming under the hammer.

▼ Quarter horse racing in Texas where these sprinters dash ¼ mile (0.5 km) at breathtaking speeds.

ON THE TRACK

Races are started with an electric starting gate. The horses wait in the starting stalls, with the jockeys ready to leap into action the moment the gates spring open. The tactics and riding ability of the jockeys, in conjunction with the trainer's instructions, often determine the success or failure of the horse. However, a good horse will be doing its best to be first as it passes the all-important finishing post. Some horses are best leading from the front. In the United States, in particular, front-running tactics are generally employed, with speed being the all-important factor. In Britain, a waiting game is more often used, depending on conditions, with a spurt of finishing speed often proving successful.

Grass tracks are the norm in Europe, but in the U.S. most races are run on a specially formulated dirt track. This consists of a firm base with approximately 4 in (10 cm) of dirt on top. Some horses run better on a particular surface, and may be shipped abroad to compete on whatever is most suitable.

▶ Closing the gates before the start at Epsom. The handlers often have a difficult task coaxing these finely-tuned animals into the narrow stalls.

Training on the turf gallops in Britain. Many trainers have their own gallops which usually incorporate some hill work. Small bushes are generally planted as a guide to the route to be followed by the jockeys.

TRAINING

In training, the flat racehorse starts at around 18 months, and by two years is joining hundreds of others in its age group on the "gallops." They learn the basics of balance and speed, and coping with having a rider on top, as they canter and gallop over various distances.

A few races are often run for two-year-olds, when the horse's ability and potential can be assessed. The stride, speed, and precociousness often tell the trainer a lot about how the youngster will develop.

As a three-year-old, the youngster must really show its worth. This is the year when superstars make their mark. Immature and backward horses never get a second chance.

In Britain, there are various centers, such as Lambourn and Newmarket, where the stables surround the tracks (public land for training horses), and these are allocated to trainers for use at certain times. Other yards have their own tracks, which is a great benefit. Many have additional equipment such as swimming pools and treadmills to help with fitness.

In the United States and many other countries, racehorses are stabled in big barns on the track (so they have access to these facilities on a daily basis). Often, whole barns move to follow the circuit around the country in hot climates, returning to winter quarters at the end of the season.

ARAB RACING

Arab racing has always been popular in the Middle East, but has recently caught on in the rest of the world. Special races catering solely to Arabs are now commonplace, with racing at all distances and huge amounts of prize money.

STEEPLECHASING

It takes enormous bravery and courage to become a champion of steeplechase courses such as the world-famous British Grand National. The stakes are high, and horses and jockeys battle it out against the odds to take their place in sporting history.

Steeplechasing came about in Britain in the 18th century as a result of new laws that allowed agricultural land to be fenced in. Hunting was extremely popular, but had previously meant jumping only over streams and ditches in pursuit of quarry. The Enclosure Acts, as they were known, now meant that horses had to negotiate much larger obstacles, such as fences, if they were to keep up with the hounds. Inevitably, the potential for sport was recognized, and before long match races started to take place. The first recorded race took place in Ireland in 1752, over a distance of 4.5 miles (7 km), using church steeples as the most obvious landmarks in the countryside (hence the name steeplechase). In 1807, the *Irish Racing Calendar* used the name of steeplechasing as a sport for the first time.

In 1839, the first Grand Liverpool Steeplechase took place at Aintree. It later became Britain's Grand National, the premier steeplechase in the world. In 1874, the Grand Steeplechase de Paris was set up at Auteuil as the richest race in the world for jumping. Canada first staged its North America Steeplechase in London, Ontario, in 1843, and the following year the first American hurdle race took place in New Jersey. By the turn of the 20th century, steeplechasing had become well and truly established as a sport—with both hurdle and steeplechasing taking place over 2–4 miles (3–6 km) in distance.

THE HORSES

Today, it is usual for steeplechasers to start their careers in hurdle races before progressing on to the bigger fences. In the United States, equine steeplechasers race younger than those in Britain, often starting out as three- or four-year-olds, although five or six is more usual for steeplechasing. While many of the horses are specifically bred for jump racing, others come to it because they have not excelled on the flat. They may have taken longer to mature, so they missed the best flat races or were temperamentally unsuitable at the time, or may have been ruled out by lameness.

Large fields make accuracy and safe jumping vital in steeplechases. Many trainers give their horses extra hunt training before they reach the racecourse to ensure they acquire a safe jumping technique.

FAMOUS STEEPLECHASERS & HURDLERS

The legendary Red Rum won the Grand National three times, and came in second twice (see p. 35). Other superstars include Mill House, the mighty Arkle from Ireland and Desert Orchid—whose five wins in the King George VI Chase captured the heart of the nation.

The United States has had many racing legends too, such as Zaccio—who earned more money than any other steeplechaser between 1979–84. American winners of the Grand National include the diminutive Battleship in 1938; the great Jay Trump in 1965; and Ben Nevis in 1980, already a superb jump horse and double winner of the Maryland Hunt Cup.

Steeplechasers tend to become better known than their flat-race counterparts, mainly because they stay around and race longer. Often, many are still racing at the age of ten or twelve.

Perhaps one of steeplechasing's greatest stories is that of the tiny Mandarin, who won the 1961 Grande Steeplechase de Paris at Auteuil even though his bit broke at the fourth fence. In an extraordinary performance with his jockey, Fred Winter, he managed to complete the remaining 22 fences of this double figure-eight course and carry off the prize.

In Britain, the story of leading jockey Bob Champion and steeplechaser Aldaniti became an inspiration to millions. Due to pair up together for the Grand National in 1979, Champion was diagnosed with cancer and Aldaniti with tendon problems. Against all odds, the pair overcame enormous health problems to score a brilliant win at Aintree in 1981.

Timber racing requires a bold horse and brave rider. Here a big jump is needed on this qualifying course for America's famous Maryland Hunt Cup.

DRIVING

Driving has been a part of human history for centuries. From the days of chariot racing to the relatively recent stagecoach era, driving has always been both a means of transportation and a spectacular sport. The skill required to control a team of horses and a carriage takes years to master. During a trial or race there are many thrills and spills that make it an exciting spectator sport.

Worldwide, driving means a popular sport and recreation activity (and, of course, is still a form of transportation in many less developed countries). Suitable for young and old, horses and ponies, it is also practiced as one of the therapies as part of the Riding for the Disabled program in Britain. For those with a strong sense of competitive spirit, there is an enormous range of events available—from showing and turn-out to obstacle classes and marathons.

DRIVING TRIALS

Probably one of the most exciting and arduous forms of the sport is the driving trials—based on the rules for three-day eventing. The first took place in 1970, in Switzerland, for teams of four horses, although now there are world and European championships which include classes for pairs, tandems, and single horses and ponies.

Like three-day eventing, driving trials comprise three separate competitions held on different days. They are designed to test the various skills required for coachmanship, as well as the quality, ability, and fitness of the horses. The three competitions—dressage, marathon, and obstacle driving—are scored on a penalty system.

Dressage Known as competition A, dressage is the first event. It takes place in a large arena 328 x 131ft (100 x 40m), with three or five judges assessing qualities such as the freedom and regularity of the paces, and the harmony, lightness, and ease of movement. They also observe the accuracy and correct positioning of the horses, presentation, and driving ability. Marks for the movements and assessments are the same as those for a ridden test. A "general impression" mark is given to cover the overall presentation and turn-out.

Marathon Known as Competition B, the marathon involves contestants driving approximately 14–27 miles (22–43km) in about two hours. It is divided into five sections, with two ten-minute compulsory halts. The last section includes eight driving hazards, which are designed to test the fitness, stamina, and general training of the horses, as well as the skill and judgment of pace of the driver.

The obedience and skills of the driver are just as apparent during the intricate movements required in the dressage phase (or competition A) as those shown in the marathon. This Hungarian team are immaculately turned out and look nicely controlled doing this phase before the more strenuous tasks ahead. The fitness and training of the horses are just as vital as those for the ridden horse.

Obstacle driving The last of the competitions, obstacle driving is designed to test the skill of the driver and the obedience and fitness of the horses after the exertions of the previous day. It consists of a driving course around anything up to 20 traffic cones, with balls balanced on top. This simple system shows when a collision has occurred, because if a horse knocks a cone, the ball falls off (so incurring penalties). Penalties are also given for run-outs and verbal help from a groom. "Drive offs" take place between clear rounds over a shortened course (sometimes with water and turns added) for special prizes. Usually, the fastest time wins.

SHOW RING DRIVING

This is particularly popular in Britain, but classes also appear in Canada, the United States, Australia, New Zealand, and South Africa, as well as The Netherlands.

In the United States and Canada, classes for driving turn-outs are basically divided into five sections. Pleasure driving is similar to Britain's private driving. There are also classes for Turn-out, Reinmanship, and Working, and these are all judged on a percentage basis for different performances.

Hackneys were the first driving horses to be established in Britain in 1885, and are still shown today in the official Harness Classes designed for them. They are judged mainly on their movement which must be high and progressive.

Combination or ride and drive Popular in Britain and the United States, these classes involve different draft (draught) horses harnessed to light horse vehicles. Competitions vary greatly, with some sections involving the horses being ridden.

Heavy harness These classes are popular in the United States and Canada. They cover a variety of breeds, including those from Europe, Morgans, roadsters, and Standardbreds, driven English-style to light, conventional four-wheeled carriages.

Private driving These classes are for horses or ponies driven in single, pair, or tandem combinations, with a variety of carts and carriages designed for the driver. Often divided by height and hackney or non-hackney types, classes are judged on the best horse correctly and attractively harnessed to a suitable vehicle.

Light trade These classes are designed for horses and ponies driven to a light-goods vehicle built to deliver merchandise or provisions. Most were built specifically for the trade that they represented. The judges give points according to requirements such as the horses' ability to stand unattended—so vital in their door-to-door delivery rounds.

The hackney, an ancient British breed, is renowned worldwide for its spectacular movement. It is extremely popular for private driving classes, which are often divided into hackney and non-hackney sections.

Concours d'élégance A special attraction, these classes are judged by artists or celebrities interested in the history of horses and driving. Exhibitors are allowed an eye-catching display of elegance and historical correctness.

Surrey Perhaps one of the most appealing driving classes, the Surrey involves ponies driven at speed in four-wheel-drive vehicles in what are basically mini-obstacle competitions. Styles vary according to different countries, but competitors from The Netherlands and Hungary are particularly successful in international championships.

The marathon phase of Driving Trials is extremely exciting and demands great skill by the driver and fitness and versatility from the horses. During this phase, the referee sits in the vehicle to judge each contestant at the obstacles. One miscalculation can mean a disaster that results in damage to vehicle or harness. It takes great tact and control to keep upset horses calm while such problems are straightened out.

HARNESS RACING

Speed and exhilaration are the hallmarks of this sport (based on the chariot races of ancient Rome and Greece), which is (almost) as thrilling for the spectators as the competitors themselves.

With hooves pounding around the track to the finish line, these "chariots of fire" make a fantastic spectacle. Small wonder the sport is so popular around the world, from Italy to Australia, from Spain to the United States. The prize money is often enormous—as is the amount of gambling the sport attracts.

Harness racing involves a lightweight, two-wheeled sulky (cart) built especially for speed. There is one reinsman (or driver), who races the horse around an oval track—either trotting or pacing. Trotting is the natural two-beat gait, which uses diagonal pairs of legs. Pacing is an artificial two-beat gait, where horses use their legs in lateral pairs. Pacing is a trained gait, especially for harness racing, although now horses have been bred that are able to pace from birth. Some champions are capable of either trotting or pacing.

TYPES OF RACE

Separate races are held for each gait. Both types are held in most countries, although these days pacing is more popular and the times are slightly faster. There are also national variations—in France, for example, some trotting races can be ridden as well as driven. In the United States, there is a slightly different starting procedure to Europe. Americans use the moving "autostart," which clears out of the way once the horses have crossed the starting line. In Europe, on the other hand, horses warm up for three minutes on an adjacent track, then have to move across to a fixed starting point—which is usually an elastic starting tape. American races are shorter too—generally about 1 mile (1.6km)—with narrow tracks catering to about eight horses at a time. In Europe, races can be 1.6–1.9 miles (2.6–3.1km) or more, and consist of up to 10 horses. There is also a handicap system in Europe.

In harness racing, horses must not break the gait. If so, they are penalized by being "distanced" or placed last in Europe or, if finishing among the leaders, put one place behind. In either case, the driver must pull to the side of the track to resume a proper gait.

Trotters may break gait for many reasons, such as un-balance, excitement, or fatigue. With pacing, special hobbles help to keep the gait established. Protective boots are used to protect the horses, especially on the inside of the knee—a particularly vulnerable area at such speed.

Harness races are breathtaking to watch because of the sheer speed and thumping of the horses on the dirt tracks. The prize money is equally spectacular.

EQUIPMENT

Over the last 100 years, the sulky has changed from a high-wheeled heavy vehicle to an ultra-light steel or aluminum racing machine with shorter shafts and smaller wheels. The spokes are covered with plastic discs, for safety reasons, and the shafts can be adjusted to suit the breadth of the horse. All control is maintained through the reins, as the driver sits low down with his or her feet secured fairly high in fixed stirrups.

The choice of bit varies, but the bridle also consists of a head pole and check rein, which encourage the horse to keep its head high and remain in the gait. A shadow roll across the nose helps to prevent spooking, as it limits the horse's view of the track. Another trick is to stuff the horse's ears with cotton (cotton wool) to help deafen the noise of spectators. Any startling as the horse turns to the finish could cause a momentary drop in speed. The shoes are also important, as they can affect balance and extension. The farrier can assist by calculating where to put a little more weight in the heel or toe.

The lateral gait of the pacer is easy to see in this picture. Some horses learn to go equally fast in both gaits, but more often than not they are trained either as a trotter or a pacer. Leg protection is important as injury could easily occur at such speed.

Horse sports are very popular in St. Moritz and none more so than trotting races. Goggles are essential to protect the driver from the snow flying from thundering hooves.

INTERNATIONAL COMPETITIONS

In the United States, where the prize money often reaches staggering proportions, breeders have spent more than a century establishing bloodlines suitable for harness racing. The imported English Thoroughbred Messenger, for example, was influential in producing several good trotting horses in the early 1800s. His great-grandson, Hambletonian, was crossed with Morgans and other suitable breeds to produce the Standardbred so successful in trotting today. Thanks to the efforts of an Iowa farmer, John H. Wallace, the Standardbred studbook became established in 1867.

Today, the most famous harness races in the United States are The Yonkers Trot, The Hambletonian, and the Kentucky Futurity, which make up The Triple Crown for trotters. For pacers, The Messenger Stakes, The Cave Futurity, and The Little Brown Jug make up the trio. International races to which foreigners are invited include The Yonkers Challenge Cup and The Roosevelt International. The French have been almost as successful as the Americans in this latter event, which is an unofficial world championship.

In France, the Prix d'Amerique, the Prix de France and the Prix de Paris are the big races under harness, and the Prix de Coinulier is for those under saddle. Some have won big races both in harness and in saddle, perhaps the most famous being Tidalin Palo in 1971 and 1972. This amazingly tough horse overcame several injuries that would have finished the careers of many, including the ghastly experience of being abandoned in a box car (railroad freight wagon) in the middle of winter when returning from a successful campaign in Italy. Eventually rescued almost dead from cold and hunger, he was found standing protectively over the body of his companion, Roc Williams, who had frozen to death during the experience.

VAULTING

Gymnastics and riding come together in this unusual equestrian pastime. The ideal is a graceful communion of the performing rider or riders and the horse moving fluidly in a continuous walk or canter throughout. To make these gymnastic feats while in motion appear so effortless takes a great deal of practice and dedication.

In Europe, vaulting or "voltige" is an accepted means of introduction to the horse. Riding may be too expensive or difficult in urban areas or where facilities are limited, but by joining a voltige class, people are able to enjoy the contact with horses and feel the rhythm and balance necessary for riding at little cost. Basically vaulting is a form of gymnastics on horseback, riders learn such things as the art of somersaulting away and landing. The balance and poise that come with voltige stand riders in good stead for the rest of their lives.

For voltige, the horse must be calm and tough, with a smooth, even canter, and ideally have a fairly flat, broad back. It must be trained to go consistently on the lunge and remain in an easy, forward rhythm. It must have a good-natured temperament and not react to outside influences or to the antics of the riders. It will require approximately six months of training to become accustomed both mentally and physically to the role intended. It is important that the horse is ridden regularly in between vaulting sessions to keep up fitness.

SPECIAL EQUIPMENT

The vaulting roller is the vital piece of specialist equipment required. This consists of a specially adapted roller with padding and two hand grips, one on either side of the withers. It may also have a loop attached between the two grips for holding. Foot loops are also usual. There should be enough padding to protect the horse but not so much that the roller is in danger of slipping around. A horse with a good wither is important.

A bridle with a simple snaffle should be comfortable and suitable. Side reins, a lunge rein, and a large whip long enough to be able to reach the back legs are important. Bandages or boots on the horse are a wise precaution.

The rider simply needs to wear comfortable sports clothes and sneakers with flexible soft soles.

It is important that the area for vaulting is safe and that the surface is constant and suitable, not slippery or deep.

GETTING STARTED

Vaulters must start by warming up well with floor work, running, stretching, and exercises on a wooden horse, if available. The horse must also be worked to ensure that it is settled and well loosened up. Exercises on the horse are done in the walk or canter. No canter session should continue for more than ten minutes without a break at the walk.

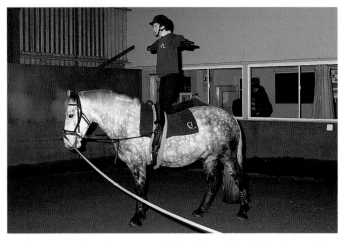

Finding one's balance becomes a priority when vaulting. This photograph shows a student learning the technique at a riding therapy center.

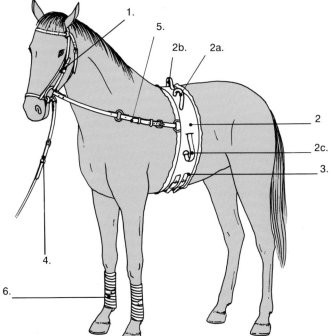

The horse ready for vaulting in bridle and lunge rein and vaulting roller (surcingle) and pad. Protective boots and bandages on the legs should also be used.

1. Snaffle bridle.
2. Surcingle—a padded roller girth around two hand grips (2a), a loop for holding on to (2b), and two foot loops (2c) for standing positions. The surcingle must not rest on the withers.
3. Pad—underneath surcingle.
4. Lunge rein.
5. Two side reins.
6. Bandages or boots.

BASIC EXERCISES

Position The vaulter's outstretched arms should form a straight line from the shoulders through the upper arms to the fingertips. The optimum height for the top of the hand is level with the eyes and ears. The shoulders should be free from tension and not drawn upward. The head should be free from tension, and the upper body erect. This is called the basic sitting position (basic seat).

Vaulting on The vaulter must run parallel to the horse and take hold of the grips, cantering in time with the horse's fore legs and looking straight ahead. After a couple of strides, the vaulter must swing the right leg up high over the horse's back while keeping the left stretched down. The hips should be swung up as high as possible, with the body forward and the weight supported on the arms. Once sitting, vaulters should pull themselves close into the surcingle with the head high, so they are ready to start any exercise.

Vaulting off Starting from the upright position, both legs are carried forward and then swung high in the air to the rear in one athletic, flowing movement. The legs are brought together and then swung to the nearside, with the arms being used to push off and away from the horse. The vaulter should land with bent knees and ankles to absorb the impact.

Dismounting Starting in the upright position, the right leg is stretched out and carried high over the horse's neck in a semi-circle to the inside. Keeping the upper body erect and as vertical as possible, the vaulter pushes off from the horse, landing softly with bent knees and ankles. With all landings, the vaulter should run out in the direction of the movement.

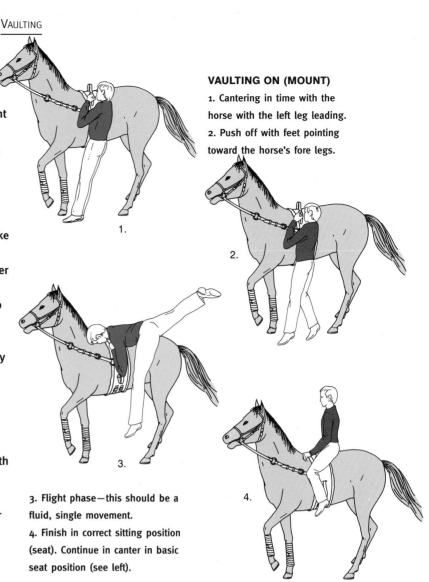

VAULTING ON (MOUNT)
1. Cantering in time with the horse with the left leg leading.
2. Push off with feet pointing toward the horse's fore legs.

1.

2.

3.

4.

3. Flight phase—this should be a fluid, single movement.
4. Finish in correct sitting position (seat). Continue in canter in basic seat position (see left).

At top level, riders perform amazing gymnastic feats while the horse canters in a steady rhythm throughout.

THE SITTING POSITION

There are various criteria for determining the correctness of the basic positions. The correct sitting position is shown with a straight line from the ear through the hip and the heel. Any movements should only be performed with your trainer who will keep the horse moving at a suitable speed. Practice makes perfect and all exercises will require some time to master.

ADVANCED WORK

All vaulting practice work should be supervised by an instructor. Once the basics have been mastered, vaulters can progress to the more difficult exercises that feature in competitions. Examples are: flag (flare)—kneeling on the horse with one leg outstretched; and around the world—turning around to face backward and then continuing around back to the starting position.

In competitions, there are single, pairs, or group sections, and there is a set format on how these are performed and judged. The trainer is vitally important to the success of individuals or teams, and hours of training are necessary to get to the top level. However, for many, vaulting may be the only opportunity of ever getting on a horse.

THE PONY CLUB AND GYMKHANAS

Ponies and fun go hand-in-hand, and nowhere is this more apparent than in Pony Club games and gymkhanas. Learning through play encourages horsemanship and team spirit, so that the sack-race champion of today could be the Olympic eventer of tomorrow.

The Pony Club was started in Britain in 1929 as a junior section of the British Horse Society. Its aim was to produce responsible riders who not only knew how to ride but also how to take care of their mounts properly. In 1953, the U.S. Pony Club Inc. was set up, and this was soon followed by similar organizations in Australia, New Zealand, and France. Today, there are more than 20 countries that have adopted the idea, and 100,000 members worldwide.

Learning through fun is one of the themes, and children are encouraged to participate in all the usual equestrian disciplines—dressage, eventing, and showjumping. Members

also hunt, ride in hunter trials, learn road safety, and participate in the myriad of gymkhana games.

Learning rallies and Pony Club camps are held throughout the year. There is a system of proficiency tests, which is structured to ensure a high standard of knowledge in all aspects of riding and horse care at the different levels.

GYMKHANAS

For many children, the most important aspect of Pony Club membership lies in the gymkhana games—a weird and wonderful array of events played as team sports. In Britain, qualifying rallies held throughout the year culminate in the highly prized Prince Philip Cup, the final of which is a highlight of the Horse of the Year Show. In 1985, a similar event was started in the United States, with its final at the National Horse Show. There is also an international program, in which teams from Britain, the United States, and Canada compete against each other. International rules have been formed by the Mounted Games Association.

The Pony Club aside, most local shows also run their own gymkhana games throughout the summer—with no membership requirements. Once you know when and where the show is to be held (usually through posters or advertisements), all you have to do is send off a stamped self-addressed envelope to the secretary for details of the events (known as the schedule). When you receive the schedule, you simply fill in the show form with the details of which classes you'd like to take part in, and send it off with the entry money before the closing date. Sometimes you don't have to make advance entries for gymkhana games, in which case you just show up and enter on the day.

Gymkhana games are divided into different age groups, and offer something for everyone. Even beginners can find at least one class they can enter. Leading-rein games (where competitors have to be led) enable very young children or nervous riders (up to the age of about eight) the chance to compete.

In the United States the word Gymkhana is most often used in relation to three western events: barrel racing, pole bending, and stake racing (each of which involves horses moving around poles).

Gymkhana games are enormously popular with children and not only teach gamesmanship and competitiveness but help with the coordination, confidence and balance so essential for all forms of riding. This photograph demonstrates all these positive aspects.

THE GAMES

The word gymkhana means equestrian gymnastics in Hindu, and was derived from games practiced by soldiers going back centuries. All modern games are based on similar principles of chasing or polo-type events, although today's organizers are always inventing new events. Modern favorites include:

Bending Competitors race in and out of a line of poles, a game that requires precision, balance, and coordination.

Sack races This involves galloping to a line of sacks, jumping off, then getting inside one, and hobbling with the pony to the finishing line.

Apple bobbing Usually, this involves galloping to a line of buckets in which apples are placed (often in water). The rider dismounts, picks one up without the use of hands (invariably in the teeth), then remounts and gallops back to the finish.

Musical poles This game may involve riders trotting around the outside of a circle of poles to music. When the music stops, the riders have to dash in and claim one. A pole is removed on each occasion, and the rider left with no pole is eliminated.

Egg and spoon Such races help the riders with coordination and balance.

Bending races are firm favorites, though passing the baton is not that easy as it requires balance and good judgement of distance.

TRAINING

Practice develops the skill and coordination of the rider for all the various gymkhana events, but good training and understanding of the pony's needs is also a vital part of mounted games.

The pony must be taught to stand still at a given point—an essential in games where something has to be picked up, secured, or put down. Eventually, the animal must be trained to canter and gallop up to a point, then stand. Often it is necessary for one or both hands to be used to tackle some problems, so the pony must learn to stay still—then respond quickly afterward.

Suppleness to perform bending races and make quick turns is vital to success. Correct schooling on the flat, so that the pony reacts to the rider's weight and slightest aids, will save valuable seconds. Stopping, starting, and turning must be practiced regularly.

The rider must be able to vault on and off the pony nimbly and safely. Practice regularly, grabbing the mane and swinging the right leg up over the saddle and settling into position.

Always remember to warm your pony up properly in a steady trot and canter before asking it to do anything tiring or difficult. Allow it to adjust to the work without strain. Ponies need to have had several weeks of fitness work before being expected to gallop and play strenuous games.

The earlier you can start in the saddle the better and easier it will be to master riding in all its forms.

OTHER SPORTS

The relationship between horse and rider has been a special bond for centuries, even millennia. This partnership has led to the development of numerous varieties of equine sports—enjoyed by riders, horses and spectators alike.

The following is a brief outline of some of the popular sports enjoyed around the world, which all display this special partnership.

POINT-TO-POINTS

In Britain, at the more amateur level of steeplechasing, point-to-point races are run by the hunts. To be eligible, horses have to appear on the hunting field on regular occasions until they are considered "qualified," and receive a certificate enabling registration to race.

Point-to-points in Britain take place after Christmas until the end of the spring. They are hotly contested, and usually take the form of a course of natural and chase fences over ordinary farmland countryside. There are races for members of adjacent hunts, opens, maidens, and ladies' events. Often, good point-to-pointers graduate on to the steeplechase scene if they show promise after a season.

TEAM CHASING

Another popular sport is team chasing. Again, mostly run by the hunts. There are generally two classes, novice and open. The event consists of teams of four galloping around a course more like a cross-country event than a steeplechase. It may be

Hunting has taken place for centuries with the quarry generally being the fox, deer, or wild boar. Horses and riders need to be fit as a full day's hunting may involve six to eight hours in the saddle.

judged on speed or a bogey time, and many courses include one or two knock-down fences carrying penalties. The team with the lowest score wins.

HUNTING

Hunting has existed since time immemorial, and is the oldest surviving sport on horseback. It is just one of the many leisure pursuits available to lovers of horses.

Today, hunting flourishes as never before, although modern farming methods and animal-rights lobbyists have caused restrictions in certain areas. Still enormously popular in Britain and Ireland, it has an enthusiastic following in France, the United States, Canada, and Australia.

Foxes, hares, or stags are the usual quarry. By far the most prolific is the fox, and there are over 240 packs of foxhounds in Britain alone. In France, wild boar are also hunted in the great forests. Coyote is the quarry in parts of the United States —especially in the western regions, where there are few foxes. In Australia, kangaroos are hunted, as well as other quarry.

THE HUNT

The sport is run under strict rules laid down by the Master of the Foxhounds Association. The master of the foxhounds, or MFH, is the person in charge of the hunt's affairs. Many packs have two or three, as well as whippers-in (who help to control the hounds). The field master is in charge of "the field"—the mounted followers—and makes sure that everyone adheres to the country code of closing gates, keeping off crops, and

courtesy on the roads, and deals with any accidents that may occur. The hunt secretary has the job of looking after the finances as well as handling much of the public relations, fund-raising, and day-to-day matters involving the members.

THE DAY'S SPORT

The day starts with "the meet," when everyone arrives at a pre-designated point. When it is time to begin, the Master and hounds move off to the first "cover," where it is expected that a fox might be found, with the hunt followers (usually) behind. If the fox is to be encouraged out in a certain direction, the field may be asked to line one side of the covert to ensure it does not run the wrong way. It is in everyone's interests to keep away from main roads, railroad lines and urban environments, if possible.

Once a fox gets away and the hounds find the scent, the chase is on. The master keeps up with the hounds and the field have to follow as best they can across country. "A check" is when the hounds lose the scent and need time to cast around. There are various "calls" on the hunting horn, which indicate such moments as "gone away."

A "run" can last for anything from half-an-hour to all day. If the scent is lost, the hunt master will lead the pack to another covert where a new fox may be raised.

An artificial alternative to hunting, with no live quarry, is drag hunting. This takes place around a pre-designated route, often with bloodhounds following an aniseed trail. While in no way as exciting as the real thing, it can be a fun way of following the hounds in areas where real hunting is impractical, or for people who don't care to follow live quarry.

SHOWING

Showing is derived from the original country horse fairs, where working, driving, and riding horses were judged by experts—then bought and sold. Today, showing is a huge industry, particularly in Britain, the United States, South Africa, and Australia. Showing caters to every type and breed of horse and pony, whether ridden or in-hand and is concerned with the individual animal's conformation—whether it displays the desirable qualities of the type or breed. The sport element comes in the "ringmanship" or "showmanship" of the individual competitor, who must know the correct method of presentation before the judges for each class to achieve any success.

The American Horse Shows Association governs the wide variety of classes in the United States, ranging from the hunter divisions, western, saddle horses, and Hackneys, to jumper classes and equitation. Various clubs and associations also organize relevant classes for the different breeds, such as Appaloosas, Quarter Horses, and Standardbreds.

In Britain, many independent horse shows are affiliated with various societies, and classes may be held on their behalf. Some of these classes are qualifying rounds leading up to the two biggest events in the showing calendar—the Royal International and the Horse of the Year Show.

OTHER EQUESTRIAN ACTIVITIES

There are many other equestrian activities that take place around the world, such as riding vacations, riding safaris, and pony-trekking. Other sports that are starting to become popular include handball, a type of mounted hockey.

There are sponsored rides for the less energetic, which involve a jaunt through the countryside (with or without jumps), while raising money for charity. Equestrian fun days and get-togethers of all sorts ensure that there is always something somewhere that will appeal to every type of horse lover.

Fancy dress classes are always popular with children and here at Britain's Windsor Horse Show, disabled riders in magnificent outfits take part.

▶ Players use bamboo cane mallets of varying lengths, weights, and flexibility, always played in the right hand. The head is made of hardwood and is cigar-shaped. Players use the side of the head to strike the ball. They usually have anything from ten to 20 mallets for use with different-sized ponies, depending on their positions.
◀ The players wear white breeches, long brown boots, protective helmets with chin straps, and a team jersey with their numbered position displayed.

The fast and furious game of polo is highly popular, particularly in America, Argentina, and Britain. Ponies and players require balance and split-second timing to be effective.

POLO

This adrenalin-charged racing sport is the oldest and fastest stick-and-ball game in the world. A version of it is known to have been played in around 600B.C. in China and Persia's royal courts. The name is thought to derive from the Tibetan word "pulu," meaning willow root, from which the ball was made (now it's more likely to be a plastic substrate).

The game was rediscovered during the British Raj in India, around 1850 and used as an excellent method of training cavalry soldiers. A modified version of the game was set up, and the first polo club was formed in Kashmir in 1859.

The first game on British soil was played between the 10th Hussars and 9th Lancers. The Hurlingham Club was founded in 1875 and went on to become the Hurlingham Polo Association (which now governs the sport).

Polo found its way to the United States in 1876, when a wealthy newspaper owner and renowned sportsman, James Gordon, brought a truckload of polo equipment to New York. Gordon and his friends then founded the Westchester Polo Club.

It is in Argentina, however, that polo is an all-consuming passion and national pastime. Boys learn the rudiments of the game at a very early age, and thousands of ponies are bred on *estancias* especially for the sport. The greatest polo ponies in the world are produced in Argentina, and they are sought after by every polo-playing nation.

HANDICAPS

The game has a handicapping system in which individual players are rated according to their performances. This is run on a scale of minus one (or minus two in Britain) to ten. By matching team totals or by crediting lesser-rated teams with a goal advantage, even matches are made up.

The games are also rated into three levels of play: low goal, medium goal, and high goal. To be eligible for the standard of play, the individual scores of the four members of the team are added together. Teams with a total score of 0–6 can only play in a low-goal match. To play in a medium-goal match, the team needs a total score of 9–16. To play high goal, the pinnacle of the sport, teams need a score of 16–20 and up.

THE PONIES

The "ponies," usually 15–15.2hh (150–152 cm) in height, are undoubtedly what make the game. Every one requires patient training to be able to cope with the rider's twisting and turning to perform the different movements necessary to hit the ball. The ponies must stay straight at all times, only responding when the rider asks. They must be quick and agile to stop, turn, and accelerate when required. Tough, wiry, fast, and very strong, these amazing animals are highly intelligent. Many learn to watch the ball and help the players by their quick-wittedness.

THE GAME

The polo field is 300 yards (274m) long and 200 yards (184m) wide, with two goalposts in the middle of either end. The two teams, made up of four players, await the referee to throw in the willow root or plastic ball, then the game commences.

The game is divided into "chukkas," periods of seven-and-a-half minutes with three-minute intervals in between. At half time there is a five-minute break, when spectators are invited onto the field to stamp down the divots (clumps of turf). Most low and medium-goal games consist of four chukkas, but at high-goal level there are six or even eight. If there is a tied score at the end, there is a "sudden death" chukka after a five-minute break, where the first team to score wins the match.

OTHER FORMS OF POLO

Modified versions of the game are also played most notably in the United States and Australia. In the U.S., one version involves only three players (numbers two and three are combined) in the team and a smaller playing area—often an indoor stadium. Generally, it is much slower, and an ideal introduction to the sport.

In Australia, a completely new version of polo has emerged. Called polo-crosse, it is a combination of polo, lacrosse, and netball. Although it originated from remote stations and farms in the outback using working horses for leisure, this is now an established Australian sport.

WESTERN SHOW CLASSES

There are numerous show classes, all derived from the practical use of the working horse. The American Quarter Horse Association has its own shows and classes, but various specialist associations and breed societies have Western riding classes worldwide with their own variation on these. Apart from the American Quarter Horse, Palominos, Appaloosas, as well as Arabs, are all popular for western showing.

TRAIL

In the trail class, the horse must be obedient and calm during provocation, and cope intelligently with three mandatory obstacles. These consist of a gate which msut be opened and closed; a minimum of four logs, which must be ridden over; and an obstacle which requires backing through or around. Other tests may include water, stepping through obstacles, hobbling the horse, and mailing letters. The horse's paces and fluence throughout are taken into account during the class.

WESTERN PLEASURE

These are perhaps the most popular events, and Western Pleasure classes are ideal for beginners (although at the top level the standard is extremely high). The horse must be a pleasure to ride at the walk, jog, and lope (canter), on a fairly loose rein, and it should demonstrate its obedience and smoothness of action.

There is something available for everyone who enjoys horses, whether trail riding, showing horses in traditional costume or going on a riding safari or equestrian tour. Some people enjoy owning them for others to ride or compete with so that they can just go and watch the fun.

The cutting horse, though specially trained, has an inbuilt instinct about separating particular identified calves from the herd. The rider must sit and stay with the horse's movement without interfering once he or she has indicated to the horse which calf to take.

WESTERN RIDING

Western riding tests the all-round training of the ranch horse, proving it to be versatile, well-mannered, and comfortable while performing various obstacles and a set "pattern" (course). This starts in the walk and finishes with a rein back.

REINING

Reining is the western version of dressage at speed, demanding a high degree of training from the rider; it must be performed in a fluid and smooth manner. Lead changes, transitions, timing, and gait changes are all performed with imperceivable aids from the rider. Patterns include all the western school movements—spins, rollbacks, sliding stops, slow and fast circles. In the United States, the National Reining Horse Association organizes many of the contests—including the Futurity show, which has a purse of several hundred thousand dollars in prize money.

CUTTING

Cutting is the chance for the horse to show its paces, speed, and agility in a series of skills based on the art of "cutting" on a ranch. The horse and rider approach a herd of cattle and, once one calf has been selected, it has to be "cut out" from the rest by the horse—without any assistance from the rider. Penalties are given if the calf escapes. Two-and-a-half minutes are given to perform this. Many do it well within the time and have the chance to cut out another calf. Prize money for cutting contests is among the largest for any equestrian sport in the world.

WORKING COW HORSE

The working cow horse event is designed to show the versatility of the general ranch horse, and is divided into two sections—reining and cattle working. The scores are added together to determine the overall winner.

The Stock Horse is Australia's answer to the American Cow Pony. It is tough and versatile and often covers huge distances on the ranch.

RODEO

Based on techniques perfected by the Mexican vacqueros, American rodeos were originally organized by cowboys to entertain themselves and their families in their spare time. Nowadays, rodeo has become a full-blown sport with huge pay checks for the successful professionals. However, it is dangerous, and offers an uncertain livelihood.

Rodeo has six basic competitive events:

Saddle brave riding This is based on the rough and tough methods used by early cowboys to "break" wild horses, and is considered one of the most demanding events. The cowboy must try to remain on a bucking horse for eight seconds, with only a plaited rein for security.

Bareback riding Perhaps the most dangerous of the riding contests, as there is only a hand-hold for support and the horse's head is left free. Tremendous balance and strength in the riding arm is required to remain on board.

Bull riding The danger of a 2,000lb (900kg) steer being ridden while it twists and turns, bucks and leaps, requires a tough attitude as well as quick reflexes and coordination.

Steer wrestling This event is performed with two cowboys, two horses and a steer, and the contestant. The cowboys chase the steer on horseback, then the contestant dismounts onto the steer and deftly brings it down.

Calf roping Cooperation between horse and rider is required to catch the calf. The rope is thrown after the calf and, once settled over its head, the horse comes to a quick

Rodeos, the cowboys' and cowgirls' favorite form of entertainment, are also hugely popular with ordinary spectators.

stop. The horse takes up the slack on the rope as the cowboy or girl dismounts to tie three legs of the calf. It must remain tied for six seconds.

Barrel racing Involves racing around three barrels in a clover-leaf formation. Speed and agility are particularly important, and American Quarter Horses are usually outstanding in this event.

With so much to see, do and choose from within the world of horses, it is hoped that this book has given the reader a greater understanding of this much loved and written about animal. It would take a lifetime to get to know even half of what there is to know about the horse, but it is fair to say that our lives would be the poorer if they were not around. As a pet, challenge and means of recreation, there can be few animals who give such pleasure and to whom we owe so much.

Calf roping shows the skill of both rider and horse, working together in harmony as a team.

GLOSSARY

Against the clock In show jumping — a competition or jump off decided by time, the winner being the competitor with the least number of faults in the fastest time.

Aid Signals used by a rider to give instructions to the horse, through his seat, legs, and hands.

Airs Movements, usually found in formal dressage, which are other than the normal walk, trot, and canter.

All-rounder A horse or pony which is very good at everything.

Amble A slow gait in two time in which the horse's hind and foreleg on the same side are moved forward together.

Arena The area in which a horse show or show jumping competition is held.

Artificial aids Items such as whips, spurs, and martingales which are used by the rider to help convey instructions to the horse.

Backing the horse To mount a horse for the first time.

Bit A device, normally made from metal or rubber, attached to the bridle and placed in the horse's mouth to help control its pace and direction.

Bloodline The sequence of direct ancestors, especially in a pedigree.

Bloodstock Thoroughbred horses that are bred for racing.

Blue feet Horn that is dense and blue-black in color.

Bosal A simple, bitless noseband made from rawhide.

Breastplate A device, normally made from leather, attached to the saddle to prevent it from slipping back on the horse.

Bridle A part of the horse's saddlery or harness which is placed about the head.

Cannons The lower part of the horse's legs between the fetlocks and the knees or hocks.

Cantle The upward projecting rear part of the saddle.

Carriage horse An elegant horse used for carriage-driving, usually with Thoroughbred in its ancestry.

Chaff Meadow hay or green oat straw cut into short lengths for use as a foodstuff.

Cheekpiece (a) The leather part of the bridle to which the bit is attached at one end and the headpiece at the other. (b) Side pieces of a bit to which the reins are attached.

Chestnuts (a) Small piece of horn on the inside of the horse's legs. (b) Bright brown coat color.

Chukka A period of play in polo lasting seven and a half or eight minutes, depending on which country the game is being played in.

Cinch (girth) (a) The circumference of the horse or pony, from behind the withers around the deepest part of the body. (b) A band made from leather, nylon, or webbing, passed under the belly of the horse to hold the saddle in place.

Cob A type rather than a breed. A short legged animal with a maximum height of 15hh (150 cm) with the bone and substance of a heavyweight hunter and capable of carrying a substantial weight.

Coldblood A horse, not a pony, of heavy, common or "cart" blood.

Colic Sharp abdominal pains, often with the symptom of flatulence; an obstruction created by a mass of hard food, or feces in the bowel, which can lead to a twisted gut.

Collection Shortening the pace by a light contact from the rider's hands and a steady pressure with the legs to make the horse flex its neck, relax its jaw, and bring its hocks well under so that it is properly balanced.

Colt An ungelded male horse less than four years old.

Colostrum The first milk that the foal drinks from the dam, rich in vital antibodies.

Condition The state of physical fitness and health of the horse or pony.

Conformation A horse's make-up and shape. The basic requirement is symmetry — the horse should look balanced.

Corn Bruising of the sole in the angle between the wall of the hoof and the heel.

Cow horse The horse which a cowboy rides while working cattle.

Crupper A leather loop which passes under the horse's tail and is buckled to the saddle.

Curb bit A type of bit used in conjunction with a snaffle bit in a double bridle with a curb chain.

Curb chain A metal chain which is fitted to the hook of a curb or pelham bit and lies in the curb groove of the horse's jaw.

Cutting horse A horse especially trained for separating selected cattle from a herd.

Dam The female parent of a foal.

Deep seat A good seated position on the saddle, but sitting slightly heavier than an independent seat.

Dirt track A racetrack, the surface of which is a combination of sand and soil — common in the USA.

Dished face A profile which appears slightly concave between the eyes and nostrils. Highly regarded in Arabs.

DMSO (Dimethyl sulfoxide) A substance used as medication to treat bruises and strains.

Dorsal eel stripe Found usually in dun-colored animals, this is a continuous strip of black, brown, or dun hair, running from the neck to the tail.

Double bridle A bridle consisting of two bits, a curb and a snaffle, which are attached by means of two cheekpieces and may be used independently.

Doubles In show jumping, a combination of obstacles consisting of two separate jumps.

Draft (draught) Refers to a horse drawing any type of vehicle.

Dressage The art of training horses to perform movements in a balanced, supple, obedient, and enthusiastic manner.

Driving Refers to the horse being hitched to a carriage, with the driver sitting on the carriage and controlling the horse by the means of long reins.

Equine (a) Of, or pertaining to, the horse. (b) The term used for the horse.

Extension The leg positions and gait of the horse.

Farrier A person who make horseshoes and shoes horses — often called a blacksmith.

Feather Copious hair around the fetlocks or entire lower legs.

Fender (Stirrup leather) The adjustable strap by which the stirrup iron is attached to the saddle.

Filly A female horse less than four years old.

Flexion The yielding of the lower jaw to the pressure of the bit; at the same time the neck is high and arched, and bent at the poll.

Foal A young horse up to the age of twelve months.

Forehand The part of the horse which is in front of the rider, that is, the head, neck, shoulders, withers, and forelegs.

Fox trot A gait in which the horse walks with the front feet and trots with the hind, the hind legs stepping into the foreprints and sliding forwards.

Frog The rubbery pad of horn on the underside of the hoof which acts as a shock absorber.

Gait The horse's basic movements in action. Natural gaits are walk, trot, canter, and gallop; artificial ones are the running walk, fox trot, amble, and broken amble.

Gaited horse An American term for a saddle or riding horse which can perform artificial as well as natural gaits. A three-gaited horse must show walk, trot, and canter. A five-gaited horse must also show a slow gait and a fast rack.

Gelding A male horse which has been castrated.

Groom (a) Any person who is responsible for looking after a horse. (b) To clean the coat and feet of a horse.

Gymkhana Mounted games, most frequently for children under sixteen.

Half halt The rider prepares to halt by sitting up and using the reins, but pushes the horse forward again just before stopping.

Half pass A dressage movement where the horse travels both forward and sideways in the direction of travel.

Halter (Headcollar) A hemp rope headpiece with lead rope attached, used for leading a horse when not wearing a bridle, or for tying up in the stable.

Hand A linear measurement equaling 4in (10 cm) used in giving the height of a horse.

Handicap (a) The weight allocated to a horse in a race. (b) A race in which the weights to be carried by the horse are estimated so as to give each horse an equal chance of winning.

Harness The equipment of a draft (draught) animal.

Harness horse A horse used for driving in harness rather than under saddle.

Haute Ecole/**High School** The so-called classical method of riding, practiced in many countries, said to descend from the simple, natural principles evolved particularly by the ancient Greeks. Refined and developed in the 17th and 18th centuries, *Haute Ecole* is today perpetuated most famously by the Spanish Riding School in Vienna, Austria, and the Cadre Noir at Saumur, France.

Haylage Stored forage.

Headpiece Any equipment — headstall, headcollar — worn on a horse's head.

Headstall Part of the bridle that encircles the horse's head.

Heavy horse A horse of muscular build, often tall and very strong, and best suited to heavy transportation, forestry, or agricultural work.

Hocks The region in the hind leg which corresponds to the ankle of humans, but which in the horse is elevated and bent backwards.

Hotblood Horses of desert or steppe ancestry. Normally taken as being the pure Thoroughbred or Arab breed.

Hunter A horse bred and trained to be ridden for hunting.

Hunt The sport of following different types of hound in pursuit of fox, stag, hare, or an artificial scent.

Hunting The sport of following different types of hound, either mounted or on foot in pursuit of the fox, the stag, or the hare or an artificially laid drag line if drag hunting.

Independent seat The ability to maintain a firm, balanced position on a horse's back without relying on the hands for security.

In-hand Any of various show classes in which the animals are led, usually in a show bridle or headcollar, but otherwise without saddlery (except for draft [draught] horses which are often shown in their harness) and are judged chiefly for conformation and/or condition.

In season The state of sexual readiness during which the mare is ready to conceive.

Jog A short-paced trot.

Knee roll Any bandages applied to the horse's legs.

Lateral work Dressage movements such as the half halt, counter canter and flying lead.

Lead rope A rope attached to a halter for leading a horse.

Leathers (a) Pieces of leather attached to the stirrup. (b) Slang for leather shoes worn to protect a horse's hooves while healing.

Leg yielding One of the first dressage movements to be learned whereby the horse moves forward and sideways away from the rider's leg.

Leg up A helping hand or boost into the saddle.

Livery stable An establishment where privately owned horses are kept, exercised, and generally looked after, for an agreed fee. Called Livery in the USA.

Loins The kidney are just behind the saddle.

Long in the back Excessive length of a horse's back, desirable in some breeds, undesirable in others.

Long-reining Training the unmounted horse in a paddock, using a long rein.

Lope The natural gait of the horse which resembles a canter.

Lunge rein A long, strong piece of webbing which used in training horses.

Mane The long hair growing at the top of the horse's head and down the neck.

Mare A female equine four years old or over.

Martingale A device used to help prevent the horse's head going out of the point of control. Consists of a strap attached to the cinch (girth) coming through the front legs and attached to the noseband (standing martingale) or by rings to the reins (running martingale).

Mealy nose or **mealy muzzle** Pale or oatmeal color of muzzle/nose typical of such breeds as the Exmoor.

Muck out (Skip out) To clean out a box or stall in which a horse has been staled removing the droppings and soiled bedding.

Muzzle The projecting jaw and nose of the horse or pony.

Natural aids The body, hands, legs and voice as used by the rider to give instructions to the horse.

Nearside The left-hand side of a horse. This is the side from which it is usual to mount a horse.

Neck rein To direct the horse using the pressure of the reins on the neck.

Neck strap A strap which goes around the horse's neck to prevent the rider pulling on the horse's mouth. Useful for beginners.

Noseband The part of a bridle which lies across the horse's nose consisting of a leather band on an independent head piece. There are four main types — Cavesson, drop, grakle (cross over), and flash. Designed to prevent the horse opening its mouth and crossing its jaw.

Numnah A pad placed under the saddle to prevent undue pressure on the horse's back. Cut to the shape of the saddle or in square pad form.

Offside The right-hand side of a horse.

On the bit When a horse carries its head near vertically, with its mouth slightly below the rider's hand.

One-day event A combined training competition consisting of dressage, show jumping, and cross country phases and generally completed in one day.

Over-horsed When a horse is too big and strong for the rider.

Overreach The back foot over-extends and clips the front one, causing bruises.

Pace A lateral gait in two time, in which the hind leg and the foreleg on the same side move forward together.

Pacer A horse that trots using its legs in lateral pairs, such as near foreleg and near hindleg together. The normal trot uses diagonal pairs.

Paddock (a) A grassy enclosure near a stable or house in which horses can be turned out. (b) The enclosure at a racecourse in which the horses are paraded and then mounted before a race.

Passage One of the classical high school airs, comprising a spectacular elevated trot in slow motion.

Pelham bit A bit designed to produce with only one mouthpiece the combined effects of the snaffle bit and the cube bit. Normally made of metal, vulcanite, or rubber and used either with one rein or two reins (in which case a leather couplet is used to link the two reins of the bit).

Piaffe A classical high school air, comprising a spectacular trot with great elevation and cadence performed on the spot.

Piebald (a) A British and Irish term for a horse with large, irregular black and white patches. (b) In the USA, a horse of different colors.

Pirouette In dressage a turn within the horse's length, that is, the shortest turn it is possible to make. Performed in walk or canter.

Points Normally means the mane (including forelock), tail, and lower legs. It is also used to mean "part," e.g. the points (parts) of the horse.

Poll The delicate area on top of the horse's head between its ears.

Pommel saddle A saddle with a very pronounced protuberance at the top front.

Pony A horse not exceeding 14.2hh (142 cm) at maturity.

Quarters The area of a horse's body extending from the rear of the flank to the root of the tail and downwards on either side to the top of the leg: the hindquarters.

Rack The most spectacular movement of the five-gaited American Saddle Horse, it is a very fast even gait in which each foot strikes the ground separately in quick succession.

Rein back To make a horse step backwards while being ridden or driven, often used in dressage tests.

Roan A coat pattern which is evenly sprinkled with white hairs and those of other colors.

Roller A cinch- (girth-) like device to keep a horse's blanket or rug in place.

Roman nose Describes a horse with a convex face.

Saddlery The bridle, saddle, and other items of tack used on a horse which is to be ridden as opposed to driven.

School (a) To train a horse for whatever purpose it may be required. (b) An enclosed area, either covered or open where a horse may be trained or exercised.

Seat The position in which the rider sits on the saddle and communicates with the horse.

Shoulder in An exercise to teach a horse to curve its body laterally as it advances; hand and leg pressure by the rider on opposite sides of the horse achieves this.

Silks The peaked cap and silk or woolen blouse, both carrying the colors of the owner, worn by a jockey in racing.

Sire The male parent of a foal.

Skewbald A term for a horse with irregular patches of white and any other color, sometimes more than one.

Snaffle bit The oldest and simplest form of bit, available in a variety of types but consisting chiefly of a single, usually joined, bar with a ring at each end to which one pair of reins is attached.

Square halt The horse comes to a complete stop in a good, tidy position and with no fidgeting.

Stallion Also called a "stud" or "entire," it is an ungelded horse that should be capable of reproducing the species.

Steeplechase A race of a specified distance and in which there are a number of obstacles of be jumped.

Stud (a) An establishment where horses are kept for breeding. (b) A stallion.

Studbook A book recording the pedigrees of individuals of a particular breed.

Tack Saddlery equipment used for riding and driving.

Tacking up To put all the saddlery equipment on the horse in preparation for riding.

Third eyelid A membrane below the horse's eyelid extending horizontally across most of the horse's eye.

Three-day event A combined competition taking place over three days, consisting of the dressage, cross-country, and show-jumping disciplines.

Throatlatch (throatlash) Part of the headpiece which fastens under the horse's throat to prevent the bridle from slipping over the head.

Toad Eye Mealy rim on both eyelids; it almost encircles the eye that is prominent. Found predominantly in the Exmoor pony and Appaloosa.

Tourniquet A device to stem bleeding or blood flow, e.g. a bandage twisted tight using a stick.

Trotter A Standardbred horse trained for harness racing.

Twitch A strap that is tightened over the horse's lip as a restraining device. Twitching is the term used when using this device.

Udder ("milk bar" or "teats") Mammary glands which provide milk for the newborn or young foal.

Under-horsed A horse that is too small for the size and weight of the rider.

Warmblood Breeds that are not as pure and refined as the Hotbloods (Arab and Thoroughbred) or as large and slow as Coldbloods. These breeds are used for riding, competitions, and driving.

Weaned The foal no longer takes milk from the mare but eats solid foodstuffs.

Withers The highest part of a horse's back at the base of the neck between the shoulder blades.

Zebra marks stripes on the limbs, neck, withers and/or hindquarters of horses usually of ancient breeding.

INDEX

CREDITS

Quarto would like to thank and acknowledge the following photographers and photographic agencies for kindly allowing us to reproduce copyright material.

Key: t=top b=below c=center r=right l=left

Ace Photo Agency p.56(c). **AKG London** p.16(b).
Animal Photography p.27(b), p.29(b), p.30(t&b), p.33(t), p.35(t), p.37(t), p.52(b), p.123(t), p.174(tl), p.201(t), p.213(b).
Bridgeman Art Library p.16(t), p.19(tr), p.19(b).
ET Archive p.12(t). **Joel Finler** p.54(b), p.24(l&r), p.25(r).
Kit Houghton Photography p.12(b), p.21(t), p.28(b), p.33(b), p.36(bl), p.42(t), p.46(b), p.53(t), p.74(t), p.78(l), p.79(t&b), p.94(t&b), p.101(t&c), p.216(b).
Image Bank p.127. **Image Select/Ann Ronan** p.17(t).
Bob Langrish p.7(t), p.9(b), p.10(c), p.20(t&b), p.21(b), p.22(t), p.23(b), p.25(b), p.27(t), p.31(b), p.34(t), p.35(b), p.37(b), p.38(t), p.39(b), p.40(t), p.43(b), p.44(t&b), p.45(t), p.49(b), p.51(t), p.55(t), p.57, p.60(l&r), p.61(b), p.62(t&b), p.63(r), p.64(t&b), p.65(t&b), p.66, p.67(t&b), p.69(t&b), p.70, p.71(t), p.74(b), p.75(t&b), p.76(r), p.77(t&b), p.78(r), p.81(l), p.82(t), p.82(b), p.85(tr), p.89(br), p.97(t&b), ,p.90(t&b), p.91(t&b), p.98(t&b), p.99(b), p.100(b), p.101(b), p.102(l), p.103(tr), p.105(t), p.106(b), p.107(t&b), p.108(c&b), p.111(t&b), p.113(tl&tr), p.115(b), p.116(b), p.118(tr), p.119(t&b), p.121(tl&tr), p.121(b), p.124, p.125(t&b), p.126(t&b), p.128(t), p.129(t), p.134(c), p.137(b), p.144(c&b), p.148, p.150, p.151, p.157(tl), p.163(bl), p.170(t), p.172(l), p.173(bl&br), p.174(cl), p.179(b), p.181(r), p.183(tr), p.185(b), p.197(t&b), p.186(t), p.187, p.190, p.191, p.193, p.194(t&b), p.195(t), p.198(t&b), p.199(t&b), p.200(b), p.201(b), p.203(t), p.205(t&b), p.206, p.207(t), p.208, p.209, p.210, p.211(t&b), p.213(t), p.215, p.216(t), p.217(t&b).
Only Horses p.22(b), p.23(t), p.189(t), p.203(b), p.204, p.207(b), p.212, p.214(l). **Pictor International** p.13(t), p.103(l).
Jeremy Reynolds p.2(c), p.4(r), p.6, p.9(t). **Visual arts Library** p.15(t&b), p.17(b), p.18, p.19(tl).

All other photographs and diagrams are the copyright of Quarto.